Converging Worlds

WHITE SEA

SIBERIA

SWEDEN

Archangel

Vologda

Perm

Finland

Olonets

Viatka

St Petersburg

Ufa

Novgorod

Kostroma

BALTIC
SEA

Estland

St. Petersburg

Yaros-
laval

Kazan

Orenburg

Nizhni
Novgorod

Livland

Tver

Vladimir

Simbirsk

Samara

Moscow

Kurland

Pskov

Moscow

Riazan

Penza

Vitebsk

Smolensk

Kaluga

Tula

Saratov

CENTRAL
ASIA

Kovno

Vilna

Mogilev

Orel

Tambov

GERMANY

Minsk

Kursk

Voronezh

Astrakhan

Grodno

Chernigov

Voronezh

Warsaw

Kiev

Kharkov

Don

Polish
Provinces

Volhynia

Kiev

Poltava

AUSTRIA-

Podolia

Ekaterinoslav

CASPIAN
SEA

HUNGARY

Kherson

Stavropol

Bessarabia

Taurida

Kuban

Terek

RUMANIA

Sevastopol

Trans - Caucasian
Provinces

SERBIA

BLACK SEA

PERSIA

BULGARIA

EUROPEAN RUSSIA

in 1900

OTTOMAN EMPIRE

Converging Worlds

Religion and Community in Peasant Russia, 1861–1917

Chris J. Chulos

NORTHERN ILLINOIS UNIVERSITY PRESS—*DeKalb*

Published by the Northern Illinois University Press, DeKalb, Illinois   60115

Manufactured in the United States using acid-free paper

Design by Julia Fauci

Library of Congress Cataloging-in-Publication Data

Chulos, Chris J.

Converging worlds : religion and community in peasant Russia, 1861–1917 /

Chris J. Chulos.

   p.   cm.

Includes bibliographical references and index.

ISBN 0-87580-317-2 (alk. paper)

1. Peasantry—Religious life—Russia—History—19th century. 2. Peasantry—Religious

life—Russia—History—20th century. 3. Village communities—Russia—History—19th

century. 4. Village communities—Russia—History—20th century. 5. Voronezh Region

(Russia)—Religious life and customs. 6. Russkaia pravoslavnaia tserkov'—Influence.

7. National characteristics, Russian—History. I. Title: Religion and community in

peasant Russia, 1861–1917. II. Title.

HD1536.R9C478 2003

281.9'4735—dc21

2003051160

To Tanja Saarinen

Contents

Acknowledgments

$\mathcal{B}$efore the mid-1980s scholars of Russia paid little attention to the religion of peasants as they encountered modern, secular, and urban culture in the last half century of tsarist rule. When peasant religion was noticed at all, it was mostly discussed in terms of cultural backwardness, an obstacle preventing the Russian Empire from enjoying the fruits of a modern, industrial society. In this portrayal of peasant religion, Russia's rural folk was implicitly blamed for the replacement of tsarist autocracy with Soviet authoritarianism. When I began to study Russian Orthodox theology as a university student, I was struck by my professors' candid disdain for unschooled faith, "superstition" in the parlance of cultural superiority. As theologians who had trained at the best schools in the United States and Western Europe, they were unable to perceive the relevance of "uninformed" faith that existed with almost no awareness of specific church canons, ecumenical councils, and the writings of the church fathers. During weekly visitations to observe Orthodoxy as practiced in the Chicago metropolitan area, one professor snickered at university-educated parishioners for uttering prayers and crossing themselves in rote fashion without being able to cite church teachings about liturgical practice.

Having grown up in the sister tradition of *Greek-American* Orthodoxy and being at that time still largely ignorant of dogma, it was natural that I took the side of the parishioners scorned by my professor. To me, their understanding of the Christian faith was no less valid than my professor's. My own earliest memories were wrapped in the gauze of my grandparents' religious beliefs, which invested tremendous spiritual energy in practices that were not always respected by the institutional authority of the church. In the minds of older-generation Greek immigrants there was no contradiction between folk customs and theology—they were simply different expressions of the same faith, as natural as the existence of rulers and subjects who, together, represented a single ethnic heritage. For many Greek-American children the essence of being Greek was Orthodox Christianity, just as Russian peasants understood the relationship between their faith and ethnicity in the waning years of the tsarist empire. The fact that our young and sheltered minds compared our *own* Greek Orthodox *Theotokos* to our grandmothers, whose indulgence and comfort we relied on in good times and bad, in no way diminished the intensity of our faith. My decision to study everyday religious practice was as much a criticism of the arrogance of my professor and everyone who shared his prejudices as a desire to learn about one of the most mysterious corners of Russian peasant life.

I began my quixotic journey into the religious world of Russian peasants while I was a graduate student at the University of Chicago, where I received tremendous encouragement and support from believers and skeptics alike. At the intellectually stimulating graduate workshop on society and culture, which was led by Wendy Griswold and attended by faculty and students from an array of departments, I learned about the rigors of critical thinking and the fruits of interdisciplinary methodologies. Throughout my studies and beyond, Richard Hellie and Jeffrey Brooks have provided support and encouragement, even when I decided, contrary to custom, to write a book quite different from my dissertation.

In researching and writing this book I incurred a great many debts and benefited from the intellectual and academic traditions of four countries. In Russia I benefited from the astute commentary of Marina Mikhailovna Gromyko and the cohort of young scholars she gathered at the Institute of Ethnology and Anthropology in Moscow. In the northern capital of St. Petersburg, Boris Nikolaevich Mironov encouraged me during the early stages of my research, while the staff of the Archive of the Russian Ethnographic Museum (AREM) and the Russian State Historical Archive (RGIA) facilitated my reading of precious archival documents and generously imparted their knowledge of Russian culture and society. At the latter institution, Serafima Igor'evna Varekhova deserves special gratitude. Her love of history and archives, combined with an acute sensitivity to the multitude of difficulties that can hinder the work of foreign researchers in Russia, has benefited an entire generation of scholars.

The helpful staff of the Newspaper Collection of the Russian National Library in St. Petersburg assisted me with the gargantuan task of identifying, locating, and reading late-imperial dailies; their kindness hastened my work, their smiles brightened my days. The staffs of the State Archive of Voronezh Oblast (GAVO) and the Voronezh University Library welcomed me with great enthusiasm at a time when foreigners were usually viewed with suspicion. Viktor Mikhailovich Abakumov of the Voronezh University Library shared his wealth of knowledge about his beloved Voronezh *oblast'* and, with his wife, Stefaniia Geronimovna Tarasinskaia, displayed characteristic Russian hospitality at a critical time in my research. In Finland I am indebted to the entire staff of the Slavonic Collection of the University of Helsinki Library, particularly Saara Talasniemi and Irina Lukka. For seven

Illustrations

Figures

Maps

years the Renvall Institute for Area and Cultural Studies, along with the Academy of Finland, provided me with a regular institutional setting and research and writing support. Among the many Finnish scholars at these fine institutions who demonstrated the utmost professionalism, integrity, and openness toward my work on an unlikely topic, I am especially grateful to Timo Vihavainen, the dean of Russian studies in Finland; Marjatta Hietala, an unflagging supporter of Russian studies and academic exchanges; and René Gothóni, a paradigm of international scholarly cooperation. I was fortunate to count among my colleagues and friends Niilo Kauppi, Johannes Remy, and Marina Vituhnovskaja, who imparted a unique wisdom, combined with companionship, over many sips of strong Finnish coffee.

For all too brief a time, the history faculty at the School of Slavonic and East European Studies at the University of London offered stimulating intellectual commentary on later versions of this book. The final touches on the manuscript were completed at the Kennan Institute for Advanced Russian Studies at the Woodrow Wilson International Center for Scholars in Washington, D.C., a paragon of research environments with its unique linkage of serious scholarship with the world of public affairs. While writing the book, I presented numerous chapters at the annual meetings of the American Association for the Advancement of Slavic Studies, the American Historical Association, and the British Association for Slavonic and East European Studies and benefited immeasurably from the commentary I received.

A list of all the individuals who have unsparingly given assistance and advice over the years would be a chapter in itself. A few deserve special mention. Richard Stites has generously read almost everything I have written with his famously critical eye and careful attention to style; Gareth Popkins has shared his insights on village society and culture, his profound knowledge of sources and archives, and his enthusiasm for a vast number of topics near and far from Russia; and Eugene Clay has encouraged me to study popular piety of all sorts in Russia—tsarist, Soviet, and post-Soviet. Simon Dixon, Gregory Freeze, Jacqueline Friedlander, Elena Hellberg-Hirn, Tuomas Lehtonen, and Roy Robson gave me invaluable commentary at various points in my work. As I put the final touches on the manuscript, Margaret Paxson provided brilliant anthropological insight on village culture and everyday life. My brief research trips to Chicago would have been far less productive without the help of June Farris, whose encyclopedic knowledge of Slavic sources in the University of Chicago Library and beyond enabled me to conduct weeks' worth of research in a few short days. Thanks to generous funding from the Academy of Finland, my research in Finland and Russia was greatly advanced by intelligent and talented assistants: Julija Azbel, Timo Haapanen, Ulla Hakanen, Arja Leinonen, Kirsikka Saari, and Leena Suvanto. Special gratitude goes to Ulla Hakanen for her assistance with maps that gave geographic context to my research. For their friendship, stimulating conversation, sense of humor, and hospitality, Zhenia and Ania Zablotsky, my unofficial hosts in St. Petersburg for more than a decade, stand out as exemplars of integrity and intelligence.

On a personal note, my family deserves commendation: my parents, John Chulos and the late Rita Chulos, for providing the secure environment needed for intellectual creativity; my siblings, Nicholas Chulos and Margaret Steinhagen, for their unfailing support in my academic and other travels, as well as for their ceaseless logistical assistance during my regular trips between the continents. More recently, Nikos Santeri and Iannis Akseli have brought me unimagined delight as I completed this project. With the naive and curious eyes of children, they daily challenge my preconceptions and force me to look at the world anew. Most of all, my wife, Tanja Saarinen, has stoically accompanied me on countless trips to Russia's capitals and countryside, has endured innumerable versions of the manuscript, and has assumed sole parenting responsibilities for long stretches of time that enabled me to complete my research and writing. This book is dedicated to her, my chief interlocutor and companion.

Passages in chapters 2 and 5 are modified versions of paragraphs from articles that have appeared in Jeremy Smith, ed., *Within the Limits: Space in Russian History and Culture* (Helsinki: Finnish Historical Society, 1999); and Chris J. Chulos and Johannes Remy, eds., *Imperial and National Identities in Pre-Revolutionary, Soviet, and Post-Soviet Russia* (Helsinki: Finnish Literature Society, 2001). Research and writing for this book was funded in part by a Fulbright-Hayes Doctoral Dissertation Fellowship, the International Research and Exchanges Board (IREX), the Finlandia Foundation, the Academy of Finland, the Ministry of Education (Finland), the Finnish Institute for Russian and East European Studies, the University of Helsinki Chancellor's Office, and the Kennan Institute for Advanced Russian Studies. None of these organizations is responsible for the views expressed in the following pages.

Author's Note

All books have their stylistic idiosyncrasies, and mine is no exception. In most cases I have used the Library of Congress method of transliteration. Well-known family and place names follow conventional usage: Tolstoy instead of Tolstoi, Archangel instead of Arkhangel'. Except in the footnotes, I have adhered to the orthographic conventions of today, which is to say that I replaced the old "th" with "f" so that "Theodor" becomes "Feodor." References to the mother of Jesus differ in the Eastern Orthodox and Catholic traditions. In Eastern Orthodoxy, Jesus' mother is seldom called the Virgin Mary, but instead is known either as the Birthgiver of God (the Russian *Bogoroditsa* is from the Greek *Theotokos*, literally, God Bearer) or the Mother of God *(Bogomater')*. For stylistic simplicity, except when giving the name of churches, monasteries, or holidays, I refer to Mary as the Mother of God. All dates before February 1918 are given according to the Julian calendar used in Russia at the time, which was twelve days behind the Gregorian calendar in the 1800s, and thirteen days behind in the 1900s. Unless otherwise noted, all translations are my own.

Converging Worlds

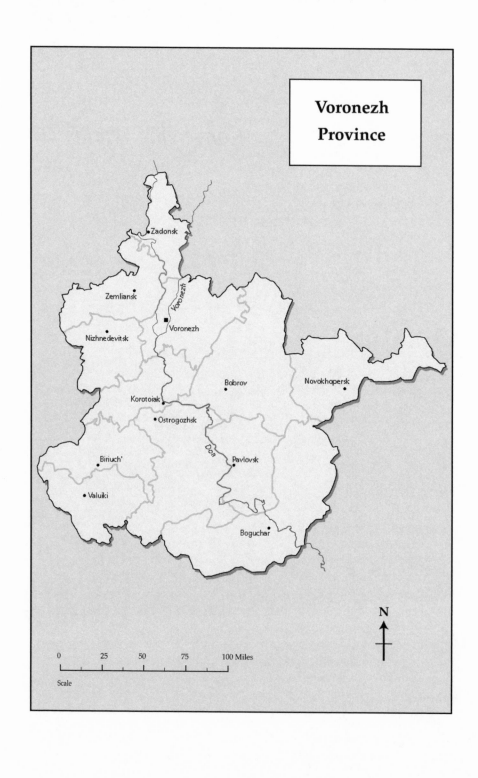

Orthodoxy, Russianness, and Local Identity

O n a hot August morning in 1861, more than three hundred thousand newly freed serfs converged on the small town of Zadonsk to witness the canonization of Archbishop Tikhon, who had been laid to rest nearly eighty years earlier in the Birthgiver of God Monastery. Weary after their long journeys on foot to this sacred place in the southern Russian province of Voronezh, dusty from the dry earth, and weak from self-imposed fasts, these peasant believers waited with anxious hope to witness the miraculous powers of their beloved holy man's relics. The event itself justified the long-suffering patience of their parents and grandparents who, since Tikhon's death in 1783, had trekked annually to the Birthgiver of God Monastery to pray in the shrine of their local holy man, experience the aura of his relics, and, occasionally, receive spiritual and physical healing. This spontaneous recognition of Tikhon's sanctity led diocesan officials to request that the ruling body of the Russian Orthodox Church, the Holy Synod, send its investigators to verify miracles attributed to the holy man and to confirm that his remains were uncorrupted. The somber black-robed members of the Holy Synod were reluctant to acknowledge, however, that the Zadonsk holy man was exceptional until, as if they had been waiting for a historically symbolic moment, they dispatched an investigative team in 1861 and immediately announced that Tikhon would be canonized as a sign of divine approval of the emancipation of the serfs and the new modern path upon which Russia was embarking. Voronezh provincial officials beamed with pride that their outback province had been singled out for such a momentous occasion and immediately set into motion an enormous frenzy of activities that would prepare their corner of the empire for a celebration of this magnitude. As Voronezh peasants enthusiastically assisted in the canonization preparations, they, too, rejoiced at the official confirmation of what they, their parents, and grandparents had long before accepted as fact.[1]

In the 1861 ceremonies honoring Tikhon, the absorption of provincial achievement into the narrative of modern Russia contrasted sharply with the images projected at the jubilee of his canonization in 1911. For more than a year, Voronezh officials worked closely with the newly established provincial church historical and archeological committee to publish commemorative works by and about Tikhon and to erect markers at places important to his ministry. Interested mostly in celebrating a provincial son and his shining ministry in life and death, Voronezh officialdom promoted a new type of regional identity that stood independently of the empire. The more than one hundred thousand believers, mostly peasants from Voronezh, who visited Zadonsk in August 1911, also focused their attention not on the empire, but on a local hero whose achievements now represented the distinguished heritage of the province. With the empire crumbling under the weight of political and civil unrest, and with the imperial court under the mesmerizing sway of Rasputin, officials and peasants in Voronezh preferred to celebrate the contours of provincial achievement represented by the life and wondrous works of St. Tikhon of Zadonsk.[2]

Despite the uniqueness of St. Tikhon's story, late-tsarist Russian history is filled with celebrations of religious and secular heroes whose singular feats deeply touched their communities. As peasants throughout Russia embraced and fêted an expanding array of holy people, they explicitly and tacitly expressed a desire to locate their seemingly ordinary villages within the greater framework of empire and nation. As the number of celebrations like the jubilee of St. Tikhon proliferated throughout the Russian countryside, producing a cacophony of local self-admiration, how did ordinary peasants view the relationship between Orthodoxy, Russianness, and local identity, and how did their understanding of this relationship evolve in the last half century of tsarist rule? In terms of religious history, what consequences did the development of a semimodern, faith-based local pride have on the Orthodox Church as an institution and on praxis at the parish level? This book is about the role of religion among Orthodox peasants in Voronezh province as Russia set out on the bumpy road toward modern nationhood after 1861. As modernization and industrialization began to tear at the social and cultural fabric of village life, most peasants took comfort in religion. Reformers, heralding progressive secular ideas rooted in the Enlightenment tradition, did not always appreciate the consoling role of religion, but as village and urban cultural worlds converged, belief and practice stood near the center of an ongoing and complex negotiation between educated Russians and peasants. As the great reforms of the 1860s and 1870s introduced radical changes in the educational, judicial, and military life of the village, no area of the empire was untouched by these dramatic changes, not even predominantly agricultural and putatively backward provinces like Voronezh.

The benefits of modern life that Voronezh peasants took advantage of were framed by the "age-old" rituals, customs, and beliefs of the village.

The hybrid culture that emerged was best found in celebrations like the Tikhon jubilee, which localized religious and secular symbols of the empire, and in the process helped to create a mosaic of unequal and adjustable parts that came to signify Russia.[3] In the minds of educated Russians who thought at all about Voronezh, the province was a symbol for lost potential, a laboratory for reformers struggling to enlighten the peasantry, and an ideal of starry-eyed romantics longing for a fictional bygone golden age.[4]

Reform and the Fate of Peasant Religion

The emancipation of the serfs unleashed a torrent of reform activities, often confused and contradictory, that inadvertently helped peasants to create bridges between new and traditional ways of thinking. For village culture, the most important consequence of the great reforms of the 1860s and 1870s was the spread of literacy and its reinforcement of a religion-based identity through an imagined community of believer-readers. Essential to this new version of local identity were provincial newspapers, which tacitly drew the peasantry into discussions about national identity. As a forum for expressions of local identity, newspapers were popular, and often populist, in orientation. Serving as provincial billboards, newspapers announced and reported about religious festivities, pilgrimages, canonizations, and civic festivals, assuring peasants that they were united with their fellow countrymen who participated in similar events throughout the empire.[5]

Nowhere was the connection between local faith and Russian identity clearer than at religious shrines. Before the emancipation of the serfs, restrictions on movement imposed by serfdom and hardships of travel had prevented pilgrimage from becoming a widespread phenomenon. The canonization of St. Tikhon in 1861 offered sufficient proof of an unintended consequence of the emancipation—the rise in travel to sacred shrines as peasants took to their feet to attend public celebrations in honor of newly discovered relics or to visit long revered shrines and favorite saints. This explosion of peripatetic energy was seized upon by religious and secular authorities who promoted and regulated pilgrimage sites as convenient venues for infusing old symbols of Orthodoxy and Russianness with new meaning. If participation in the life of shrines and civic celebrations helped to establish networks of communication between villages, towns, and cities, bringing an end to the social and cultural isolation of the peasants, such festivities also reinforced the fundamental structures of rural life.[6]

Studies of interactions between peasant villages and the outside world have tended to concentrate on moments of dissonance when relationships between communities or between communities and representatives of provincial and state authority break down.[7] While not ignoring conflict, this book focuses on the influence of post-emancipation social and cultural reforms on village religious life and peasant responses to challenges to their traditions. One result of reform was a growing sense of empowerment among the weakest members of society. As peasants acquired the confidence they needed to question openly autocratic authority and its patriarchal mores, they sought greater independence in the way they conducted their religious life. Using their newly acquired literacy to learn about administrative procedures, village communities flooded local and national church offices with petitions and complaints designed to bring greater control over parish management. Although church authorities remained sensitive to local religious needs, they often interpreted peasant activism as a negative consequence of secular enlightenment that ultimately would harm the Orthodox faith through the dilution of its traditional hierarchical principles. Chief among religious leaders' concerns was the unmonitored influence of the written word, especially when it took the form of personal interpretations of biblical texts that might have led to the heterodox belief that religious authority lay in Scripture rather than church institutions. Worried about a popular revolt by the literate faithful, church leaders further alienated ordinary believers from the clerical hierarchy by delaying a complete translation of the Bible into modern Russian until 1876. The reluctance to publish a comprehensible version of the basic text of Christianity also provided ammunition to critics who argued that the Orthodox Church was an institution concerned primarily with its survival at the expense of the faithful's spiritual advancement.

The 1905 edict on religious tolerance fueled the fears of most leading churchmen about the inability of Orthodox Christianity to compete favorably in the emerging religious marketplace; the task of enhancing the public image of the faith proved, however, impossible as long as the church remained subordinated to the monarchy. Keenly aware of the damage done to its prestige as a result of its official status, and humiliated by the Rasputin affair in the last decade of autocratic rule, Orthodox hierarchs concentrated their reform efforts on the separation of church and state as a means of salvaging the prestige of their ancient faith, improving clergy-laity relations, and revitalizing parish life.[8]

Peasant Religion as a Historiographical Problem

The history of Russian peasant religion in the last half century of tsarist rule has suffered from the secularized nature of scholarly research. If Soviet historians delighted in condemning belief and practice as mysterious pages from the annals of a defunct pagan past, historians elsewhere reveled in demonstrating the utter irrelevance of faith to the processes of modernization and industrialization. Both sets of historians, ensconced in their own comfortable worlds, built upon the solid foundation of knowledge laid by their nineteenth-century predecessors, the creators of modern scholarly disciplines. These academic pioneers in Russia and elsewhere created binary models of the world that held national achievements in the arts and sciences (of the small, but influential, educated minority) in direct opposition to the ignorant backwardness of the "dark masses."[9] In Russia, as elsewhere in Europe, cultural enlightenment was considered to be a panacea that would cure rural folk of their superstitious ways. Although nineteenth-century scholars and intellectuals must share a portion of the blame for creating this stereotype of peasant religiosity, the parish clergy, who were in daily contact with the peasantry, made their own contribution to this biased portrait, which proved to be just as important. Taken as a whole, the clergy's prolific writings on religious practice in the village resemble a work in progress with few coherent objectives or conclusions, except for their disparagement of peasant religion.

Until the late–twentieth century, Russian clergymen's portrait of benighted village belief and practice was widely accepted in academic, cultural, and political spheres. This view came under scrutiny only in the 1980s when a shift in the focus of social and cultural research elsewhere in Europe began to move peasant religion from the distant margins to a point much nearer to the center of Russian studies. Almost no aspect of religious life remained untouched as scholars moved away from the familiar pious-pagan dichotomy to explore peasant religion in the context of village social structures, power relationships, and cultural activity.[10] While these new interpretations are turning many generally held assumptions on their heads, basic questions about religious life remain unanswered because Russian scholarship has yet to fully reconsider the word *dvoeverie* (dual faith) and the closely related term *perezhitki* (survivals), both widely used to describe village piety. Few peasants understood these words, nor would they have agreed with their usage.[11]

Dvoeverie first appeared in medieval Russian sermons to describe the transposition of Christian beliefs and practice onto the indigenous pagan religious culture. By the late–nineteenth century, the term was widely used to emphasize tension between institutional Orthodoxy and peasant religious praxis. Ethnographic jargon elaborated this distinction by using the ambiguous *pover'e* to refer to folk piety, and the imprecise *verovanie* to describe church religion, thus creating an artificial gap between two contradictory, yet compatible, elements of peasant Orthodoxy. The term *perezhitki* entered into common currency during the last decades of the tsarist regime as a way to describe folk piety as an impediment to modern change. After 1917 antireligious propaganda expanded the meaning of *perezhitki* to include all folk culture, with religion serving as a key obstacle to a bright future. Thus the Soviet image of the pious or pagan peasant became firmly associated with extremely negative aspects of traditional life: peasants (and believers in general) were considered to be either too simple-minded to understand religion as a false ideology, or were cast as victims of clerical exploitation. According to the Soviet model, success in eliminating religious belief among the peasantry required that history be rewritten and memory be obliterated, literally through books and education, and physically through the destruction of religious buildings, objects, and believers. The result was an excessive interest in religious aberrations, dissent, conflict, and alienation. Following the collapse of the Soviet Union, *dvoeverie* and *perezhitki* became taboo words as scholars have sought more complex interpretive models to understand peasant religious life.

"Peasant Orthodoxy" and "popular Orthodoxy" in this study encompass a wide range of practice whose adherents considered themselves to be members of the official church, or followers of its teachings.[12] The belief of the faithful remains less clear than the expressions of it and the ways religion gave meaning to everyday life. I have tried to strike a balance between elements of Orthodox Christianity that united diverse communities of believers, and competing voices among the faithful. My goal is to provide a nuanced understanding of the religion of Russian peasants by examining one province, while also drawing general conclusions about Orthodox folk piety throughout the empire.

Voronezh Province as a Symbol of Backwardness and Essential Russianness

The focus of this book is Voronezh province, which is located approximately five hundred miles south of Moscow (see map on page 2). When the city of Voronezh was created as a fortress outpost of Muscovy in 1586, local inhabitants spoke of it as "the gold mine," a metaphor for the freedom and natural abundance embodied in its rich black soils and dense forests.[13] Throughout the sixteenth and seventeenth centuries, the untamed and exotic frontier land out of which Voronezh province was eventually shaped became the nearest thing to a state-guaranteed haven from enserfment and led to the prospering of the *odnodvortsy,* small landowners of peasant or petty-service origin who employed little or no dependent labor to farm their freestanding estates. As its territories were settled by Russians fleeing serfdom and Ukrainians escaping the bloody wars over Ukrainian independence, Voronezh acquired a reputation as a restive frontier susceptible to insurgence. It was swept up first by the Moscow uprising of 1648 and then by the most violent and widespread seventeenth-century peasant revolt, led by Stenka Razin (1670–1671), the Cossack leader who soon became immortalized as a great folk hero. The church schism of 1666–1667 added a religious dimension to provincial dissent, and Voronezh once again became a haven, this time for Old Believers fleeing to the margins of the empire in the name of faith. In 1682 the aims of the state were irreversibly imposed on the idiosyncratic social order and religious dissent through the establishment of the diocese and the appointment of Mitrofan (canonized 1832) as the first bishop of Voronezh. After his death, oral legends and hagiographic literature created the image of Archbishop Mitrofan as a provincial

Fig. 1—Cover of *St. Mitrofan the Wonderworker, First Bishop of Voronezh*

pioneer whose stern leadership and imperturbable self-confidence led Voronezh on the path toward religious conformity, while his friendship with Tsar Peter the Great was portrayed as symbolizing the intersection of imperial and provincial interests (see figs. 1 and 2).[14]

Throughout the eighteenth and nineteenth centuries, economic growth and cultural development in Voronezh followed the patterns of the empire at large as bustling cities and towns along popular trade routes and railroad stations sprouted up all over the countryside. By the mid–nineteenth century, residents of the city of Voronezh looking for entertainment could choose from a variety of plays, concerts, and operas, or they could read a growing variety of locally written fictional works. After the emancipation of the serfs, urban culture was gradually brought to the peasantry through a network of secular and religious primary schools, popular literature, and rural reformers. Peasants did not always welcome urban-educated schoolteachers and reformers, but in time villagers' curiosity contributed to the rise in literacy and led to a small, but steady, emigration to other parts of the province and empire. Elsewhere in Russia, movement away from the natal village helped to ease the demographic explosion from which Russia suffered in the decades following 1861 and led to a radical change in the household structure as younger males increasingly requested their allotments of arable communal land before the death of the patriarch. In Voronezh, however, the younger generation was less likely to challenge tradition, and household sizes remained unusually large.[15] Struggling to cope with cramped living space and barely able to make ends meet, Voronezh peasants did not always look favorably upon villagers returning from the cities with their newly acquired urban dress, manners, ideas, aspirations, and consumer products.

More than three hundred years after Voronezh had evoked images of frontier freedom and religious dissent, its backwardness bedeviled or beguiled educated Russians searching for solutions to their country's unusual historical development. By the beginning of the twentieth century, lower than average literacy and emigration rates, an impoverished agriculture-driven economy, and its location away from the major cultural and political centers had helped to create in the minds of many educated Russians an image of Voronezh as a symbol of backwardness. The assumed deprivation of Voronezh, however, was also a source of inspiration for reformers, who never lost their zeal to transform its villages with knowledge and economic improvement. In the world of culture, Voronezh peasants came to represent a sense of Russianness that was less dependent on ethnic purity than Christian spirituality, hard work, and long suffering.[16] Voronezh natives such as the painters Nikolai Ge (1831–1897) and Ivan Kramskoi (1837–1887) drew their inspiration from local peasant life, while village folk songs found their way into famous collections by Mikhail Stakhovich (1824–1858) and were used by Rimsky-Korsakov, Tchaikovsky, and Mussorgsky. In his successful popular concerts featuring a "people's choir"

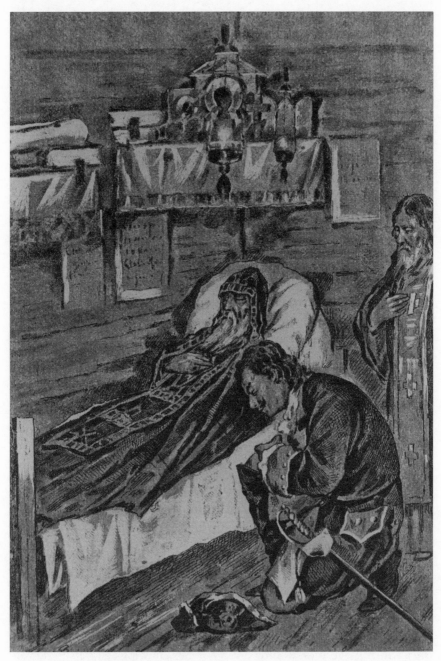

Fig. 2—Peter the Great paying last respects to Mitrofan of Voronezh

made up of peasants, Mitrofan Efimovich Piatnitskii (1864–1927) immortalized his native Voronezh village in an idealized version of folk singing.[17] When Evgeniia Eduardovna Linëva took the first phonographic recorder to the Russian countryside to record peasant songs, she went to Voronezh.[18] Faced with the prejudices of their cultural superiors, Voronezh peasants entered the stormy twentieth century keenly aware of the distinctions that set their little corner of Russia apart from the rest of the empire. Until the end of tsarist rule, this awareness of difference colored Voronezh peasants' constructions of their own Russian identity, whose main components were almost invariably religion, community, and local pride.[19]

Organization of the Book

The first half of this book sifts through the muddy waters of popular piety to establish the relationship between liturgical life, parish organization, superstition, and belief. Chapter 1 seeks to unravel the most puzzling riddles of the wide range of practice falling under the rubric "Orthodox piety," whose influence lasted long after peasants left the village, the prominence of women in keeping the faith alive, and the margins of acceptable belief and practice. The influence of religion on peasant conceptions of historical and human time is the subject of chapter 2. As the pressures of seasonal work, migration to towns and cities, and generational changes increasingly threatened to fragment village life, communities continued to renew their sense of identity and connection to their past through a procession of holidays and life-cycle rituals. The subject of chapter 3 is villagers' understandings of their sense of history through tales about their ancestors' mythical and real encounters with great figures of the empire. The physical reminders of their heroic past were often found in the parish church and its wondrous icons. Chapter 4 examines the role of parish institutions in local identity. Although parish relationships were not always harmonious, a sense of unity emerged in struggles against diocesan and synodal officials, who were unwilling or unable to heed the increasing demands of believers who wished to take control of local religious administration.

The extension of this community-centered perspective to the world beyond the village is the subject of the last half of the book. In chapter 5 I argue that liturgical uniformity enabled the faithful to *imagine* their coreligionists were following the same traditions, something that was confirmed during visits to neighboring parishes, shrines, or wherever hierophantic essence was discovered. Although participants shared terms, symbols, and rituals, their usage and meaning diverged, thus allowing believers to tolerate each other's differences in ways that often created the illusion of harmony. Chapter 6 considers the myth of the peasant aversion to change, something that proves untrue in the light of the transformation of emancipation-year peasants from allegedly idyllic, passive, and retrograde tillers of the soil to ambiguous, active, and future-oriented rational actors whose choices and demands were given full expression during the revolutionary year of 1905, and again in 1917. For many reasons, 1905 was a pivotal year for peasant religion, first, because of the effects of revolution on traditional life, second, because of the new political freedoms, which included religious tolerance. Chapter 7 compares attempts by parish clergymen and peasants to reform grass-roots Orthodoxy in order to make it more responsive to local needs. At the center of this reform activity were calls for the revitalization of parish life, but long-standing mistrust and misunderstanding between peasants and clergymen prevented a common reform program and had fatal consequences for the Orthodox Church after 1917. The conclusion contrasts the swift collapse of the Orthodox Church as an institution with staunch peasant defenses of their most sacred places and traditions, which endured as highly localized shrines preserved in the private realm of faith and memory.

Varieties of Piety

That's what our fathers did and that's what we do.

Whether or not you believe it, *domovye* exist.

—Peasant proverbs, Voronezh Province

*M*ore than half a century after the Russian peasantry was freed from the legal bonds of serfdom, village culture continued to be bathed in the customs, practices, and beliefs of "the grandfathers" *(dedki)*, the semimythical spiritual forebears who, even in death, exerted influence over everyday life. The patriarchal hierarchy of the grandfathers paralleled the divine order at whose helm stood the Russian God, a stern, yet benevolent, fatherly figure who watched over his temporal and incorporeal creations. As the supreme elder, the Russian God demanded honor and obedience that was best displayed through conformity to ancient norms of behavior and social order. Violators of this cosmic scheme risked immediate punishment and, for the most egregious offenses, eternal damnation. As rising literacy rates and physical mobility slowly brought urban culture to rural society in the last half of the nineteenth century, most villages were divided between the majority of residents, who adhered to the inherited customs of the grandfathers, and a small, but growing, number of *new peasants* who questioned the validity of age-old traditions.[1]

The predicament of the new peasant is illustrated in the lively memoir of Ivan Stoliarov (1882–1953).[2] Standing on the divide between the illiterate village and the literate city, Stoliarov's life represented one type of success story that was created by the emancipation and great reforms of the 1860s and 1870s. Fraught with personal and professional frustrations and sympathetic to the spiritual world of the peasantry, Stoliarov dedicated himself to the improvement of the people he left behind as he evolved into a highly educated Russian émigré in Paris, longing to return to his beloved homeland. As the youngest son of a large peasant family from Karachun, one of the thousand small villages scattered about Voronezh province, Stoliarov was an unlikely candidate for advancement until his mother, wishing to end her family's cycle of poverty, enrolled her son in one of the new parish schools that began to sprout up in the mid-1880s. To promote her son's intellectual curiosity and diligence in his studies, young Ivan's mother encouraged him to read the popular religious series *Troitskie listki,* which she had received as a gift from a group of nuns she met while visiting the capital of Voronezh.[3] As a teenager, Stoliarov's desire to improve the lot of fellow villagers led him (with a generous stipend in hand) to the district agricultural school, where, like his contemporaries in other professional schools, he soon became attracted to revolutionary ideas. Stoliarov's interest in political and social change was more than a youthful infatuation, and in 1905, with the help of one of Voronezh province's largest landowners and member of the Kadet party, Countess Sophia Panina, he threw his lot in with the ill-fated Peasant Union, a decision that would later haunt him.[4] The following year he traveled to Paris, where he enrolled at the Sorbonne (see fig. 3). After the toppling of the tsarist regime in February 1917, Stoliarov returned to Russia to work at the Ministry of Agriculture and continued in his position after the Bolsheviks rose to power later that year. By 1928 his agricultural expertise and knowledge of the French language had won him the position of supervisor of the Soviet Union's Paris office for purchasing agricultural equipment to be used in the newly initiated collectivization campaign. When, two years later, he was summoned back to Moscow without explanation, he feared that his earlier support of the Peasant Union would jeopardize his life and chose to remain in Paris with his family in an impoverished, self-imposed exile until his death in 1953.[5]

The biography of this admittedly obscure personage in Russian history is important because of what it reveals about the intersection of village tradition and urban enlightenment, as well as about the lasting influence of communal norms and ways of thinking even among those peasants who benefited most from education. A combination of tradition and opportunity had led Stoliarov's mother to act on her ambitions because, as the youngest son of a large peasant family, he was not obligated to support his parents in their old age and was free to devote himself to his studies in the new rural schools. Tradition also served as a narrative device as he explained his autobiographical shift from "peasant" to "educated" Russian and then cosmopolitan extraordinaire in the terms of the village and its traditional customs. Standing between village and city, Stoliarov appreciated the functional and psychological purpose of the grandfathers' tradition: it provided villagers with a cognitive framework, deeply embedded in religion, with which to understand the world around them, their suffering and impoverishment, and their joyous moments. Religious belief was so

Fig. 3—Ivan Stoliarov, 1911

(From *Zapiski russkogo krest'yaniana*, © 1986, Paris: Institut d'études slaves)

intricately woven into personal and social identities that, despite his absorption of secular urban culture, Stoliarov's devotion to revolution had the trappings of a religious life: he became a revolutionary out of a deep sense of obligation to the peasantry and its customs. Like many other erstwhile peasants, he spent the rest of his life paying the price for his dedication.

This chapter offers glimpses of the religious underpinnings of village life by unraveling some of the most puzzling "riddles" (in Stoliarov's words) of popular Orthodoxy, its lasting influence long after peasants left the village, the prominence of women in keeping the faith alive, and the margins of acceptable belief and practice.

The Geography of Piety

Peasants divided their world into sacred and profane spheres that echoed Orthodox theological writings about earthly life as an imperfect image of the paradise that was constantly being resacralized as part of the Kingdom of Heaven. Like Eliade's mythical center where heaven and earth meet, the geography of Russian peasant piety linked the temporal and the extraterrestrial. The peasant village was an enchanted world in which the sacred could be encountered anywhere from the bathhouse to the parish church. What remained constant was a direct contact with the supernatural in its more tangible forms close to home, as well as in the distant and sometimes strange dogma and rites of the Orthodox Church. By uttering the correct saying, maintaining a certain order in one's daily routine, or avoiding things that could invoke unclean forces, peasants hoped to protect themselves from ordinary harm that usually threatened the natural biological processes of birth, life, and death.[6]

In this localized religion, the peasant cottage (izba) served as a miniature shrine where the sacred and profane spheres of life overlapped, allowing peasant believers a greater level of comfort vis-à-vis things holy than was ordinarily permitted in the parish church and its strictly defined liturgical acts.[7] Most important to the welfare of the household were the house spirit (domovoi), a male figure who watched over the family, and the icon shelf (bozhnitsa) in the sacred corner (krasnyi ugol), a domestic altar, reliquary, and memorial to the ancestors. On the shelf were icons of the patron and other favored saints of the household, ritual towels (sing., polotentse) and belts (sing., poias), holy water from church (sviataia voda), blessed Easter bread (artos), incense (ladan), church candles (svechki), votive lamps (svetil'niki, lampady), and other objects collected during religious holidays or on pilgrimages.[8] In the revered space of the sacred corner babies received their first blessing from family members before being baptized, children bid farewell to their parents before departing for the sacrament of holy matrimony, and the deceased were laid out for the last time as part of the funerary ritual. The sacred corner is also where the family came together to share daily meals and experiences, finalize agreements, and settle differences.

According to peasant belief, the general welfare of the household was secured by the correct observation of customs about building a new home and moving. A household whose fortune had been particularly calamitous avoided a building site too near the old one, and a home replacing one that had burned down was never to be built on exactly the same place lest it, too, would burn. On the night before moving, peasants offered bread and salt, the traditional symbol of hospitality, to the house spirit as an invitation to the new home. Placing a coin under the floor in one corner of the new cottage was thought to ensure wealth; burying a piece of wool in another corner was thought to guarantee warmth in the winter months; and placing incense in the corners of the rooms was expected to counteract the malevolent powers of the evil eye and all types of wizardry. An alert peasant was always on the lookout for auspicious signs or omens that foretold misfortune, such as black cockroaches, which were a sign of wealth and were welcomed in moderate numbers, or red cockroaches, which foretold poverty and were to be gotten rid of immediately.[9]

Beyond the protective walls of the cottage, the natural world teemed with the benevolent and malevolent spirits of the forest *(leshii)*, hills *(gornyi)*, and water *(vodianoi)*. Villagers were wise to be on guard against frolicking devils *(cherti)*, who constantly schemed their next trick, or the dreaded evil eye *(glaz)* that could be cast upon unwitting recipients by fellow peasants possessed by unclean spirits.[10] Travel away from the protective walls of the cottage was considered to be a time of heightened vulnerability to malevolent forces. To ensure that the journey bode well, the entire household might sit in the sacred corner and pray for a few minutes on the morning of the departure or perform a ritual sweeping of the floors to brush away harm.[11]

Related to the risks of being harmed while away from the familiar environment of hearth and home was the fear of an encounter with the Antichrist, a bogeyman figure that was associated with strangers visiting or residing temporarily in the village. When F. A. Shcherbina and his data collectors arrived in the Voronezh countryside in the 1880s to gather information for what became the most detailed microstudy of the prerevolutionary peasant economy, villagers divined "evil signs indicating . . . if not the Antichrist, then, in any case, unclean forces."[12] Despite having recruited his team from among the peasantry and requiring what amounted to sensitivity training for nonpeasant members of his cohort, religion-based fears of strangers made it extremely difficult for Shcherbina to penetrate the proverbial wall surrounding the village.[13] In preparation for Shcherbina's visit, old women busily sewed crosses onto clothing or used other religious objects to ward off malevolent forces that the outsiders were expected to bring with them. They also "tried to insert crosses in the drawers of those tables at which the registrars wrote, used chalk to mark the benches and floor with crosses, sometimes even marked the spine or sole of the registrars' boots with crosses, said prayers, [and repeated] charms."[14]

As village contacts with the outside world increased, the psychological lines around communities often sharpened. In 1915 a rumor spread throughout several villages in Valuiki District that the leaders of recently opened kindergartens were agents of the Antichrist.[15] Hearsay about the Antichrist afflicted mothers the most as they sought to protect their children from the mark of the devil or feared that registering them at school was somehow demonic. In 1916 murmurings about the Antichrist spread through Kozlovka and nearly triggered a riot when a peasant woman named Malakhina burst into the local zemstvo school in tears and begged that her children be allowed to go home. After one teacher tried to convince Malakhina that the children would not be branded with the mark of the Antichrist but simply were being enrolled in the school, "three peasants burst into the school building while one of them waved a stick and shouted: 'Children, run away from the school.' Raising an unimaginable panic, the children, without their coats or hats, began to jump out of the window and run away." One of the women urged the swelling crowd of onlookers to beat the teachers. In the end, public order was restored when the priest arrived, but this did not prevent the rumor from spreading to the neighboring district of Boguchar.[16]

Not all strangers were unwelcome. The historical narrative of late-imperial Russia was filled with the perpetual movement of religious people as improvements in overland travel enabled them to roam the countryside in a "reversed pilgrimage."[17] These religious travelers, the spiritual wanderers *(stranniki, podvizhniki)* and holy fools *(iurodivye)*, who created a human web of communication between disparate villages, challenged the traditional stationary geography of peasant piety and captured the imagination of villagers, who were fascinated by their strange appearances and tales about faraway lands.[18]

One such hero was Ioann, the "Sezenovskii Wanderer" (1791–1839), a serf from Voronezh province. Early on Ioann displayed an uncommon solitude, contemplative disposition, and desire to visit the holy sites in Kiev. At the tender age of fifteen Ioann became a holy fool, chained himself to his friend (the son of his lord), shirked all work responsibilities, and ran away to the Kiev Monastery of the Caves to became a novice. Monastic bliss was cut short abruptly when, after two years, a peasant from his natal village arrived in Kiev on a pilgrimage, recognized Ioann, and promptly informed their lord. To avoid extradition, Ioann began a six-year period of wandering before being invited to live in a solitary hut in Sezenov village (in neighboring Tambov province). Despite his extremely antisocial behavior, which included the homoerotic act of physically binding himself to his friend, word of Ioann's spiritual aura spread to other communities and brought many admirers to Sezenov long before his final resting place, the Sezenov Ioanno-Kazan women's monastery, became a center of peasant pilgrimage.[19]

More sedentary rural versions of wandering holy people were peasant lay nuns *(derevenskie monashki)*, a relatively new phenomenon in village society.[20] Pledged in childhood by their parents or by their own vows made during adolescence or early adulthood, lay nuns dedicated themselves to a life of poverty, chastity, and learning. While formally shunning monasticism, some of these devout women organized their own communities complete with an "abbess."[21] In order to support themselves, they read prayers for the dead and taught village children to read and write. As with so many aspects of folk piety, the activities of these pious laywomen occupied the ambiguous domain between local and universal religion and implicitly challenged clerical authority, especially through their prayers for the dead and instruction about the faith.[22] Being from the peasantry, lay nuns enjoyed widespread popularity because they understood villagers' conceptions of the world as a stage for the "cosmic drama in which good triumphed over evil."[23] When the machinations of the animated spirits of nature were beyond the purview of spiritually motivated Orthodoxy, peasants turned to community members who possessed special powers, brewed secret potions, and cast spells.

Magic, Healing, and Women's Special Knowledge

Although peasants' belief in the powers of sorcery, witchcraft, and healing derived from their conception of the world as inhabited by benevolent and malevolent forces, the lack of medical and scientific personnel in rural Russia led most villagers to depend on magical cures and herbal treatments for their physical and psychological well-being.[24] The most ostensible practitioners of magic and herbology were sorcerers (m. *koldun*, f. *koldun'ia*), witches (m. *vedom*, f. *ved'ma*), and "knowers" or herbal healers (m. *znakhar'*, f. *znakharka*).[25] As peasant counterparts of medical and scientific specialists, these sorcerers, witches, and healers ministered to the physically and psychologically afflicted members of the community, dispensed personal advice, and assisted with veterinary and agricultural problems. Just as doctors, nurses, midwives, therapists, veterinarians, and agronomists were set apart from the rest of society by their education and professional attire, practitioners of magic and healers distinguished themselves by their lifestyle, appearance, and aura. Settling on village outskirts and moving about in the dark of night, they dispensed magical potions and practiced secret rituals behind darkened windows and locked doors. To these peculiar habits could be added distinctive physical traits that putatively included excessive body hair, unusual birthmarks, and extremely disagreeable personalities. When good and evil forces in the village remained in balance, sorcerers, witches, and healers lived in precarious harmony with the rest of the community. When village fortune appeared to be inescapably doomed, sorcerers, witches, and healers became easy targets of peasant malice.

Before they turned to sorcerers, witches, and healers, peasants in need of a cure first consulted with adult female relatives, the most immediate sources of knowledge about folk remedies. As domestic specialists, women advised household members about curatives and provided psychological comfort. Fevers, among the most dreaded of common ailments because of their quick onset and seemingly endless variety, were especially difficult to treat. A popular cure required that a series of powerful words be written on a piece of paper and worn around the neck for six weeks before burning and drinking it with holy water. Another prescription called for the construction of a dozen dolls, representing the twelve sisters of fever, to be hung under the fire of the stove.[26] To reverse the effect of or protect against the evil eye, which caused all sorts of physical and psychic trauma, a charm might be uttered that invoked the name of the Lord, the Mother of God, and the saints, followed by the sign of the cross and the word "Amen." Simply mentioning the Holy Trinity and Mother of God was thought to affect an outcome.[27] Toothache, a common affliction with many possible cures, could be alleviated during the Sunday liturgy: "when the deacon says 'receive the body of Christ [while giving out communion],' one must say 'and take my painful teeth.'"[28] These and other remedies were part of women's special knowledge that was passed through the generations by mothers anxious to prepare their daughters for married life and parenting responsibilities.

As in most agrarian societies, the generative powers of women featured prominently in folk healing and was related to popular beliefs about the sacrality of Mother Earth. As a result, Russian peasant women were often depicted and treated as highly localized earth mother cum domestic Mother-of-God figures, who diligently guarded village spirituality and morality.[29] As problem solvers in the domestic sphere, peasant women may not have possessed the same powers or aura as magicians and healers, but their overall contribution to the well-being of the household was unmatched.[30] Young mothers relied on the advice of more experienced women of the household on matters ranging from prenatal care and "birth training" (a mixed bag of superstition and practical information) to herbal interventions. To the fortunate 50 percent of children who survived their first five years of life, mothers, aunts, and grandmothers were also a source of knowledge about the world, which was conveyed at every turn and reinforced by the lullabies they sang, the stories they told, the games they played, the clothes and ritual fabrics they sewed, and the behaviors they cultivated. Despite all of the problems of traditional peasant child rearing and folk remedies, women mostly succeeded in creating a modicum of safety and security in a world fraught with uncertainties and dangers. In their capacity as upholders of folk piety and protectors of household welfare, peasant women represented the embodiment of village morality, and, despite their dependence on magical and herbal treatments for common ailments, they regularly earned the praise of church leaders, who held them up as moral beacons in an otherwise dark village landscape.

Heresy and Otherness

Considering the wide range of belief and practice that fell under the broad umbrella of Orthodox piety with its ample room for spiritual wanderers, witches, "knowers," and domestic healers, who were the heterodox and heretical in the eyes of late-tsarist church leaders? Strictly speaking, practitioners of any faith may be labeled heterodox if their beliefs and practices do not conform to dogma. The Russian Orthodox Church seldom resorted to such designations and instead pragmatically included the heterodox practices already described in this chapter, even while considering peasant piety to be little more than paganism dressed up as Christianity.[31] As Archbishop Anastasii observed in 1890 during his first parish visits as prelate of Voronezh, Orthodox Christianity remained a purely external *(vneshnii)* matter rather than one of deep internal *(vnutrenii)* conviction for most peasants. As he pointed out two years later, "The simple people *(liudy prostye)* in general . . . are not capable of giving an intelligent answer about their faith."[32]

Following this line of reasoning, official Orthodoxy defined heretics as those current or erstwhile members of the faith who renounced the teachings and the authority of the church, yet remained religious. In the parlance of educated believers, these were the followers of the so-called false teachings *(lzheucheniia)* of Old Believers *(starovertsy, staroobriady, raskol'niki)*, Flagellants *(khlysty)*, New Israelites *(novo-izraeltsy)*, Milk Drinkers *(molokane)*, Pashkovites *(pashkovsty)*, and Tolstoyans *(tolstovsty)*.[33] At the beginning of the twentieth century, nonbelievers—atheists *(ateisty)* and "the godless" *(bezbozhie)* were added to this group, although these terms did not enter peasant linguistic currency until revolutionary propaganda began to dominate public discourse after overthrow of the tsar in February 1917.[34]

The precise number of heretics in rural Russia remains a matter of speculation. Before 1905, when the law of religious toleration cleared the way for members of all confessions to profess their faith without the threat of persecution, church officials considered anyone baptized in the Orthodox faith as one of their own. The use of infant baptism as the standard by which to count members meant that conversions to other faiths later in life or the widespread practice among sectarians to observe the rituals of Orthodoxy in order to stave off harassment by local authorities and neighbors did not make their way into official statistics.[35] Comprising about one percent of the population, Old Believers had limited success in converting the population to their faith and instead preferred to live quietly among the Orthodox. Nonetheless, Orthodox clergymen viewed the followers of Old Belief to be an invidious presence in need of being uprooted. To be sure, the church's response to its unidentical twin was a carry-over from the original schism two centuries earlier, but jealousy also motivated late-imperial clergymen as they, along with a significant portion of the lay population, were impressed with the sober way of life, literary skills, and astute knowledge of religious texts (especially the Holy Scriptures) characteristic of Old Believers and most sectarian groups.[36]

Given the widespread admiration for Old Believers and sectarians in Voronezh province, how did religious difference play out at the village level? The answer to this question, like so many others in Russian village history, was determined by boundaries, in this case between spiritual insid-

Fig. 4—Old Believer Church of the Veil, Valuiki District, 1906

ers and outsiders. Most information about peasant perceptions of Old Believers and sectarians was elicited in inquiries about otherness, which created the false impression that antagonisms between the Orthodox and heretics were the result of religious difference.[37] When it came to literacy, Orthodox peasants admired Old Believers' ability to read because it provided immediate access to teachings of the faith and thus lessened their dependence on cultural superiors for religious knowledge. Peasants also considered literacy to be an impetus for the nontraditional economic activity of Old Believers, which helped to release them from the grip of poverty that was caused by subsistence farming. Some Orthodox peasants even adopted Old Believer customs, such as the two-finger cross or deep prostrations, without understanding why variation in practice should separate adherents to what was, at least in the minds of most villagers, a common faith.[38] In some communities, Orthodox peasants tolerated the most obvious displays of heretical faith—houses of worship—such as the Church of the Veil, which belonged to the Old Believers in Valuiki. Favorable relations with the local Orthodox population allowed Old Believer parishioners of the Church of the Veil to renovate and enlarge their church first in 1879, and again in 1906, in order to meet the needs of a growing congregation (see fig. 4).[39]

Orthodox peasants' tolerant attitudes about Old Belief and sectarianism was regularly noted by diocesan missionaries as a significant obstacle to their proselytization efforts. In the Voronezh, Novokhopersk, and Bobrov Districts, where sectarian groups were especially active, regular public debates between the diocesan missionary and Old Believer and sectarian leaders usually ended in humiliation for the proponents of Orthodoxy, whose strongest argument was blind faith in the state religion. When this tack failed, some clergymen turned to bullying and enlisted the assistance of the local police. The irony of the situation may not have escaped peasant notice, as the very same church leaders who fought against the irrational superstitions of the village were now proposing an emotional-spiritual defense against sectarian logic.[40] The two unequal sides in the struggle for souls became so embattled that in a synodal decree of 1895 Archbishop Anastasii was ordered to explain to his clergy that the best way of fighting the "false teachings" of sectarian groups was not through coercion, but through clerical surveillance of their propagators, spiritual instruction connected with church services, and religious lessons in the primary schools.[41]

Despite church authorities' anxieties about the rising apostasy of the peasantry, confessional records indicate that Orthodox Christianity was the faith of at least 99 percent of the Voronezh peasantry throughout the late-imperial period, even after 1905. The notoriety of local sectarian groups, however, proved a constant embarrassment to local religious authorities, who struggled to explain why their predominantly Orthodox diocese proved a conducive spawning ground for the heterodox. One of the most famous outbursts of sectarian activity in Russia occurred in Voronezh province during the 1880s and 1890s as peasants gathered around Vasilii Fedorovich Mokshin, a prominent Flagellant activist and self-proclaimed living Christ. Mokshin, a peasant from Dankovo village in the district of Voronezh, the main "nest" (gnezdo) of the Flagellant sect in the diocese, rejected the Orthodox Church and its sacraments and icons. His own experience of peasant piety led him to condemn its most salient aspects, including the widespread reverence for saints' relics, which he dismissed as a form of idolatry. The alternative religious experience offered by Mokshin contained monastic overtones and required followers to embrace true Christian living based on respect and compassion toward others. In place of the Orthodox liturgy was a charismatic worship service led by Mokshin, at which, according to police investigations, his followers sang until "[t]hey became quite unlike their usual selves."[42]

Diocesan missionaries were deeply troubled by Mokshin's claims and his followers' behavior, especially their open violation of prevailing sexual norms. Parish clergymen and Orthodox peasants were less prudish and instead worried about Mokshin's claim to be the Messiah, his prayer meetings with followers, who were known as "apostles," a certain virgin named Agrafena (with whom he was particularly close) being called "the Mother of God," and his rejection of secular authorities. In 1880, after being found guilty of spreading the Flagellant heresy among peasants and of renouncing the church and its sacraments, Mokshin was exiled to the Caucasus, where he continued to preach while supporting himself by working as a tailor. After a few years, Mokshin was allowed to return to Voronezh Diocese, where he settled in a village in the Bobrov District. What undid him was not his preaching, but his conviction for adultery in 1889 and his alcoholism. A man of all trades, who was not easily deterred, Mokshin opened a successful public house, which he apparently ran until his death from alcoholism in 1894. Despite the lack of a successor, the Flagellant supporters of Mokshin remained strong, something that Archbishop Anastasii attributed to the dark morals of the village and the appeal of urban youth culture among peasant adolescents and young adults.[43]

What made this self-proclaimed messiah so attractive to peasants? According to one Roman Riabykh, a loyal follower, it was Mokshin's charismatic presence and his ability to perform miracles. In addition to his charisma and wondrous powers, the appeal of Mokshin's teachings was a nonsacerdotal, deritualized Christianity that offered unmediated communication with the divine, direct knowledge of the Gospels and other holy writings that were inaccessible in the church Slavonic of the liturgies, and active participation in religious services, particularly group singing.[44] If church officials knew so much about Mokshin and his teachings, why was he allowed to preach openly? As long as their official numbers remained low, heretics did not warrant harsher methods by clergymen preoccupied with the revival of the clerical estate, the dwindling number of seminarians taking the priestly vows, the establishment of a parish school system, the rise of new and difficult-to-supervise forms of lay spirituality, and the demands of peasant parishioners for parish reform. Most important was the fact that the religious activity of Mokshin and his followers had deep roots in folk beliefs about the forces of nature, the powers of special people, and direct communication with the supernatural.

When antagonisms arose between Orthodox and non-Orthodox peasants, the cause was usually cultural difference rather than religious antagonism, such as Old Believers' shunning of tobacco and smoking, predilection for their own utensils even when eating and drinking in public, and insistence on praying only to their own icons.[45] Another point of friction between these two groups was conversion from one side to the other, which was usually a matter of convenience to allow mixed marriages to be performed. Marital reasons for conversion between Old Belief and Orthodoxy were viewed, however, with suspicion by the two communities, and converts were expected to revert to their previous faith upon the arrival of their firstborn.[46] Conversions of convenience inevitably led to tensions that extended beyond the family, and the community was left to decide whether religious reversion was something that had been intended all along or was a more contemplative transformation. In the end, the line between tolerance and intolerance depended on Orthodox peasants' willingness to embrace non-Orthodox believers.

Beginning in the late 1890s, the relations between Orthodox and sectarian peasants took a new and violent turn.[47] A typical example comes from

Boguchar District in 1903 when Orthodox peasants turned their hostility toward a small group of Flagellant peasants who regularly met to discuss their faith, pray to icons, and sing psalms. For unexplained reasons, the local Orthodox suddenly decided to put an end to these private meetings. Unsuccessful in their attempts, the Orthodox villagers asked the diocesan missionary and the township elder to organize a public interrogation of the Flagellants. More than three thousand people attended the event and watched as the twenty Flagellant defendants refused to answer questions about their faith and their reasons for leaving the church. Several Orthodox villagers became impatient and began to taunt and hit the accused, who ran for cover in the township administration building. When a group of enraged Orthodox faithful reached the building, they broke down the door and dragged the Flagellants outside to finish the job in full public view. At the last moment, the diocesan missionary and parish clergy arrived and, on humanitarian grounds, pled for the lives of the Flagellants. In the end, the missionary left the parish, having accomplished nothing, and the Flagellants returned home.[48]

While Orthodox peasants generally maintained a healthy curiosity in their confessionally different fellow villagers, church leaders reacted with an increasingly exaggerated trepidation that was finally confirmed by the law on religious tolerance in 1905. For the next twelve years, the Orthodox episcopate intensified its efforts to bring folk piety in line with institutional praxis rather than grapple with the troubling secularism of civic-minded zemstvo workers and returning seasonal laborers or the effects of rising literacy rates and the growing popularity of literature for the people. As church leaders fought to preserve their narrowing authority and privilege in religious, social, and cultural spheres, they depended on local civil authorities to provide additional support in the form of surveillance and missionary work, all in the name of defending two main pillars of autocracy, Orthodox Christianity and the peasantry, with the purported goal of improving the lot of the people.

Clinging to the Faith

Throughout the post-emancipation period, the household and community remained the fundamental structures of the peasant world. Although oppressive at times, communal norms provided villagers with a broad social net that was based on a division of the world into sacred and profane spheres whose uneasy relationship led to endless calamities. Organizing their temporal space in this way, peasants searched for effective ways to channel benevolent supernatural forces in an attempt to control the uncertainties of life. By combining what they accepted as the most essential elements of institutional and noninstitutional Orthodoxy, peasants were able to preserve traditions that reinforced communal spirit and an understanding—

however unrealistic—of the village as an autarkic organic whole, even as their communities slowly became economically and psychologically dependent on the outside world. Thinking themselves to be Orthodox in every way, peasants did not consider their enchanted view of the world anything less than Christian. Nor were peasants alone; vestiges of superstition could be found in urban culture and among educated Russians.[49]

The presumed irrationality of peasant piety did not fit into the tidy intellectual frameworks of the newly created scholarly disciplines. Although high-minded explanations of peasant piety might have been useful for the readers of secular and religious publications, they included few genuine attempts to comprehend its complexity, particularly the peaceful coexistence of diverse expressions of Orthodox faith, even within households and individuals. By the mid-1890s, Orthodox leaders concerned about the effects of literacy blamed the popular press for its negative influence on peasants with enough education to be able to read. In the words of Archbishop Anastasii, "a coldness toward the faith," an expression that until this time had been used by Voronezh bishops only to describe the irreligiosity of educated Russians, was being planted in the minds of the people.[50] After 1905, this "coldness" was framed in terms of a growing antichurch and antireligion movement that purportedly was caused by the general moral decay of village life.[51] If peasants held firmly to their age-old religious beliefs, church leaders like Archbishop Tikhon demonstrated equal loyalty to traditional stereotypes of peasant piety.

Why were church authorities and educated Russians unable to view traditional peasant piety as a means of providing comfort and meaning to villagers as they adjusted to modern life? Trained in the Enlightenment tradition, it was natural to reject anything that challenged logical and rational thought. A less articulated explanation is that the ascetic and eremitic traditions of the faith, which emphasized independent piety, resonated with the peasantry, and challenged the institutional authority of the church.[52] Left with few other supports to help them cope with the unsettling prospects of modern life, for many peasants, new and old, the supernatural sphere offered the most assured source of hope for the future.

Telling Time—*Eternal Truths, Mortal Fates*

The difference between [urban and peasant Russia] appeared in the way the
year was delineated into customs marking the procession of everyday life.
With the reform of Peter the Great, the city received a civil calendar that
divided the year into months and days. Peasants [however] still based everything on church events and church holidays.

—Ivan Stoliarov, *Zapiski russkogo krest'ianina*

*W*hen printed calendars intended for the peasantry
were introduced at the end of the nineteenth century, they tacitly acknowledged the dual function of agro-Christian holidays, which marked human and historical time in a way that
reaffirmed the beliefs, traditions, and morals of the community.
Taking the form of a farmer's almanac, these calendars were
adorned with illustrated covers that depicted hard-working
peasants using primitive tools to work the land. In the distance
behind the fields stood a church, its crossed domes and implied
liturgies alluding to the semireligious nature of farming in
late-tsarist Russia. Framing this scene was a border of tiny
words listing important events in church and state history.
Turning the page, the peasant reader discovered a dozen or so
pages providing the main religious holidays for each month,
almost like a sacred partner to the agricultural timetables
found on the succeeding pages.[1] By connecting the repetitious performance of sacred life with the mundane reality of
agricultural schedules, calendars intended for the peasantry
assimilated popular conceptions of eternal and human time,
the former constructed around grand tales and mythical heroes, the latter rooted in the progressive stages of human and
communal life.[2]

While the peasant ritual year was filled with holiday observations of the changing seasons, at less fixed times of the year peasants marked the stages of human life with celebration or mourning that defined expectations for personal fates and forecasted prospects for communal prosperity. Metaphorically, rituals and customs that accompanied birth, marriage, and death represented the future, present, and past of a household and provided a community with a cultural genealogy that became embedded in peasant cosmology.[3] As rapid industrialization and seasonal labor routines began to affect village demographics, birth and death customs changed little because peasants remained vulnerable to debilitating diseases and some of the highest infant mortality rates in Europe.[4] Marriage customs proved, however, more flexible as education and seasonal labor began to replace traditional matchmaking with individual choice.[5] For different reasons, calendric holidays and life-cycle rituals provided regular opportunities for the eternal truths held by communities to be merged with the mortal fates of individual lives.

Holidays: From Fasts to Feasts

In late-tsarist Russia, the Orthodox year was divided into two main fast and feast periods—St. Philip's fast *(filippovki)* and Christmastide *(sviatki)*, and Great Lent *(Velikii Post)* and Easter *(Paskha)*—and twelve major feast days (some of which were preceded by shorter periods of abstention and prayer).[6] A second category of religious holidays was observed by each community and honored village churches, saintly patrons, and wondrous icons. Celebrated at the initiative of local believers, these lesser-known feast days constituted a flexible and productive "little" tradition with "its own calendar of sacred times" that complemented the official tradition of the Russian Orthodox Church.[7] If fasts (including Wednesdays and Fridays), holidays, and Sundays are counted, between two-thirds and nine-tenths of the year were imbued with religious meaning by Voronezh peasants and helped to create a sense of timelessness. As the same calendric rotations churned eternally, at times like background music, at times like a main chorus, individuals entered and departed from the stage of village life without fundamentally altering the rhythm (see appendix table 1).[8]

According to Orthodox tradition, the peak of the ecclesiastical year, Easter, serves as the focal point for the remainder of the religious calendar. While church sermons and holiday preaching reiterated the preeminence of *Paskha* in the festal year, peasants took a more egalitarian approach and designated equal status to Christmas, which they termed the "winter Easter." In anticipation of Christmas, entire villages observed the St. Philip's fast, forty days of strict abstention from meat, fish, dairy products, alcohol, and sexual activity. During this period, fish was permitted only on two special occasions: the day of the Presentation of the Mother of God in the

Temple on 21 November and the feast of St. Nicholas on 6 December. Although fasting was an individual matter, pressures from family and friends meant that this form of spirituality also had its social aspects, and members of the community who did not follow the strict regime could expect to be shunned, chastised, or mocked by fellow villagers. By mid-December, as peasants grew weary from fasting and the effects of winter darkness, they anxiously awaited the grand showcase of the Christmas Eve liturgy, whose completion launched a twelve-day period of Yuletide festivities.[9]

As a much needed period of merriment during the darkest and coldest time of the winter, when socializing was conducted mostly indoors, Yuletide brought people out of their physical isolation and onto the streets for *narodnoe gul'iane*, a winter carnival of excessive revelry.[10] Yuletide began with the "abundant" *(bogatyi)* Christmas Eve *(sochel'nik)*, peaked on New Year's Eve, and ended with the "meager" *(golodnyi)* night before Epiphany (5 January, also called *sochel'nik)*. The religious sobriety of church services was followed (and sometimes accompanied) by drunken abandon; the "famine" of Lenten fasts was followed by the "feast" of celebration, and in good times and bad, peasant tables were laden with seasonal delicacies for human consumption and ritual offering. Adult trepidation about the future was allayed by a playful belief in the magical formulas of children's fortunetelling games *(igry)* and adolescents' "divination" *(gadanie)* about their prospects for marriage in the upcoming year. Carolers earned pocket money as they walked around the village *(koliadovat'* or *khodit' Khrista slavit')*, and clergymen visited all the homes in the parish to offer blessings and collect gifts.

If Christmas celebrated life in the dead of winter, the New Year holiday looked cautiously to the future. Whatever happened on the first day of the year was considered to be an omen for the next twelve months, and measures were taken to ensure prosperity and good fortune. On New Year's Eve families said prayers in the sacred corner of the peasant hovel, after which the household head appealed to the forces of nature; walking into the yard, he invited Winter, personified as a frost-covered man, to join in the fun. At midnight an elderly man from the community announced the new year before the church bells were rung to signal the calendric change and to welcome beneficent supernatural forces to the parish. On the following day village boys filled their mittens with a variety of seeds, which symbolized the generative powers of nature, and later scattered them in the sacred corner before sprinkling the mixture around the village.[11] The reproductive and magical powers that brought forth life were the focus of divination that was popular among girls who hoped and dreamed of suitable marriage partners.[12]

Epiphany marked the end of Yuletide and lent itself well to the promotion of communal prosperity in the form of a good harvest. Just as the baptism of Christ symbolized the death of the old Adam and the birth of the new eternal life, blessings of local water sources were expected to benefit the spiritual lives of believers, as well as transform the dead ground, frozen under the winter snow, into vibrant fields of grain several months later.

Water blessed during Epiphany liturgy was taken home in vials and buckets that believers brought with them to church, and these vessels of sacred liquid were stored in the sacred corner except when they were used for spiritual and medical emergencies.[13] Upon returning home from church, the eldest male symbolically invited good fortune to the household by sprinkling its members, farm and domestic animals, and buildings with a few drops of the blessed water. As a precaution against unclean forces, crosses were then drawn on gates, doors, and windows, all marginal spaces that were key points of entry into the peasant domicile. The family then gathered before the icon shelf to beseech deceased relatives to protect the household against misfortune before each member swallowed a bit of the sacred water, which symbolically broke the day's strict fast.[14] Peasant eagerness to obtain the water occasionally led to unruliness during blessing services, requiring the intervention of the local police. When a priest in the Pavlovsk District refused to bless the local water source on Epiphany because he had forgotten to obtain police authorization for an outdoor ceremony, peasants raised a ruckus until, "at the demand of the parishioners who were acting out of misunderstanding and rudeness," the priest was escorted to the river bank and forced to perform the service.[15]

The communal jollity of Yuletide was not to be experienced again until *maslenitsa,* or Shrovetide, set into motion a week-long carnival that began on the eighth Sunday before Easter.[16] As elsewhere in Europe where Shrovetide preceded the onset of Great Lent, *maslenitsa* was a time of abundance that contrasted with the lean and somber weeks of abstention that lay ahead.[17] Popular nomenclature expressed these excesses by referring to *maslenitsa* as the week of "gluttony," "drunkenness," and "ruinousness." Debauchery among adults had its more innocent parallel in youthful courtship rituals that included mixed-sex sledding, skating, and tobogganing, each providing moments of privacy that allowed young girls and boys to circumvent traditional matchmaking by appealing directly to their beloved.[18] When festivities ended on "Forgiveness Sunday" *(Proshchennoe Voskresen'e)* with a spiritual cleansing similar to confession and absolution in Catholic traditions, a profound religious solemnity fell upon the village like a wet blanket dousing a fire as peasants shifted their attention to spiritual matters.

Public expressions of Lenten spirituality included the fulfillment of annual confession and communion obligations, regular church attendance, and fasting. Private devotion emphasized prayer and, for the literate, religio-moral readings.[19] Despite the heavy burdens of spring field work, women were inclined to embark on pilgrimages to revered and wonderworking objects in nearby villages, towns, and cities, as well as to the shrines of local Saints Mitrofan and Tikhon, the Kievan Monastery of the Caves, the Holy Land, and the capital of ecumenical Orthodoxy, Constantinople. Because Great Lent coincided with the start of the spring sowing season, peasant communities expected their clergy to bless the fields and animals as part of the ritual driving of the cattle to pasture on the feast days of St. Eudocia (1 March) and St. George (23 April). The Annunciation to the Virgin Mary on 25 March merged the agrarian motifs of St. Eudocia and St. George with human fertility, which not only looked ahead to Christmas nine months later, but also recalled the burdens and responsibilities of bringing new life, in any form, into the world.

With the arrival of Holy Week, the approaching celebration of Easter was keenly felt not only because of the imminent conclusion to a long period of abstention, but also because this Christian holiday, more than any other in the Orthodox calendar, held out the dual message of hope and salvation. Holy Week began with Palm Sunday *(Verbnoe Voskresen'e)*, which antici-pated both the death and resurrection of Christ and exalted his triumphant entry into Jerusalem. Symbolically reenacting this biblical moment, bleat-ing sheep were led to the village church while the faithful waved pussy wil-lows, a symbol of nature reborn, and shouted "Hosanna! Hosanna!" Palm Sunday also launched the strictest fast period of Great Lent, when food be-came even more modest or was foregone altogether, and when the rigors of spiritual examination forbade even the exchange of glances with fellow vil-lagers. On Holy Thursday peasants went to church to hear the twelve Gospel accounts of the last days of Jesus' life. Returning home with lit can-dles symbolizing the victory of light over darkness, the household head would "mark in the form of a cross the gate of the household compound, walk around the yard, and go into the animal shed and all dark corners."[20] Then a cross was burnt into the door of the peasant cottage, the ceiling, and tie beams before scrutinizing all corners to determine if prosperity (mossiness) or deprivation (dryness) lay in the future.[21]

Easter gathered diverse members of the community in a week-long festi-val that brought the spring holiday cycle full circle from Shrovetide to Bright Week *(svetlaia sed'mitsa)* following the Resurrection. Just as Christ broke the chains of hell when he rose from the dead, the evil hold of spells was thought to be broken, and believers were given a new start on life. An-ticipation and excitement mounted as the hands of the clock neared mid-night on Holy Saturday, when every light was extinguished except for a solitary candle held by the priest from whose flame the entire community would be illuminated anew. At the stroke of midnight, as if a match had been set to firewood, villages suddenly ignited in a social and cultural resur-rection of joy and festivity that lasted for fifty days until Pentecost. With church bells ringing in the background, the air was filled with exclamations of "Christ has risen!" shouted by the faithful. A customary breaking of bread at church after the Resurrection service formally concluded the Lenten fast and reinforced the sense of unity created during the long period leading to Easter.[22]

Throughout the fifty days following Easter, the message of Christ's resur-rection was relived in rituals aimed at ensuring a good harvest and commu-nal well-being. Bright Week began with visitations to each household by

the priest and was as important for his income as it was for the popular belief that his blessing would bring good fortune. Throughout the week Easter
eggs, holiday foods, and wine were taken to the graves of departed family
members with the hope that the deceased would protect the crops and live-
stock. Idiosyncratic family customs were supplemented by communal
memorial services in the village cemetery when the priest arrived with
icons to say general prayers while ritual lamentations were performed by
local professionals.[23] During the fourth week of Easter, special prayers were
said over wells and water sources, whose blessed properties would serve as
facilitators of an abundant harvest. From Ascension Thursday *(semik)* until
Pentecost *(Troitsa)*, many communities remained wary of the beautiful water nymphs *(rusalki)*, who they believed suddenly came alive during this
brief period *(rusal'naia nedelia)*. Although the sirenlike beauty of the
nymphs threatened young men who, according to popular belief, would
drown if they were seduced, *rusalki* were more associated with fertility. Two
widespread practices sought to transfer the mythical aura of *rusalki* to the
community. The first took place in a festival of maidenhood when young
girls decorated the parish church with wreaths they wove using local green-
ery. The second began with a parade through the village with a straw
rusalka doll which ended with a ritualistic burning, mock funeral ceremony, complete with prayers by the village priest and ritual lamentation by
peasant women, and burial in a corner of the grain fields so that its special
powers would fertilize the soil.[24]

Although the remainder of the year was filled with alternating fast periods and feast days, the Yule and Easter cycles were the most important in
the peasant holiday calendar. Each fast and feast had its individual moments of devotion, but in late-imperial Russia indications of private religiosity were critical public markers that defined peasants, regardless of their
motivations, as members of a community. The passage of time as a personal
experience distinguished holidays from life-cycle rituals.

Life-Cycle Rituals and the Passage of Human Time

Ritual in illiterate cultures reminds people of their past while giving
meaning to the present and purpose to the future. Although the majority
of Russian peasants probably devoted little time to existential questions or
programs for personal development, few were willing to surrender themselves to the whims of fate and relied on superstitious rituals to ward off
evil forces, prevent the spread of disease, and ensure abundant harvests.
From cradle to grave and beyond, signs and omens portended the future,
customary acts and behaviors warded off evil, and magical incantations
and potions effected desired results. Three moments in life carried special
significance for the individual's transition from one stage to another: birth,
marriage, and death.

BIRTH AND BAPTISM

Pregnancy came as a mixed blessing despite the prevailing wisdom that a large household was a measure of wealth. The road to that wealth was fraught with many obstacles, but by following social and cultural conventions peasants could at least hope to brighten their prospects. The arrival of another "mouth" (edok) to feed required workloads to be reassigned and resources to be redirected to the mother and baby.[25] Despite the best intentions of the mother and other household members, the newborn child had only a 50 percent chance of surviving the first five years of life. The precariousness of life led peasants to play a game of hide-and-seek with evil forces that involved secrecy and suspicion. During childbirth, which usually took place behind the locked doors of the bathhouse, a trusted midwife and female relatives assisted in the safe delivery of the child and defended against the powers of nature that were especially active during the vulnerable transitional moment from prenatal to postpartum existence. Doors to the bathhouse were guarded, incantations repeated, prayers uttered, but all of this could prove fruitless if evil forces were alerted by a scream or shout escaping from the lips of the laboring mother. To ease the pain of labor, other family members, including the laboring father, prayed, lit church candles, and performed folk rituals that symbolized the release of tension, the relaxation of muscles, and the opening of blockages.[26] Once the child was delivered, physical characteristics were noted for what they might reveal about his or her fate much the way a midwife today counts the fingers and toes of a newborn.[27]

Because of high mortality rates, infants were baptized a few days after birth to ensure a place in the Kingdom of Heaven and to protect against misfortune.[28] Through the rite of baptism, babies were formally accepted into the parish and village communities, but usually in the absence of their parents, who waited at home until the child returned from church in the arms of the godparents.[29] In some parishes, the newborn received a name from the priest, who may have fulfilled his role symbolically by honoring the parents' wishes or by acting as a spiritual father and giving a name that would serve as a role model. Upon their return from church, the godparents ceremoniously returned the infant to the mother, who placed the baby in a cradle or bed sprinkled with coins for good luck. The celebratory dinner following the baptism honored the midwife for guiding the child safely into the world and for relieving the new mother of her usual domestic duties during the first week after the birth. As a reminder of the mother's suffering during childbirth, the midwife served the father a bitter dish of heavily salted boiled wheat. Toasts to the mother and good wishes for the baby's health were followed by a ritual exchange of gifts between the parents and godparents, who presented the baby with a sacred towel that served as a conveyance for protective powers until death. The completion of the festivities marked the mother's resumption of normal domestic responsibilities and the first stage of the child's integration into the household.[30]

Already from birth the family distinguished between the social value of boys and girls, who were to be treated differently. The sex of the newborn child was, after all, critical to the future of the family, whose fortunes could improve with the survival of enough sons or could be destroyed with the birth of only daughters, who were often treated as temporary guests and as another mouth to feed until they wed and moved away from home.[31] The predicament of first-time parents was aptly put in two popular proverbs: "If the first child is a boy, then the husband will respect his wife," and, "If the first child is a girl, then the husband and wife will never get along."[32] Although child rearing was the general responsibility of both parents, a greater burden was placed on mothers, whose carelessness, overindulgence, or misjudgments would be blamed when their children came of marriageable age.

MATCHMAKING AND MARRIAGE

Unlike birth or death rituals, matchmaking and marriage customs usually occurred at designated times of the year, with most weddings taking place between the end of the harvest and the onset of the St. Philip's fast, at the end of Yuletide, or just after Bright Week. These were convenient times of general communal festivity that coincided with abundant food supplies, but they also adhered to church restrictions on marriage during fast periods, Yuletide, Bright Week, and the twelve major feast days.[33]

If baptism was an Orthodox birthright, then marriage signified peasant youths' tacit acceptance of communal norms, their passage into adult life, and the acquisition of new responsibilities, the most important of which was the establishment of a new family unit that would serve as the basis for a new household, tax unit, and communal landholder. Despite changing attitudes toward matchmaking as a result of increased contacts between urban and rural areas in the last decades of the nineteenth century, courtship and individual choice were regularly overruled by the mutual economic and social interests of the commune and household.[34] Following one's heart and ignoring society's norms could result in being ostracized, ridiculed, or disowned by the community and family; in extreme cases, parents reacted to the wayward amorous inclinations of their children by contracting a marriage with someone more suitable to household interests, often with disastrous results.[35] One consequence of traditional matchmaking rituals was that the life of adolescent peasant children was focused on marriage as an event that would have the greatest influence on their adult (and eternal) life.[36]

Matchmakers *(svaty, svakhi)* were seldom the initiators of a union and instead acted as symbolic deal makers who performed a service for the parents while lending a sympathetic ear to the wishes of the children. To assess characteristics and qualifications of village adolescents of marriageable age (sixteen for girls, and eighteen for boys), matchmakers and parents chaperoned parties and dances that offered venues for acceptable social contact between the sexes.[37] These occasions also provided opportunities for young girls and boys to find their own partner. Once a boy found a suitable girl, with the backing of his parents, a matchmaker brokered a deal and conveyed the terms of the dowry and bride price.

The highly ritualized ceremonial agreement to a match reinforced the patriarchal foundation of peasant life in the crude terms of a property transaction. At the start, the young girl's subordinate status as an object to be manipulated was depicted in her parents' symbolic offering of her as desirable "merchandise" for the inspection of the prospective in-laws. In a nod to the church's exhortations against forced marriages, which dated to the Middle Ages, the soon to be betrothed were asked for their assent, to which they gave their ritual replies.[38] Then the family of the boy "paid" for the girl with cash and gifts, sealing the deal with a ritual handshake or handclasp that signaled the beginning of a celebratory feast and drinking spree. Many communities sandwiched in a prayer for the couple before the festivities began, and most betrothed couples made symbolic prostrations of appreciation and respect before their respective parents.[39] Between the engagement party and the wedding itself as much as a year might pass. During this time the girl focused her attention and activities on the impending loss of the familiar and relatively carefree maiden life she had enjoyed thus far and the difficulties she would face as an outsider once she took up residence with her husband's family. The engagement period reached a crescendo with the hen *(devichnik)* and bachelor *(mal'chishnik)* parties a few days before the wedding, a last opportunity for the girl's friends to perform ritual laments and bid her farewell as if she were never to be seen again, and a final chance for the groom to carouse with his mates without having to account for his whereabouts.[40]

On the day of the wedding, the young bride stood in mourning as her girlfriends again sang lamentations that spoke of the transition from the familiar comfort of her natal home to the unfriendly residence of her in-laws.[41] Then, without looking back, she departed for the church, with icon in hand, on a carriage sent by her in-laws as her mother sprinkled it with coins and grain for luck.[42] Meanwhile the young groom bid his parents farewell and received their blessing before leaving for the matrimonial ceremony. During the journey to the parish church, which was fraught with danger (real and imagined), the couple could be spoiled or given the evil eye. To protect the bride from the evil eye, a special cloth was tied to her clothing, and jingling bells were hung on the horses to frighten away lurking demons. The bride's godmother or the matchmaker accompanied her to the church while guarding a container holding the earrings, bracelets, and ornamental headgear that would soon become the decorative reminders of her status as a married woman.[43] During the church rite *(venchanie, venets)* a blessed ritual towel (usually made by the relatives of the girl) was given to the couple as a veil of protection to be kept in the sacred corner and to be used during the baptism of children produced by the union.[44] A portion of the towel followed the couple to their graves and in this way provided eternal protection, as well as a sense of continuity between the living and the dead.[45]

The week-long communal celebration that followed the church rite proclaimed the changed status of village society, warned of the hardships of married life, and reminded the new couple of their obligation to procreate. To encourage the immediate creation of a new member of the village, on the night of the wedding the bridal couple was led by the best man and the matchmaker (or a female relative of the girl if the matchmaker was a man) to a specially prepared wedding hut in an outer building of the household. Calling them "prince and princess," an allusion to the church rite that crowned them as heads of their new family, the best man helped the groom to undress, and the matchmaker assisted the bride. Then they were led to their bed, which was covered with a quilt that earlier had been placed under the icon shelf. Their friends were invited into the chamber, where they sang and toasted the couple as the best man and matchmaker shook a large ritual cloth over the bed. Finally the matchmaker kissed the girl three times, unbraided her hair (symbolizing her departure from maidenhood), said a few prayers, and blessed the couple, before joining the best man in an all-night vigil outside the hut. The next morning the matchmaker and the best man would conduct a ritual sheet check to attest to the consummation of the marriage and report on the compatibility of the new couple.[46]

At the end of the festivities the newlyweds assumed their social responsibilities and began their normal work routines, although they usually lived apart from the rest of the household during the first few months of their marriage while they adjusted to their new life together and enjoyed a singular opportunity for private intimacy.[47] The young peasant woman now began a new life that, according to one observer, was "filled with entirely undeserved reproach, verbal abuse, and very often rude punishment, all of which are flung at her not only by her 'God-given' husband, but sometimes also by her father-in-law and brother-in-law."[48] Maltreatment was meted out, however, mostly by her mother-in-law, who assigned the daily chores and often berated the young bride. Such cruelty might be expected in the tight living quarters of the peasant cottage, which frequently reawakened the sexual feelings of an aging father-in-law or brothers-in-law.[49] The situation usually eased with the arrival of the first child, especially if it was a boy, but the inequities of married life continued as part of the larger inequalities between the sexes that were never far beneath the surface of village life.

As the social climax of their youth slowly faded into the past, the young couple became full members of the adult community. With the arrival of their own children, they would be expected to adhere to social norms governing baptism and soon enough would begin the process of identifying suitable partners for their own sons and daughters. In time and with good fortune, the once youthful couple would assume the mantle of elderly members of the household less important for their physical labor than their link with the disappearing past as they awaited the final moment of life.

DEATH AND THE AFTERLIFE

Death is one of the basic organizational motifs of life, and peasant beliefs about this final moment and post-mortem existence reveal much about the temporal reality of the village. Just as Jacques Le Goff's purgatory was about the "spacialization" of thought that related parts of a twelfth-century intellectual revolution with radical social changes, Russian peasant utterances about heaven and hell spoke about the human struggle to attain the good life.[50] In the idiom of the village, the afterlife was painted in materialistic hues that reflected peasants' struggles to influence, mollify, and gain control of the fates belonging to the chaotic and unknown "other world." The result was an order that mirrored religious, political, and social distinctions of earthly existence divided into three categories: the good (we), the bad (they), the not-so-good/not-so-bad.[51] Key to this other existence was the *geography of the afterlife,* or how peasants mapped heaven and hell.

Words provide a sense of this cosmic geography. *Rai* (literally, Paradise, or Eden, related to *raion,* region, or area) was a more educated way to refer to heaven, while *zagrobnaia zhizn'* (life beyond the grave), *tot svet* (the other world), and *budushchii vek* (the coming age) were more common expressions of concrete distinctions between two states of being. Working through the archeology of peasant beliefs leads to ancient myths about the Moist Mother Earth, whose warm embrace nestled those who had honored her by upholding the timeless laws of nature.[52] Orthodox peasants adhered to this vision of the sacred earth while searching for heaven in or above the clouds or beyond a rainbow, "a radiant place, where trees with beautiful fruits . . . flowers, and berries grow." In this scheme, heaven was the permanent residence of redeemed souls, who were escorted there by the angels and the saints and thereafter lived under angelic guard far from the suffering of demonic spirits. For the damned, hell was "a dark, terrible place in whose depths burned an inextinguishable fire" guarded by devils, demons, and goblins who prevented anyone from escaping. Located in the nether regions of the earth, hell was likened to a boiling cauldron of unbearable heat and darkness. This was the place to which sinners were led directly after death, under the escort of unclean spirits gleefully shouting: "One of ours, one of ours!"[53] For souls whose eternal status was unclear, a sort of purgatory *(chistilishche)* existed on a large precipice between good and evil. Russian purgatory, like its Western counterpart, gave the not-so-saintly/not-so-damned an opportunity to expiate their sins before the final judgment, usually with the prayers of their loved ones. In addition to the three regions of the afterlife, peasants also distinguished between the national and religious characteristics of the soul: Russian Orthodox Christians having a purer, more radiant content; followed by non-Orthodox Christians and members of other major religions living within Russia's borders *(inovertsy)* having mildly tarnished essences; and, finally, nonbelievers *(neveruiushchie)* and the condemned *(osuzhdennye).*[54]

Death itself was considered a natural part of life that could be avoided for only so long with the assistance of ruses or tricks, but as the popular saying admitted, "We'll drink and be merry, and then death will come and we'll die."[55] Superstition warned of the consequences of an improper death and urged peasants to heed signs that gave due warning to put one's affairs in order. Abnormal behavior in animals was particularly ominous. "When a dog digs a hole in the yard or an owl hoots on the roof, then there will be a death in the home." "If a cat or hare runs across the road, the nearest person will die." "If a woodpecker pecks in the icon corner, then death will come to that home or to a near relative."[56] Broken mirrors were more than bad luck, they portended death.[57] Virtually anything that violated what peasants considered to be the natural order of things could be considered portentous. "Whoever breaks something on the first day of Easter will die that year." "If something falls from the ceiling, the person it lands on will die soon."[58]

Such beliefs placed a great emphasis on the final moments of life, the place, and the manner of death, all of which determined the fate of the spirit, at least in its immediate post-mortem existence. Prolonged suffering, incapacitating illness, sudden or premature death, and suicide were feared precipitants of wandering and disturbed spirits whose unwanted visits would cause harm to the community. As in most traditional societies, the best place to die was within the comforting and protective walls of the peasant cottage near the icon shelf, for it was believed that a peaceful death reflected a gentle life and a restful death. Although death separated peasants physically from their living friends and relatives, the spiritual relationship between the deceased and their survivors was treated with great care. Upon death, and sometimes just before, the corpse of the deceased was washed and dressed in new clothes (unmarried girls were dressed in the traditional wedding costume) that served as "identity cards" in the next life, marking gender, class, social, and marital status. As soon as news of the death was conveyed to the parish elder, the church bells performed a "ringing of the spirit," which announced this important shift in communal composition. Coins, vodka, and food were gathered and buried with the dead to help their passage into heaven (as payment for sins, possibly a reflection of the way absolution was usually dispensed after payment to the confessor); magical cloths and belts were also enclosed in the coffin to protect against unwanted encounters with evil spirits. The body was then moved to the sacred corner of the peasant cottage, where it remained until the funeral the same or the next day. Aside from the grief felt at having lost a household member, the presence of the deceased in the home was considered to be especially inauspicious for the living. To protect against unclean forces that might attempt to enter the corpse peasants opened the chimney and called the late relative by name three times.[59] The only people allowed close contact with the body were the priest, deacon, literate peasants who read psalms and prayers, and female relatives who performed ritual and authentic laments.[60] When it came time for the funeral and burial, the body was transported to the church in an open coffin while grain was sprinkled in the path of the procession as a symbol of life and as an antidote to death. At the graveyard the coffin was nailed shut as ritual lamentations were sung and final farewells were bid.[61]

Although physical separation between the household and the departed began with the burial, contact between the two was believed to continue for thirty-nine days while the deceased walked the earth before beginning eternal life on the fortieth day (just as Christ ascended to heaven after forty days of wandering among his friends and relatives). Throughout this period, the needs of the deceased were considered to be nearly the same as in earthly life, and special porridges were left at the icon shelf or on the table, cups of water were left on the window sills, chimneys and *fortochki* were left open, and the bedding of the deceased was moved to an outer building, all so that domestic life would not be disrupted when the dead person returned every night after a day of wandering.[62] Memorial services on the ninth, twentieth, and fortieth day after death, as well as on the six-month and subsequent anniversaries, reinforced links between the living and the dead. In addition to private prayers, remembrance of the "forefathers" was often passed from generation to generation in the form of communal commemorations of the dead on the Saturday before *maslenitsa*, on Easter, on the second Tuesday after Easter *(radonitsa)*, on St. Dimitrii's Saturday ("Relatives Saturday") at the end of October, and on other days according to local custom.[63] These memorials took place in church graveyards and were accompanied by gifts of food and drink as well as fellowship and merriment that strengthened communal and family bonds by supporting the idea of eternal unity and permanence of the group over the individual.

Eternal Rhythms of Mortal Fates

As Russia sputtered its way from serf society to modern industrial empire in the last decades of the nineteenth century, the dependable rhythms of village holidays and personal celebrations offered a sense of stability and comfort to millions of peasants as their traditions slowly unraveled in the face of urban culture. To many peasants, city living, with its cold, calculating, profit-driven, individualistic ethos represented the opposite of the warm, genuine, survivalist, communal spirit of village life. The stuff of village dreams, romance, fantasy, and fiction was based on such dualistic perceptions of Russian society, but peasants were joined in their idealism by urban elites, whose disaffection with the superficiality of city life engendered an appreciation of the countryside as a pristine world of unalienated and direct interpersonal relations. Seeking escape from the demands and formalities of urban living, the chiefs of government, industry, and culture strove to create what Priscilla Roosevelt has termed "the cultural Arcadia," the retreat from official life to a space and time of freedom.[64] Beyond the façade of the cultural Arcadia was a longing for signs of eternity that would lessen the anguish of human mortality. In Orthodox Russia, the constant flow of peasant holidays offered educated Russia a glimpse of the eternal past imperfect, drenched with the backwardness and stench of handheld plows and manure-filled farm yards.[65] Tsars, war, famine, revolution, and politics came and went, but peasant tradition created the illusion of a palpable social timelessness that contrasted sharply with the clock of industrial life with its dehumanized eternal mechanism dragging Russian society into the future.

CHAPTER THREE

Mythical Origins, Magical Icons, and Historical Awareness

At the turning point from the big road to Karachun village stood a post.

To it was nailed a board with the inscription: "Karachun village, Voronezh

province, Zadonsk district, Sennovskaia township." Beneath the inscrip-

tion a figure indicated the number of male and female "souls."

—Ivan Stoliarov, *Zapiski russkogo krest'ianina*

*B*efore ethnographers began to record local histories in the second half of the nineteenth century, peasant notions of the past were stored in collective memory, a social process with communal mechanisms suggesting what is worth remembering and forgetting. The maintenance and modification of communally relevant memories were supported by oral tradition and its rituals, as well as monuments and wondrous objects that, together, evoked public reminiscences about village history.[1] At the center of these memories, or "histories according to the people," were the parish church, a symbol of eternal truths, whose presence dated to the early days of the community, and the village signpost,[2] a brief catalogue of local identity that alluded to secular developments in population size, jurisdictional assignment, and nomenclature.[3] Although most village biographies featured spectacular beginnings that included mythical visits of a tsar, the appearance of wondrous icons, or encounters with holy people, subsequent events were the less heroic struggles against natural and man-made disasters and achievements, such as droughts and fires or the construction of mills and schools. As these moments were collectively honored, their memory was preserved through stories about bygone years, celebrations, and commemorations.

By viewing history as both mythical and mundane, peasants were able to create seamless links between their humblest ancestors and the mightiest leaders of the Russian Empire. Out of respect for previous generations' interpretations of the past, public recollections followed a general outline, but allowed for pragmatic modifications, however small, to the basic story line.[4] While peasant versions of history were simpler than the well-articulated and erudite treatises produced by the country's leading thinkers, village legends also claimed a piece of the imperial myth by placing their destiny under the ambiguous umbrella of Russian identity. Aspirations to a supra-village identity were expressed most vividly in origin legends and tales about wonder-working icons.

The Way It Was

When asked to speak about the early days of their village, elderly peasants typically began their tales with the phrase, "That is the way it was" *(tak bylo)*, and then recited a chronology of events that demonstrated how the progression of Russian history had contributed to the uniqueness of their community. Tales about villages that had been settled in the century following the creation of Voronezh in 1586 spoke of the erstwhile Tatar threat to the Muscovite princes and of political refugees fleeing Polish-ruled Ukraine, beginning in the 1630s.[5] One story told of the fairy-tale adventures of Tatar princes who roamed the forests of Orlovo village in the mid–sixteenth century and named the nearby river Usman', a Tatar reference to the beauty of a young princess who drowned herself as a result of an ill-fated romance.[6] Ukrainians and Cossacks fleeing Polish oppression left their mark on local history by constructing fortresses and towns such as New Cherkask (Novyi Cherkask; 1652), which was soon renamed Ostrogozh and later became the district capital.[7] Dozens of smaller settlements and villages preserved their non-Russian names and heritage, such as Kazatsk (1660s), named after its Cossack founders, or the fortress and later district capital of Korotoiak (1647–48), which derives from the Turkic for black *(kara)*, hill *(tau)*, region/shore *(iak)*.[8]

Legends about villages settled in the late–seventeenth and early–eighteenth centuries were dominated by Peter the Great, who stumbled upon many small communities as he complemented his work in the naval shipyards of Voronezh with leisurely travel throughout the province. Hunting and fishing in the woods and rivers of Voronezh, Peter and his retinue etched themselves into the local memory of one village after another as they enjoyed the hospitality of local peasants, ordered the construction of churches, or bestowed names on anonymous communities. In the case of Kon'-Kolodez', which was settled on the eve of Peter's ascendancy to the throne, collective memory dated the village's origin to the second of two visits by the tsar, during which he changed its name. The momentous event occurred in 1709, after

Peter the Great and his companions became disoriented while hunting in a nearby forest.[9] Unable to find its way out of the woods, the royal party wandered around for more than a day before it decided to follow the instincts of one of its horses, who brought the group to a well near the banks of the Don River. As Peter walked along the river he noticed a group of peasants rushing forth from a cluster of nearby hovels. At the same time Peter's humble subjects were offering their assistance, an imperial ship under the command of Vice Admiral Naum Akimovich Seniavin approached in search of the tsar.[10] While Peter rejoiced at the turn of events, his horse wandered off unnoticed. Following an extensive search, the poor equine was discovered lifeless next to a well from which Peter had earlier drunk. The death of such a valued horse so moved Peter that he commanded Vice Admiral Seniavin to found a village on that spot and to name it Kon'-Kolodez', literally, "Horse Well."[11]

Physical evidence of the tsar's second visit began with the village church, a stone construction built in the early 1730s to replace an earlier wooden building that dated to the first decade of the eighteenth century. In the minds of Kon'-Kolodez' villagers, liturgical books published in 1692, 1707, and 1711, along with a now lost antimension, were implicit reminders of the influence of Peter the Great on their community, but an inscription inside a 1711 edition of the Gospels reading, "During the time of the Sovereign Peter Alekseevich," was explicit proof that the royal visit had actually taken place.[12] A recent testimonial to Peter the Great was the village's stone pyramid that stood eight meters high and was topped off by an iron horse rearing up on its hind legs.[13]

When Peter was not part of the origin tale, the role of esteemed founder was played by less distinguished figures of Orthodox Christianity and imperial Russia. The village of Dmitrievskoe took its name from the parish church, which, by honoring St. Demetrios of Salonika (d. 306), established a spiritual link to the early history of Christianity.[14] But Dmitrievskoe was also connected to one of Russian Orthodoxy's own luminaries, St. Tikhon of Zadonsk, who blessed its church while he was archbishop of Voronezh (1763–1767). The transformation of this local holy man into an all-Russian saint during his canonization in 1861 simply reinforced the bond between Dmitrievskoe peasants and the imperial narrative.[15]

Changes in village and parish boundaries, as well as the subdivision of large communities of believers, required that origin legends be modified to reflect new realities. The village of Bol'shie Lipiagi traced its roots to the early days of Voronezh history, yet the most remarkable aspects of its origin legend were acquired only in the middle of the nineteenth century when a devastating fire destroyed its parish church and removed a central part of its communal identity.[16] The parish of Bol'shie Lipiagi had not always been independent, and for nearly two centuries, from the late–sixteenth century until 1772, villagers had traveled to the district capital of Valuiki to worship in a wooden cathedral that was built with a generous donation from Peter the Great. To eliminate the hardship of travel to the capital, the residents of Bol'shie Lipiagi constructed their own church and in 1772 established their independence from Valuiki. For almost ninety years Bol'shie Lipiagi villagers were served well by their church until an improperly extinguished candle led to its fiery demise. Immediately after the fire, villagers received permission from Archbishop Ignatii of Voronezh to collect money for a new church, but upon learning that the Valuiki parish had begun construction on a new stone cathedral, Bol'shie Lipiagi residents expressed interest in purchasing the old wooden structure because that is where their ancestors had worshiped. The parishioners of the Valuiki cathedral agreed to the offer and petitioned the diocesan consistory for its approval. When the consistory refused to permit the sale, the Valuiki parish appealed to the Holy Synod, cleverly including a request for funds to maintain the church if its request was turned down. At the beginning of 1861, the Synod approved the sale, and the church was transferred to Bol'shie Lipiagi, along with a piece of history that now physically connected villagers to their ancestors as well as to their legendary brush with Peter the Great.[17]

When village origins were attributed to secular events, Orthodox Christianity proved no less important to historical memory. Meniailova village was founded at the beginning of the nineteenth century by Ukrainian petty itinerant traders known as *meniailova* or *meniaily*, a reference to their frequent travels.[18] In the place of an origin tale of epic proportions, Meniailova residents viewed the construction of its parish church in 1861 as a turning point in their history. Before the construction of the church, villagers had belonged to the parish of neighboring Alekseevka, a large, sprawling village. The completion of their own church was marked by a donation of a four-panel icon from Jerusalem, which was followed a few years later by another gift, a copy of a famous icon from Mt. Athos. Standing three yards high, measuring twenty-eight inches in width, and covered with gold leaf, the icon from Mt. Athos was escorted into its new community by a group of elderly men and women, who were met in ceremonial fashion by a cross and banner procession surrounded by parishioners. Following the obligatory prayer service and liturgy in its honor, villagers declared it their own sacred object, and the icon became the centerpiece of many special services recalling its origin. Together, the sacred images from Jerusalem and Mt. Athos connected the unpretentious daily existence of Meniailova with the physical and spiritual centers of Orthodox Christianity.[19]

In portraying themselves as part of the greater phenomena of Orthodox Christianity and the Russian Empire, villagers were also keenly aware of their different physical traits, dress, and speech, but these, along with their achievements, were painted in patriotic tones that praised local monuments to cultural and economic achievements.[20] An exemplary case is the large village of Alekseevka, which was founded by a certain Boyar Faddeev in 1691. Originally consisting of a mill and a few dozen Ukrainian peasant cottages, the village slowly prospered under the relatively amenable and free administration of the Sheremetev family, who acquired Alekseevka in the early–eighteenth century.[21] Over the years, the Sheremetev family made regular contributions to village cultural and social life, the most important being a school constructed by Count Nikolai Petrovich Sheremetev in the 1730s and, opposite the school, a fire observation tower, built in 1864. Villagers themselves constructed three almshouses (bogadel'nia) for the poor and elderly; a zemstvo hospital, which had one doctor, two medics, a pharmacy, and a veterinarian; and nine primary schools. These institutions served a burgeoning population, which, by the late–nineteenth century, had grown to the considerable size of ten thousand residents. Beginning in 1902, a cultural club for residents of all social backgrounds featured local and traveling performers. In the eyes of Alekseevka residents, their cultural needs had been nearly met, and only public reading rooms and a library could provide further uplift.[22]

Despite the importance of these economic and cultural achievements, Alekseevka villagers drew particular satisfaction from their church and its influence on communal life. Built in 1691, the same year the village was formally established, and situated on Bazaar Square, the church had been at the center of public life in Alekseevka throughout the eighteenth century. By 1800, the steadily growing population of Alekseevka had outgrown the small wooden structure, but not until 1812 had sufficient funds been raised to erect a stone replacement. The ceremonious opening of the Byzantine-style, triple-altar church on Bazaar Square in 1820 left such a deep impression on the community that the event was recalled several generations later, in 1905, as if it had just happened. Standing next to its wooden predecessor on Bazaar Square, ample space was available for outdoor religious processions and large communal blessings; its location in the heart of the village also symbolized the confluence of spiritual and economic life, most notably during Sunday markets, as well as during seasonal fairs that were held on major religious holidays.[23] The presence of the sacred in secular spheres of public life was viewed by villagers in Alekseevka and throughout Russia as natural and inseparable because, as Vera Shevzov has argued, the "ultimate reference points [in the village] were not social, political, or economic, but ones that concerned God and human salvation."[24] Success and failure were impossible without relating them to the divine as represented in the parish church.

Less positive moments in village life also gave shape to local identity. All communities, vibrant or sleepy, faced the constant threat of natural disasters, moments that were burnt into the memory of contemporaries and their descendants and shaped the way that historical time was perceived. Every village knew about the fires, epidemics, droughts, crop failures, and famines that had threatened its very existence. Communal survival in the face of calamities inevitably required divine intervention, often through the intercession of favorite saints and wondrous icons. Vowing everlasting appreciation for this secular salvation, communities and individuals made "contracts with the divine," which subsequent generations fulfilled lest they invoke the wrath of God. For peasant communities, historical and ordinary time intersected in the ritual fulfillment of communal vows in commemorations that were sprinkled across the peasant calendar as constant reminders of the past.[25]

Iconic Symbols of Identity

Throughout Russia, followers of the Orthodox faith believed that the magical powers of wondrous icons and sacred objects offered the most reliable protection against calamity.[26] Peasant reverence for these holy objects was in keeping with Orthodoxy's high esteem for icons, yet church leaders saw a conflict between this vibrant manifestation of grass-roots piety and the preservation of episcopal authority. Adopting a moderate position, the Holy Synod deemed this form of religious initiative to be acceptable only when sanctioned by the church, requiring believers to apply for an official stamp of approval for their beloved objects.[27] To ensure that regulation was effectively carried out, in 1893 the Holy Synod ordered diocesan bishops to compile detailed descriptions of specially revered and wondrous icons.[28] As a result, local communities of believers were forced to engage with the formal institutions of church administration if they wished to receive official recognition of their icons, a designation that could draw large crowds of pilgrims willing to donate to the parish coffers. But by requesting an official decision, a community also ran the risk that their icon could be declared fraudulent, thus limiting pilgrim-related income and possibly diminishing the image's spiritual essence. Once the decision was taken to submit an icon for synodal approval, a parish was required to transport the image to the district cathedral or a nearby monastery where it would be thoroughly inspected. If it was declared to be wondrous, the icon was returned to its home parish, where it was to remain except for brief periods when it was loaned out to other communities.[29]

The struggle for control over local religious life was often over the use of wondrous icons, and interference in the use of holy images was not easily tolerated by peasant believers. Voronezh diocesan officials claimed seventeen wondrous icons, whose shrines attracted thousands of pilgrims each year and, despite bishops' discouragement of loans, circulated in parishes near and far (see appendix table 2 and fig. 5). The pages of provincial newspapers were filled with stories of these sacred images, one of the most popular being the icon of St. Nicholas the Wonderworker (see fig. 6), which was normally housed in the Valuiki Dormition Monastery. For several generations, the villagers of Urazova, not far from the monastery, had enjoyed a special relationship with the icon. According to legend, when the icon had "spontaneously appeared" *(iavlenie)* to the first Romanov tsar, Michael, shortly after his ascendancy to the throne in 1613, he commanded that a monastery dedicated to the Dormition of the Mother of God be constructed on the very site.[30] The popularity of the St. Nicholas icon meant that it spent most of the year on visitations to nearby villages like Urazova, which, in the 1830s, had successfully petitioned the Holy Synod for an annual loan. The relationship between Urazova and the Dormition Monastery remained intact until 1871, when monastic officials, faced with a growing number of disappointed pilgrims, cancelled all loans of the object. Despite this decision, the Urazova faithful attempted to negotiate new terms, but in 1887 their patience ran out, and they appealed to the Synod to reinstate the annual loan.[31]

Urazova believers' attempt to reinstate the use of the St. Nicholas icon began as an exercise in communal memory recall. When villagers began their appeals in 1887, they remembered the sequence of events, but not precise dates, and placed the first loan sometime in the 1830s, a decade in which Voronezh experienced six individual years of crop failures or cholera epidemics.[32] Communal memory proved more elusive when it came to remembering the reasons for the loan being canceled. At some point between the 1830s and 1871, considerable discord had developed between the clergy of Urazova and monastery officials over the division of income generated during the icon's visit to the village. Monetary squabbles, compounded by increasing demands for loans, had led monastery officials to impound the icon within their own community. Undeterred, Urazova residents filed one petition after another to diocesan authorities, who denied the requests, citing the unresolved dispute over income generated by the sacred object; but the ruling also noted that Urazova was only four and one-half miles away from the monastery, a distance easily traveled on a good road connecting the two communities. The cholera epidemic of 1891 added an element of urgency to their request, and villagers finally received special permission to bring the icon to their village one more time.

As the epidemic again ravaged the village in 1892, Urazova believers appealed once more to diocesan authorities, this time bolstering their claim with more than two hundred signatures or their proxies. Barely masking their exasperation, the authorities cited Suffragan Bishop Veniamin's report of his visit to Urazova that year in which he vaguely noted "undesirable" morals in the village, as well as certain "improper" behavior near the church during the liturgy. Moreover, diocesan authorities expressed their doubt that their refusal to permit the icon loan had precipitated the epidemic. Villagers believed otherwise and claimed that the icon was also able to cure diphtheria, typhus, feebleness, and cholera. Moved by the suffering of village children, who were especially vulnerable to the epidemic, diocesan authorities agreed to a single one-month loan, on two conditions: that the civil authorities guarantee safe passage of the icon and that the icon visit all three churches in Urazova, thus avoiding accusations of favoritism. Before making its final decision, and ever concerned about its image in the eyes of the faithful during times of hardship, the diocesan board, with the

Снимокъ съ Чудотворной иконы Божіей Матери, Троеручицы, находящейся въ Воронежскомъ Алексѣевскомъ Акатовомъ монастырѣ. Празднованіе Ея 12-го Іюля.

Fig. 5—Wonderworking Icon of the Three-Handed Mother of God, Voronezh Alekseevskii Akatov Monastery

support of the monastery abbot, agreed to permit the icon to be loaned to Urazova three out of every four years for no more than three weeks at a time.[33] For its part, the parish was required to seek annual approval from the bishop of Voronezh, who reserved the right to cancel the loan if Urazova villagers failed to demonstrate "appropriate reverence," "sublet" the icon to other believers in the district, or if civil and monastic authorities disagreed with the arrangement (which they did not). Had the case ended here, the village of Urazova would have scored a significant victory for their twenty years of perseverance. Villagers, however, deemed the proposal unacceptable and filed an appeal to the Holy Synod, which reverted to its 1871 decision.[34]

This case demonstrates how the wonderworking icon of St. Nicholas shaped the history of Urazova village, as well as reinforced communal identity as villagers rallied around it to guarantee public welfare. In drafting its petitions, this local community of believers depended on collective memory to write its village history, at the center of which was the annual commemoration of a specially revered icon. An important psychological consequence of the act of remembering was the implicit linkage of the village to the icon's miraculous origin and the first tsar of the Romanov dynasty.[35] Beyond religion, the case reveals Urazova peasants' astute knowledge of church procedure for petitions and appeals, as well as their skilled use of the system to attain a favorable decision, even though, by pushing too hard, they ultimately failed in their quest.

The approval of an icon loan set into motion elaborate preparations for its arrival, which mimicked the pomp and ceremony normally reserved for visits by dignitaries. As an anthropomorphized guest of honor, upon its arrival in the village a wondrous icon was met by the local clergy and the faithful, who flocked to greet it. During welcoming services in the parish church and at the nearby water source, joyous praise was addressed to the icon itself, as if it could not only hear, but also silently respond with benevolent acts. When the faithful were allowed to individually approach the icon, they expressed their reverence by crossing themselves, bowing their heads, and kissing the sacred object with tenderness and affection that was ordinarily reserved for beloved family members. Prayer services and expressions of reverence were repeated throughout the loan period as the icon was carried to the local fields, public buildings, and individual homes for special blessings. When the time came for the icon's departure, the ceremonial farewell service was punctuated by exclamations of sorrow by the weeping faithful.

Villages less successful in obtaining icon loans were keenly aware of their place in the hierarchy of mobile spiritual essence. Such was the case of the Noven'kaia and Userd villages in Biriuch district. Their stories began during the epidemic of 1847, when the Userd wonderworking icon of the Tikhvin Mother of God saved Biriuch from devastation while on loan to the city. For the next twenty-two years, Biriuch city officials diligently petitioned diocesan authorities and the Synod for an annual loan of the icon. Finally, in 1869, permission was granted.[36] Biriuch's good fortune soon became the envy of Noven'kaia villagers, who had unsuccessfully bid for the icon. Situated along the route from Userd to Biriuch, the tiny village of Noven'kaia attempted to turn defeat into victory by becoming an unofficial stopping point for the procession, but even this modest request, which was taken all the way to the Holy Synod, failed. Instead, the village was forced to serve as

Fig. 6—Icon of St. Nicholas the Wonderworker, Valuiki
Dormition Monastery

an unofficial rest stop for the weary members of the icon procession.[37] The
fates of Biriuch and Noven'kaia would have remained local news had the
communities not chosen to use the pages of the diocesan press to express
their sense of exalted or injured pride. The first story was written by a
member of the Biriuch community on the fourth anniversary of the procession, and it described an effervescent pleasure in having secured a regular
icon visit. A year later, a representative of the Noven'kaia community responded directly to this article in terms that conveyed a deep wound, not
only in being overlooked in the description of the icon procession, but also
in having lost their bid to obtain a loan.[38]

When a wonderworking icon was housed far enough away to prohibit a
loan, villages ordered reproductions to be made and treated their arrival as
they would have the original. Just as the villagers of Meniailova had integrated

into their identity the reproductions from Jerusalem and Mt. Athos, surrogates of famous icons were quickly absorbed into the history of the small village of Khvoshchevatoe, whose elders ordered a copy of the wonderworking Kozel'shchinskaia Mother of God icon from the Kozel'shchinsk Nativity of the Mother of God Monastery in Poltava province.[39] When it finally arrived by train, a delegation from the village met the icon in the capital of Voronezh and accompanied it through numerous villages before it arrived in Khvoshchevatoe. With the church bells ringing, the icon was met at the entrance to the village by the clergy and local faithful. After a ceremonial prayer service in the church, parishioners filed past the icon to pay their respects while the choir sang hymns of praise to the Mother of God and a festive troparion in honor of her birthday, which fell on that day.[40] By obtaining a copy of the icon, the faithful of Khvoshchevatoe had created a symbolic link between its parish and the Kozel'shchinsk Nativity of the Mother of God Monastery. Henceforth, the original icon would serve as a reference point for the Khvoshchevatoe community, which, at least in terms of the icon, had become the monastery's spiritual dependent.[41]

Throughout rural and urban Russia, icons served first and foremost as special protection against calamities, and secondarily as media of communication between groups of believers and the institutions of church administration. Although they were not always aware of it, history and historical understandings involving religious images reminded both literate and illiterate Russians of the basic cultural values that bound them together as members of the empire and as inheritors and creators of its central narratives.

Religion and Historical Awareness

As village society began the transition from oral to literate culture in the last decades of the nineteenth century, the historical rhythms of myths and legends helped peasants to shape new views of the world that gave equal credence to events verifiable by historical documents and to tales dependent on oral tradition.[42] Whether or not Peter the Great actually named a village mattered less to peasants than the symbolic link between their tiny corner of the globe and the Russian Empire as represented by the tsar. In a less formulaic way, village residents structured their understanding of the past with events that depended on physical reminders to reinforce their significance. With Orthodox Christianity embedded in the foundation of peasant society, gatherings at churches and around wondrous icons offered a semblance of unity as Russian society began to feel the effects of increased mobility, literacy, and freedom of expression.

As the familiar frameworks of village life began to crumble, believers found comfort in their sacred spaces and drew strength from their wondrous icons. Rather than abandon the faith, which a growing number of educated Russians portrayed in villainous hues, peasants looked to religion for solutions to contemporary problems. Church officials, preoccupied with a battery of assaults on their authority and with internal divisions about how to respond to the needs of a restless society, struggled to maintain their control over local religious life while recognizing that acceptable forms of independent spiritual activity were essential for the survival of the faith. With their strict regulations on wondrous icons aimed at streamlining the process of identification and approval, they sent another more discouraging message to loyal peasant believers who, in the generation since the emancipation, had become active in the construction of rural Russia's new public institutions and had come to view parish life as a logical extension of that sphere of activity.

CHAPTER FOUR

Uncompromising over Parish Authority—
The Church, Its Clergy, and the Peasantry

After [my] announcement, noise and shouts erupted and were accompanied
by raised fists, which could not be suppressed even by the *volost'* elder.

—Clerical superintendent's description of a dispute about the

selection of a parish elder, 1901

*A*t the spiritual center of post-emancipation village
life towered the church *(khram)*, the sacred temple of God,
whose shimmering domes, golden crosses, and mellifluous bells
reached for the heavens while uniting believers in common
worship.[1] In the eyes of worshipers, the parish community
(prikhod) consisted of a spiritual realm of living and deceased Orthodox Christians and a physical territory comprising land,
buildings, and sacred objects.[2] Peasants worked diligently to
support their houses of worship and clergymen in the belief that
their efforts, combined with regular participation in sacred rituals, would win them eternal salvation. Although this devotion to
the parish church and belief in everlasting redemption outlived
the Romanov tsars, the spread of literacy in the last decades of
the nineteenth century brought with it a self-empowering access
to knowledge that altered the dynamics of local religious life.
The most radical consequence of the self-empowerment of literate peasants was an unprecedented grass-roots religious activism
that transformed the ancient institutions of the parish assembly
and village commune into councils for public action against
episcopal decisions and clerical behavior that threatened to im-
pede the road to Paradise.[3]

Literacy proved to be an ineffective weapon against the
church hierarchy. From their distant offices in the diocesan capi-

tals and St. Petersburg, steeped in prejudice about peasant ignorance, church officials interpreted the rising tide of petitions and complaints flowing in from the villages as a sign that urban intellectuals were duping the masses with their secular teachings. But a more balanced reading of the documents would have revealed the presence of a strong traditional tone in these demands, in which peasants firmly declared their devotion to the faith and meticulously distinguished between the imperfection of individuals and human institutions and the perfection of the divine sacraments. Between the episcopate and the faithful stood the parish clergy, whose own precarious status in village life oscillated between that of revered spiritual fathers capable of understanding the needs of their flock and reviled outsiders donning the cloak of urbane aloofness.[4] Ultimately, the struggle over parish authority divided the episcopate, the clergy, and the laity, the three basic constituencies of the Orthodox Church, and transformed the parish into a contested space that deterred agreement on religious life and prevented a united front against the most serious threat to their faith: modern secular culture.

The Church and Its Clergy

Many problems of post-emancipation Orthodoxy can be traced to the reforms of Peter the Great, which abolished the patriarchate and placed church institutions under the secularized leadership of the Holy Synod. With the sweep of his autocratic hand, Peter the Great created a hybrid institution that was stripped of much of its secular power while vesting it with broad authority over internal administrative and canonical matters. Preserving the Muscovite system of dual secular and religious jurisdictions, the central institutional apparatus of the Petrine church was reproduced in the provinces, where governors supported and reinforced the authority of bishops.[5] As the chief religious official of the province, the diocesan bishop supervised an administrative board (eparkhial'noe upravlenie) made up of ordained and lay members and was responsible for all clergymen assigned to his episcopal see. The bishop was assisted in his administrative duties by a network of lesser officials known as superintendents (blagochinnye), senior members of the nonmonastic clergy responsible for between fifteen and twenty parishes. It was through the superintendents that ordinary believers first encountered church bureaucracy, turning to it with their concerns about parish life.[6] The hierarchical and bureaucratic structure of Russian Orthodoxy was not always efficient; still, it provided parish clergymen and ordinary believers with a functional mechanism to conduct business with diocesan authorities and, when necessary, the mother church in faraway St. Petersburg.

At the parish level, the clergy was differentiated according to function and rank. Chief among them were the rectors (nastoiateli), senior priests (protoierei) of a parish, who supervised junior clergymen (sviashchenniki, ierei) and deacons (diakona). The ordained clergy (sviashchennosluzhiteli) was further divided into those who had regular positions *(shtaty),* which made them eligible for the prerogatives of the estate (the most important being job security and pensions), and those who occupied nonpermanent, super-numerary posts *(vneshtatnye).* Next in the pecking order were members of the unordained clergy *(tserkovnosluzhiteli,* literally, "church workers"): readers and chanters *(diachki, ponomari, prichetniki, psalomshchiki),* church elders *(starosty),* wardens *(storozha),* sacristans and keepers of the keys *(kliuchari),* and bakers of the communion bread *(proskurni/prosfirni).*[7] Among the unordained, the church elder was charged with the preservation of lay decorum during reli-gious services, and he was expected to maintain and protect church buildings and cemeteries, refurbish bells and icons, stock communion wine, procure fresh liturgical bread, order church candles, and raise funds for any special needs of the parish. Beyond the walls of the church, the elder served as medi-ator between disputing parties and often wrote or coauthored petitions and complaints on behalf of the parish, as well as mobilized communal action.[8]

The clergyman's duties were defined by his performance of religious rites, but a priest in Russia had always done more than recite prayers at the altar table. As the chief parish administrator, the priest created and maintained parish records on births, marriages, and deaths in the community, as well as oversaw all of its economic transactions. Undertrained in the area of homilet-ics, rural clergymen were thrust by seminary reforms in the 1860s into their new role as pulpit preachers; at the same time the primary school initiative of 1864 directed them into the classrooms of the new secular village schools as catechism instructors. By the beginning of the twentieth century the list of priestly duties had expanded to include expertise in agronomy and finance.

The ever expanding duties of clergymen were hindered by their dire eco-nomic circumstances of service in a village parish. To address clerical poverty, the Holy Synod introduced a new village-level body, the parish council *(prikhodskoe popechitel'stvo),* which was to be made up of ordinary believers charged with the improvement of clerical finances, upkeep of church buildings, restriction of the influence of secular ideas, and elimina-tion of fractiousness among believers.[9] From St. Petersburg, the new coun-cils may have appeared to be the best way to provide for the parish clergy's financial needs, but in parishes throughout Russia, the new institutions were viewed as unnecessary because existing village and parish institutions already performed these tasks.[10] By 1905, when the Holy Synod acknowl-edged the redundancy of the new councils and issued a resolution that in-troduced the hyphenated term *tserkovno-prikhodakaia obshchina* (church-parish commune), an array of grass-roots organizations of the faithful—brotherhoods *(bratstva),* religious circles *(kruzhki),* and church so-cieties *(obshchestva)*—each with overlapping spheres of activity, brought to-gether members of the clergy and laity to perform many of the tasks origi-nally imposed on the parish councils.[11] Fifty years after their creation and with Russia about to enter World War I, only 17 percent of Voronezh parishes had functioning parish councils.[12]

As with most of its attempts to reform parish life, the Orthodox Church lacked the administrative apparatus and financial resources that could put significant changes into practice. Had synodal and diocesan authorities chosen to work with local communities of believers, they would have found that peasants were eager to assume the responsibility for parish administration and programming that would have agreed with the episcopate's initiatives. The means to the common end, however, would have been very different. Whereas the episcopate relied on its code-oriented institutions, the peasantry solved its problems and created its strategies through its own popular assemblies that adhered to unwritten rules of peasant social justice.

Religion and Peasant Social Justice

Peasant notions of social justice were based on what villagers perceived to be their natural rights, duties, and obligations that enabled communal life to function within an atmosphere characterized by petty, envious, disputatious score settling.[13] Written law played a small role in the day-to-day function of village life; instead, peasants survived by balancing their own interests against those of local officials, landlords, and anyone associated with them, including, at times, clergymen.[14] When disagreements about faith and praxis broke out within households, between neighbors, with communal leaders, and between villages, peasants first sought informal resolutions through negotiation, popular justice *(samosud)*, or, infrequently, protest; but when these tacks failed, they took their cases to the village or parish commune, township courts, or higher religious authorities. In the end, justice was restored, however temporary, and the rhythms of everyday life continued as before, with minor adjustments. What peasants sought was not an end to religion, but fairness in matters concerning the everyday practice of Orthodox Christianity.

Tensions among the faithful and between the clergy and laity in post-emancipation Russia centered on three violations of peasant religious norms: liturgical errors, immorality and corruption among the clergy, and denied requests to construct new churches. When peasants organized a petition or complaint against their clergymen or in protest of an administrative decision, they did so at tremendous expense, usually paying for the services of a local scribe who had mastered the formulaic style of the genre and was well versed in procedure.[15] Once diocesan or synodal religious authorities deemed a case worthy of consideration, they usually ordered an investigation that could last months as sworn statements were taken from hundreds of parishioners. The more complicated the case and the more contentious the charge, the more likely were contradictory testimonies that left investigators and higher officials unable to pronounce judgments.

The process of filing petitions and complaints reinforced among parish-ioners a sense of communal identity as large groups of men and women, often as many as several hundred, attempted to exert greater control over the administration of parish life.[16] On the seldom occasion when the prob-lems of village parish life grabbed national attention, the Holy Synod moved quickly to find a resolution. Such was the case in 1858 when an exposé writ-ten by Fr. I. S. Belliustin, a parish priest from the central Russian province of Tver, was published in Paris on the eve of the emancipation. The book sent shock waves through the upper echelons of the church and state, and the scandal that followed underscored the ideological entrenchment of the reli-gious elite, the professional resolve of rank-and-file priests, as well as the prej-udices of educated Russia when it came to peasant capabilities. Writing about the corruption and moral abasement of the rural clergy, Belliustin poignantly described the church's inability to bring order to local religious life.[17] Bel-liustin argued that the creation of a unified and harmonious parish commu-nity would be possible only after clerical poverty had been eliminated and pastoral training had been improved so that future priests would be better prepared to serve their future communities. Although these ideas had previ-ously circulated among the urban and rural episcopate, the Holy Synod re-acted swiftly, sentencing Belliustin to exile in the far northern Solovetsk Monastery. Only the intervention of Tsar Alexander II saved Belliustin from his frosty punishment, while the problems of clerical reform and parish life were again relegated to the cool chambers of the Holy Synod.

LITURGICAL ERRORS, CLERICAL IMMORALITY, AND CORRUPTION

Over the next decades, the Belliustin affair cast a long shadow over synodal deliberations about local religious life. Beginning in 1869, five years after the introduction of the parish council, church leaders addressed the inadequate training of the rural clergy by introducing a seminary curriculum that empha-sized theological instruction, rather than pastoral training, that would have prepared seminarians for the day-to-day needs of their future spiritual charges. That same year, in order to improve the economic well-being of the clergy, the Synod consolidated small parishes and increased the clerical land allotment, which was to be taken from communally held fields.[18] The results frustrated rural believers as their priests became better educated, their churches were closed, and their communal land was confiscated. To make matters worse, all of this occurred at the very moment when the church faced a growing short-age of priests as fewer clerical sons chose the priesthood over secular careers, which led to a precipitous increase in the ratio of priests to believers from 1,586:1 in 1870 (the year after the closures were ordered) to 1,833:1 in 1888, nearly twenty years later. By the beginning of World War I, this number had reached 2,178:1. The Holy Synod's decision to streamline the lower clerical or-ders, with whom the peasantry had the most regular contact, further aggra-vated an already desperate situation (see appendix tables 3 and 4).[19]

The dearth of rural priests helps to explain peasants' willingness to tolerate incompetent, immoral, and corrupt clergymen—they preferred an inferior servant of the cloth to none at all—but another consequence of the severe staffing problem was the episcopal lenience toward clerics with repeat offenses. Of the more than three hundred surviving petitions and complaints filed by Voronezh peasants between 1859 and 1917, slightly more than half were about liturgical errors, and all of them included additional accusations of clerical immorality.[20] The most common violation of the peasant moral code was inebriation while performing religious rites. Most of the accused clergymen had long histories of excessive drinking, and for the most part believers possessed a titanic reserve of patience for clerical drunkenness.[21] Such was the case of a group of parishioners who endured Fr. Aleksandr Belozorov's insobriety for decades before lodging a complaint, in 1906, after he repeatedly failed to perform religious services because of his perpetual state of drunkenness. The straw that broke the proverbial camel's back was Belozorov's failure to appear for vespers on the feast day of the local holy man, St. Mitrofan of Voronezh. For more than an hour villagers stood in church waiting for their priest, when he finally wobbled in stone-drunk and uttering profanities. The service proved too difficult for Belozorov, who could hardly stand up straight or speak clearly, and finally he slumped onto the altar table and fell asleep. Still wanting to have their service, these determined believers forced Belozorov to complete it, but when his condition prevented him from anointing them with the customary blessed oil, the congregation allowed him to return home on the condition that he agree to complete the service the next morning. When Belozorov failed to respond to the church bell on the following day, parishioners set off for a church in a neighboring village. (Belozorov did eventually arrive four hours later, but again he was roaring drunk.) The case did not, however, end here. Charges of sexual harassment and excessive fees to perform confessions were also lodged. In the end, the diocesan administration agreed with the forty-three petitioners who filed the original complaint, demoted Belozorov to the rank of psalmist, and transferred him to another parish, but not before the wily cleric had mobilized thirty-five peasants who claimed that none of the charges was true.[22]

Allegations of liturgical errors that were not a byproduct of drunkenness were usually the result of peasants' frustration with their priest's lack of sympathy for their dire economic circumstances. When Fr. Aleksandr Nikolaevich Savitskii of Aleksandrovka village failed to perform in a "timely" and "reasonable" manner the funeral rite for a young peasant woman, her father, Feodor Koltunov, perceived this to be a blow to his honor and filed a complaint with the diocesan administration. Two weeks before Koltunov's daughter died of typhus, his son had succumbed to the same illness and had received a proper burial. But when the second misfortune struck the impoverished Koltunov, who had yet to pay the entire emolument for his son's funeral, he claimed that Fr. Savitskii refused to bury the young woman before the accounts had been settled. Grieving and ill themselves, the Koltunovs sent a friend to fetch the priest, who, witnesses claimed, replied: "Tell Feodor to get together all the money for [the funeral of] his son and daughter. . . . Otherwise . . . I will not bury them." Undeterred by this rebuff, they sent another person to plead their case, but again Fr. Savitskii refused, noting the bad condition of the cart. Finally, Koltunov himself went to the priest, who allegedly berated him for impertinence, shouting: "Throw off your hat, you rude pig!" Despite this outburst, this time Fr. Savitskii agreed to bury Koltunov's daughter, but, according to the girl's relatives, when he failed to appear at the cemetery, the body was moved from the church to the priest's house. When the service was finally performed in the evening, it was too dark for the grave diggers to close the burial pit.[23] By performing the funeral after dark, Fr. Savitskii had violated a long held peasant prohibition against burial after sunset, a time when unclean forces were actively about.

In its investigation of the case, the diocesan administration found that the cart sent by Koltunov indeed was unsuitable, since it was normally used to haul manure. Investigators also questioned Koltunov's behavior when eyewitnesses testified that he arrived at Fr. Savitskii's house inebriated and threatening to harm the priest physically. This part of the story was corroborated by a telephone call made by Fr. Savitskii to the local police to report Koltunov's threatening behavior. Once the commotion had settled, Fr. Savitskii buried the girl, but only her sister attended the service, and not her parents. These circumstances, combined with Savitskii's previously "exceptionally good behavior," was enough for diocesan authorities to rule that the charges against the priest were groundless. Koltunov's appeal to the Holy Synod ended in the same way.[24]

As church investigators fastidiously questioned the accused parties and gathered sworn character references from parishioners, an invisible line was drawn that separated the parish into one group who vouched for the cleric's moral purity and another who held him to be guilty.[25] Implicit in these divisions was the existence of long-standing factions and cliques aligned in favor of and against the priest. Whereas alcoholism appears to have contributed to the commission of liturgical errors, illicit sexual behavior was associated with the overall moral degeneration of the church's representatives and thus potentially more destabilizing to communal propriety. When a group of peasants of Pokrovskaia Church accused their priest, Nikolai Tairov, of having an affair with the widow of another priest, they also reported that he had insulted parishioners and extorted money for religious services. Many of the fifty-six peasants who gave sworn statements confirming that Tairov had extracted higher fees to perform the rites of confession, communion, and holy matrimony also claimed to have seen the priest in bed with the widow Shislova. With more than twenty-four improper acts verified by investigators, the diocesan administration ordered a two-month monastic penance and transferred the priest to another parish. Fr. Tairov appealed the decision to the Holy Synod, which upheld the diocesan ruling. This prompted six parishioners (possibly at Tairov's urging, as rumor had it) to petition in defense of their priest, but in the end he served out his sentence, was transferred, and was removed from the priesthood.[26]

Despite the small number of parishioners who committed themselves to Tairov's defense, church investigators remarked upon the difficulties they faced when gathering evidence of the priest's alleged improprieties. One reason for parishioners' unwillingness to step forward was their fear of reprisals not only from their peers, but from their only priest, who could refuse them essential rites and other religious services. Case materials suggest another, equally compelling, reason that peasants hesitated to testify against their priest: in order to do so, they would have tacitly admitted their own voyeuristic behavior of waiting to catch a glimpse of Tairov and Shislova in bed.

The least common moral offense was corruption, which usually referred to the pilfering of parish coffers, or aiding and abetting thieves who had stolen from the church.[27] For nearly a decade, the peasants of Bykovo village struggled to get a ruling against their deacon, Petr Nikitin, whom they accused of stealing sixty-two silver rubles from the parish lockbox, which was kept on the altar table. When Nikitin failed to appear with the key during the monthly counting of collections, accusations were lodged by two peasants who, after a recent service, had seen the deacon loitering near the box and handling its contents. After much resistance, Nikitin turned over the key and was promptly confronted by the church elder, who noticed that the box's seal was broken and its contents missing. Nikitin grimaced and equivocated until the priest and church elder asked the two peasants to denounce the deacon to the district clerical superintendent. On their way to the superintendent, Nikitin approached the peasants, admitted his theft, and offered to return one third of the money until he could come up with the rest if they agreed to drop the charges. The peasants refused, and a few days later Nikitin admitted that his dissatisfaction with his share of clerical income had motivated him to pilfer the church coffers. His confession did not exonerate him, and the denunciations were read by the district superintendent.

At this point the case took an unexpected turn when it was handed over to the secular jurisdiction of the district land court *(zemskii uezdnyi sud)*, which found Nikitin guilty, ordered him placed under surveillance, and forbade him to handle parish funds, which, it determined, should have been in the hands of the church elder. The Voronezh criminal court *(ugolovnaia palata)* then decided that evidence was lacking in the case and questioned the reliability of several witnesses. A tangle of village nepotism and corruption began to unravel that connected one of the peasant accusers to the church elder, a former member of the clergy, who had been removed from his position for an unnamed offense. Finally, Nikitin's association with other thefts in the village moved the court to query diocesan administrators about why a person with a suspicious background was in charge of the keys. Nikitin's accusers were offended by the court's suggestion that they had conspired against the deacon and appealed to the senate in St. Petersburg for a new ruling. The senate upheld the decision of the Voronezh criminal court, informed the Holy Synod, and closed the case. In response, the Synod informed the court that the Voronezh diocesan administration had already defrocked Nikitin.[28]

The case of Petr Nikitin and many others like it highlight the diverse visions of the religious life that could be found in all communities, as well as the contentious inner workings of the peasant village, tensions between the genders, and generational conflict. The cleric who was given to drink or swearing or was lax in some of his liturgical duties had to be mindful of local religious norms lest he become the object of nasty, prolonged, and possibly falsified complaints. Lacking the right to select or remove their priests, deacons, and psalmists, parishioners had no other effective means than to file a complaint if they wished to rid themselves of ill-performing, abusive, or immoral clerics, or to level the parish playing field.[29] To lend strength to their petitions against their priests, deacons, and psalmists, peasant believers bundled the main complaint with secondary charges that, regardless of their veracity, might better attract the attention of higher church authorities. One consequence of "bundled petitions" was that the paper trail they left contributed to the most enduring images of the clergy as thoroughly debauched.[30] This new authority of the pen left the church's bishops trapped in a bureaucratic web that they had helped to create not for the purposes of peasant empowerment, but for the preservation of episcopal authority. Their intervention in parish conflicts forced them to take sides in a struggle that had no clear victors.

New Church Constructions

For all but the largest and wealthiest villages, the erection of a new parish church required the blood, sweat, and tears of fund-raising activities, debates about the use of communal resources, and years of perseverance. When diocesan and synodal authorities turned down requests to build new churches, disappointed believers often went to extreme measures to reverse the decision. In the unusual case of Gorokhovka village, initial diocesan approval for a church was rescinded after peasants had nearly completed construction of their new house of worship. For thirteen years, Gorokhovka peasants had endured hardships, including the crop failure and cholera epidemic of 1891–1892, to construct a parsonage, a school, and residences for two deacons. All that remained was the blessing of the church building and the appointment of clergymen. Archbishop Anastasii was, however, unwilling to allow this to happen because, in his mind, the clerical land allotment, thirteen miles away, was too far from the church itself and because not all of the buildings were ready for use. Disappointed with Archbishop

Anastasii's decision, the village assembly met some time in 1901 and drew up a petition to the Holy Synod, which was signed by 340 members. In the end, the Synod upheld Archbishop Anastasii's decision, but parishioners continued to plead their case without success as the unblessed church stood vacant and unused.[31]

Fervent religious desire also motivated the peasants of Staraia Chigla, who wished to move their old church closer to them rather than to use a new one built by the local landowner, Tulinov. Inconveniently located at the bottom of a hill, the new stone church was unreachable during the spring and autumn flood seasons. To rectify the situation, in 1858, Staraia Chigla peasants petitioned diocesan authorities to move their old wooden church (now closed) and its remaining holy aura closer to them and to re-open it for services. Tulinov considered the wooden church as his own property because his ancestors' serfs had built and paid for it more than a century earlier. The community of Staraia Chigla saw the matter differently and argued that because their forebears had built the church, it belonged to the village, and not to the serf owner. This was a bold argument to make three years before emancipation was declared, but diocesan authorities based their ruling on location and documentation. The wooden church was undeniably sitting on the property of Tulinov. Furthermore, the parish registry contained documents confirming that it was indeed the landowner's property. To satisfy the peasants' demand, however, diocesan authorities granted them permission to construct a new church on their own land, a decision they found prohibitively expensive. Staraia Chigla peasants appealed the decision to the Holy Synod, which ordered diocesan authorities to conduct an investigation. As the case dragged on, this community of believers remained firmly devoted to its wooden house of worship and sent another petition to the Holy Synod in 1861, this time asking permission to sell items from the church at the center of the dispute. Not surprisingly, the Synod turned down the request, and the case appears to have ended here.[32]

The ruling in the Staraia Chigla case was typical in land and property disputes between peasants, landowners, and clergymen until the end of tsarist rule. Ultimately, *ownership* that could be verified by documents, rather than current or previous *use*, was at stake. Although church authorities had the support of the law behind their decision about the Staraia Chigla parish, they could have struck a compromise that would have satisfied, or at least equally disappointed, both parties by allowing the peasants to use the old wooden structure without moving it. Instead, prior use that was claimed by the peasants was deemed to be of lesser importance than the rights of landowner Tulinov.

Sometimes church officials feigned ignorance of the difficulties of rural transportation, which often prevented believers from attending worship services.[33] When, at the beginning of the twentieth century, peasants from Zaval'ska and Ostroukhova villages wished to join forces to build their own church, they cited the distance from the one they currently attended, a lack of transportation to it, and a consequent decline in the moral environ-ment.[34] When their request was rejected by diocesan authorities, these peasants appealed to the Holy Synod. In addition to their moral reason-ing—"the teachings of the Holy Church are not heard, and, being cut off from the rest of the world, our fellow villagers are forced into ignorance through which morality, family, and public life from year to year all fall and fall!"—the petitioners hoped that by combining resources the 412 resi-dents of Zaval'ska and 224 residents of Ostroukhova would be able to build and staff their own church. Archbishop Anastasii turned his attention, however, to other issues, namely, his unsubstantiated claim that the major-ity of residents in both villages did not want a new church because it would be too expensive, and his reckoning that the distance between the villages and the existing church was no more than an easy three-mile walk. The Holy Synod concurred with Anastasii, but only after villagers had taken their case to the provincial zemstvo board.[35]

Regardless of the particular issue at hand, struggles between local com-munities of believers and faraway religious officials became increasingly preoccupied with questions of legitimate authority. At least until 1905 the written word ruled, social rank dominated, and religious power eluded the faithful.

Rising Tensions over Parish Authority

From the emancipation in 1861 until the outbreak of the revolution in 1905, the repeated failure of church authorities to reform the parish from above coincided with the beginning of peasants' attempts to gain broader independence in local religious life. With few exceptions, the ongoing ne-gotiation between peasants and higher church officials regarding parish af-fairs was conducted peacefully, and although the decisions of the Voronezh diocesan administration and Holy Synod favored the clergy, most villagers appeared to be convinced that the scales of justice were not tipped unfairly against them. This helps to explain why so many communities allocated precious resources to file petitions and appeals to diocesan and synodal au-thorities: parishioners believed that they had a fair chance of achieving their goals. When, beginning in 1905, peasants increasingly turned to vio-lent means to acquire more control over parish administration, they did so out of frustration with an ineffective and unsympathetic religious bureau-cracy, and not to unseat the faith that provided existential meaning to their often dreary lives. Responding to the unexpected turn of events, and out of desperation to quell agitated parishioners throughout the country-side, the Holy Synod asked bishops to submit a list of recommendations on how to reform local religious life. Not surprisingly, the responses over-whelmingly stressed the need to reinvigorate the parish community by al-lowing it greater autonomy in the everyday management of local religious life and by restoring its legal status, which would bring with it rights of ownership. Peasants were not, of course, to be granted authority over dogmatic matters, but they would be given a freer hand in administering parish finances, schools, buildings, and land and in settling internal disputes. Restoration of the elective principle *(vybornoe nachalo)*, which had been abolished at the end of the eighteenth century, also received widespread support as a means of establishing a new contractual relationship between the clergy and the laity.[36]

Although parish reform remained mostly at the level of discussion after 1905, church and secular leaders had finally, and publicly, begun to admit that their conceptions of local religious life were out of sync with village reality. As political unrest and rural uprisings rapidly eroded the foundations of village life in the last decade of tsarist rule, believers rallied around the parish church as a symbol of unity that allowed for a broad range of voices and interests. At the same time believers struggled to gain control over parish life, they also began to wander the countryside in search of sacred phenomena that infused the local community of believers with new religious excitement.

Saints, Pilgrimage, and Modern Russian Orthodox Identity

Leaning with a crook in one hand,

They move forward step by step,

Wiping sweat with their sleeve,

The Russian Orthodox people.

—Psalmist Ivan Prozorovskii, on the fiftieth anniversary

of the canonization of St. Tikhon of Zadonsk

*T*he power of Orthodox Christianity to evoke ideas of the nation lies in its rich assortment of symbols and rituals that offer regular means of interacting with and imagining ever larger communities of coreligionists. Orthodox theology itself provides the foundation for holistic identities in its teachings on the Eucharist and tradition. In its most essential form, the church reaffirms its existence and renews its unity in Christ during the Eucharistic reenactment of the Last Supper.[1] Though often ignorant of theology, ordinary believers also placed the Eucharist and the liturgy at the center of religious tradition, and, in doing so, *imagined* that their coreligionists were performing the same rituals. Proof that this imagined community existed was as close as the neighboring Orthodox parish, but for an increasing number of believers this sense of communion was also discovered during visits to Russian holy places scattered around the empire. As peasants embarked on pilgrimages with increasing frequency after 1861, religious and national identity intersected in the form of a greater community of Orthodox faithful, first vis-à-vis believers of neighboring parishes, then as members of the Russian national church, and finally as part of the Ecumenical church.[2]

Pilgrimage as a widespread religious phenomenon came to Russia later than in most European countries and emphasized physical motion, as in the Latin tradition, in contrast to spiritual renewal through adoration, reverence, and worship, which is of primary importance in the Greek tradition. The particularly Russian contribution to Orthodox Christian pilgrimage is that the hardships of religious travel equated spiritual improvement with physical sacrifice that resembles more the Western *peregrination,* with its combination of "walking and suffering [to pay] off the reward there is to be attained," than the Greek *proskinima* and its tradition of spiritual renewal.[3] Before the emancipation of the serfs in 1861, the majority of Orthodox faithful experienced religious travel much as it had for centuries: vicariously through pilgrims' tales and popular versions of saints' lives; during visits to local churches or monasteries of distinguished sacredness; or as part of an individual or group pilgrimage. After 1861 freedom of mobility, the availability of affordable train travel, a reliable highway system, and the rise of provincial commerce facilitated the growth of pilgrimage among peasants, who began to appear in large numbers at faraway holy places such as the Kievan Monastery of the Caves, the Holy Land, and Mt. Athos. On a more modest scale, religious travel gradually became an important expression of popular Orthodoxy as peasants visited local fairs and markets that coincided with the feast days of nearby churches and monasteries.[4]

Although not without some caution about the mobile and hard-to-control religious masses, church and secular authorities generally viewed the rise in pilgrimage after 1861 as an opportunity to infuse old symbols of Orthodoxy with new meaning. At holy places and during the increasing number of public celebrations of imperial history, popular and elite constructions of national identity intersected in the spectrum of local identity and encouraged peasants to expand their traditional conceptions of the world to include notions of the region or nation. When a local shrine was officially recognized as significant to the fate of the nation, it became the destination of a journey toward modern *Russian* Orthodox identity when "homeland / home region" *(rodina)* came to mean "fatherland" *(otechestvo).*[5] Similarly, when provincial residents imbued local events with national significance or, conversely, validated the importance of moments in national history by reconfiguring them as affirmations of the locale, they were etching out their new identity as Russian nationals. The result was a popular understanding of "Russia" that was ambiguously modern and equivocally national.[6]

Voronezh province was graced with two shrines that were important to late-imperial Russian Orthodoxy. The first, the Annunciation Mitrofanov Monastery in Voronezh city, housed the relics of St. Mitrofan. As the first bishop of Voronezh, St. Mitrofan was a provincial religious pioneer, whose friendship with Peter the Great and affection for the common people were embedded in local lore. The other shrine was the Zadonsk Birthgiver of God Monastery, where the relics of St. Tikhon were preserved. Although

Mitrofan and Tikhon were made saints within a thirty-year period of each other, they represent different uses of canonization by secular and church authorities. Mitrofan's elevation was a small episode in the history of the national church, whereas celebrations of Tikhon's sanctity were much grander in scale, promoted a new symbol of the national faith, and encouraged religious travel as an ideal expression of Orthodox spirituality. The Tikhon canonization set into motion an explosion of pilgrimage activity that lasted beyond 1917 as large numbers of pious commoners were drawn to beloved and newly discovered shrines.[7]

Holy People and Sacred Shrines

Many communities and individuals in late-imperial Russia were attracted to wondrous icons or religious objects because they had proven their abilities to protect against calamity, served as instruments of good fortune, or performed miracles. Knowledge of hierophantic essence first and foremost spread by word of mouth, but literate peasants also turned to published stories about sacred people and places for information about holy people and their shrines. A popular written source for these stories was *Troitskie listki,* which was used by clergymen in their weekly sermons, was freely distributed during religious holidays, and was available for purchase at many pilgrimage destinations. The contents of *Troitskie listki* appealed to newly literate peasants interested in spiritual feats, philanthropic activities, and wondrous works of people who began their lives in circumstances familiar to most villagers. In addition to portraying these spiritual heroes as struggling to balance the often conflicting demands of the secular and religious roads they traveled, the tales in *Troitskie listki* also held out the possibility of spiritual and physical rewards that could be obtained during visits to sacred shrines.[8]

One such hero was Andrei the Holy Fool (1744–1812), the son of a small landowner in Kaluga province, who renounced his privileged heritage. Early on, the contemplative Andrei displayed the peculiar habits of walking around naked (in the tradition of holy fools) and roaming about with a knout and axe tied on his left shoulder. Despite being ridiculed by local children who called him Andrei the Axe, he rejected his upbringing and helped out in the fields. At the age of thirty-five, Andrei moved to the district capital, where he quickly gained a reputation for his spirituality and good works. Toward the end of his life he entered the Meshchovsk Monastery which, after his death, became a pilgrimage destination for many seeking the benefits of his healing powers.[9]

The story of Anastasia Semenovna Logacheva (1809–1875) held up the ideals of determination, perseverance, and faith that were common in the holy person's biography. A peasant from Nizhnii Novgorod province, at the tender age of twelve Anastasia was abandoned inexplicably by her parents.

Left to fend for herself, Anastasia decided to visit the famous local spiritual elder, Serafim of Sarov, to ask for his blessing on her decision to begin an eremitic life. Instead of giving his approval, Serafim advised Anastasia to witness the holy relics in Kiev and to reconsider her decision. Upon arriving home from Kiev, she discovered that her parents had returned just as suddenly as they had departed, and once again Anastasia decided to call on Serafim. This time Serafim reminded her of her filial obligation to care for her parents and urged her to postpone entering the religious life until after their death. For twenty years Anastasia dutifully provided for her aging parents by reading the Psalter for the Dead, working in the fields, and spinning. After their death, she dug a cave where Serafim told her she would smell the scent of burning palms and, finally, began her long anticipated spiritual life. As word of Anastasia's residence in the cave spread, Orthodox faithful from all social backgrounds began traveling to her humble abode. Following a pilgrimage to Jerusalem, Anastasia finally settled into the new Nikolaevskii women's monastery in Tomsk province (central Siberia), where she was tonsured and later appointed Mother Superior. After her death, rumors about the healing power of her relics attracted many pilgrims to her grave in the monastery.[10] Although Anastasia upheld tradition, she did so reluctantly and only at the insistence of Russia's most famous holy man and with seemingly little feeling for her parents, who had, after all, capriciously turned their back on her.[11]

As the reputations of holy people became widely known through published lives, their shrines became popular destinations for pilgrimages. When one of these holy people was canonized, the additional publicity brought by commissioned biographies, laudatory remarks spoken in sermons by ordinary clergymen, and personal accounts of those who attended canonization events increased the number of pilgrims visiting their shrines. The story of Mitrofan of Voronezh is an example of a holy man whose tremendous popularity eventually led to canonization. Soon after his death in 1703, and long before the church officially recognized his sanctity, pilgrims began to stream to his grave at the Annunciation Mitrofanov Monastery in search of spiritual or physical succor.[12] Reports of wondrous healings at the grave of Mitrofan attracted a growing number pilgrims, especially after 1830 when his uncorrupted remains were accidentally discovered by then Archbishop Antonii of Voronezh (1826–1846) and monks of the Annunciation Mitrofanov Monastery. Soon as many as fifty thousand pilgrims visited the wondrous remains.[13] Curious suspicion moved the Holy Synod to investigate the discovery and, in the spring of 1832, to declare that Mitrofan's remains were uncorrupted and to confirm that he was the source of tens of confirmed miracles. A public ceremony marking the canonization of Mitrofan was set for 6 August 1832.

To create the proper atmosphere for the ceremonies, the governor of Voronezh, D. N. Begichev, ordered two public announcements to be read in all the churches instructing local officials and residents how to decorate public buildings and private residences. The instructions also established protocol for maintaining public order during the ceremonies, authorized the construction of separate spectators' sections corresponding to social estates, arranged for adequate housing and victuals for the expected crowd of fifty thousand, commanded all building custodians to remain at home at all times and to lock up if they needed to leave (to prevent theft), and appealed to all local residents to take special care in preventing fires.[14] Despite the flow of pilgrims from all parts of Russia, the canonization of Mitrofan remained a local event: Mitrofan's sanctity was not described in terms of national destiny or history, but as a manifestation of the Russian people's reverence for the extraordinary spiritual and thaumaturgic characteristics of a provincial hero who happened to be a religious paragon. As the life of Mitrofan was written and rewritten dozens of times, corrections and embellishments were made, but two things remained constant: his fondness for commoners and his association with two important moments in Russian history—Muscovy's fortification of the southern border against the Crimean Tatars in the sixteenth and seventeenth centuries and Peter the Great's construction of a modern navy in Voronezh.[15]

The canonization of the other Voronezh saint, Tikhon of Zadonsk, less than thirty years later represents a different type of sanctification, one that celebrated historical figures as influencing or validating the uniqueness of Russian history and the essence of national identity. Whereas Mitrofan's canonization scarcely referenced the nation, celebrations of Tikhon's sanctity promoted the saint as a new symbol for a reform-oriented Russia free of serfdom and on the road to social and economic development. Dubbed the "people's saint" (narodnyi sviatitel'), Tikhon was, however briefly, portrayed as a protector in whom the Russian Orthodox faithful could place their hopes and dreams.

The basic story of Tikhon's life was not very different from that of the saints featured in Troitskie listki. Like some of them, Tikhon defied his humble background and climbed the ecclesiastical hierarchy; once he became bishop of Voronezh, he had no qualms about renouncing the fineries of episcopal life and enthusiastically associated with commoners. Born into a large and impoverished deacon's family of Novgorod province during the last year of Peter the Great's reign, he should have expected little more than to follow in his father's footsteps. Soon after the death of his father, Tikhon began his training for the deaconate at the Novgorod religious school and then at the diocesan seminary. He excelled in his studies and seemed destined for the priesthood until he was miraculously saved from certain death when the railing at the top of a bell tower at a local monastery suddenly broke and crashed to the ground while he was leaning against it.[16] A short time later, Tikhon had a second wondrous experience, an "ecstatic" sensation that culminated in a mystical vision, while gazing at the evening heavens, contemplating his good fortune and the mysteries of eternity. Convinced that the strange force and premonition were signs of his special mission in life, Tikhon took monastic vows and began a rapid advancement up the clerical hierarchy that culminated in his appointment to the bishopric of Voronezh in 1763. During his brief tenure as bishop of Voronezh (he retired to the Zadonsk Monastery in 1767), Tikhon earned a reputation for his vigorous reform of the clergy, strident opposition to Old Belief, and preaching against nonstandard Christian practices. In his later years, Tikhon won a special place in the hearts of peasants who came to regard him as one of their own.[17]

Soon after his death, stories about Tikhon and his wonderworking abilities began to attract a loyal following that cut across all social strata, catapulting him into the exclusive cohort of wonderworker superstars.[18] His place in elite and commoner collective memory was assured by the 1796 biography written by Evgenii Bolkhovitinov, the metropolitan of Kiev and a prominent historian of the region, whose work would serve as a model for all subsequent scholarly and popular lives of the saint.[19] By the time of Tikhon's canonization in 1861, Bolkhovitinov's biography had been reprinted ten times and matched the popularity of simpler versions of *The Life of St. Tikhon* that began to appear at the beginning of the nineteenth century.[20] Alongside literary representations of Tikhon was an evolving praxis at his shrine in the Zadonsk Monastery, which peaked every year on 13 August, the date of Tikhon's death, when Voronezh bishops, governors, local landowners, and pilgrims (mostly from the privileged classes) attended memorial services.

A devoted following of believers was not enough to propel Tikhon along the road to sanctity, and he might have remained no more than a beloved local holy man had Archbishop Antonii, Archimandrite Simeon (rector of the Voronezh theological seminary), and Abbot Serafim (of the Zadonsk Monastery) not accidentally discovered Tikhon's uncorrupted remains in 1846.[21] As word of the discovery of Tikhon's uncorrupted remains spread, pilgrims seeking cures and special blessings from the deceased prelate now turned their restless energies toward Zadonsk.[22] As the shrine's popularity gained strength over the years, the Holy Synod finally agreed to send an investigative team to Zadonsk in May 1861.[23] Led by Metropolitan Isidor of Kiev, the clergymen described the body of Tikhon from head to toe, revealing a morbid satisfaction that the Synod's men had not been sent in vain.

> Despite the fact that [the corpse] has been in the grave for 76 years, the body of Saint [*sic*] Tikhon . . . has been preserved uncorrupted, except for one big toe on the left foot, which has been subjected to decay by the unalterable determination of the Creator and Lord, according to which if not the entire body of a person, then at least some part of it, should be returned to the earth from which it was taken. The flesh on all the limbs of the body is preserved, hardened and clinging to the bones, its color darkened and similar to the color of the famous preserved uncorrupted relics of the Holy Saints. The shoulder and knee joints of the arms and legs are a little detached, though they are not entirely separated . . . several limbs lack agility sufficient enough to be moved.[24]

The team also verified at least forty-nine miracles attributed to the Zadonsk holy man since 1820, when a monastery register listing earlier wondrous works was purloined by a pilgrim.[25] Among those listed in the register, all but five were from Voronezh and its neighboring provinces. Peasant women were most likely to be cured (14), followed by women of the landowning or service classes (11), men of the landowning or service classes (6), women of the lower urban and merchant classes (5), peasant men (3), merchants (2 men, 2 women), monks (2), nuns (2), one priest, and one man of the lower urban and merchant classes. These numbers attest to the diverse social background of pilgrims visiting the relics, as well as the local, rather than national, appeal of Tikhon. By using the canonization ceremonies to praise the autocracy for emancipating the serfs and by promoting Tikhon as an emblem of modern Russia, the Holy Synod, at least for the moment, transformed this provincial holy man into a national symbol.[26]

The Canonization of Tikhon of Zadonsk

Anxious to portray harmony between popular and official sentiment during the canonization ceremonies, members of the Holy Synod explained their selection of the Zadonsk holy man as the first post-emancipation saint as the convergence of divine will and popular sentiment. To encourage newly freed peasants to attend the event, a synodal order required that parish priests throughout European Russia announce the ceremonies in due time to allow for travel arrangements to be made.[27] Printed announcements of the canonization events, along with oral reiterations, helped to reinforce the Synod's recognition of Tikhon as an all-Russian "people's saint" whose officially recognized sanctity manifested God's way "to bless Holy Russia" as it moved away from traditional life and serfdom toward modernity and freedom.[28]

With these images in mind, the governor of Voronezh ordered Zadonsk to be cleaned up, collected donations from merchants for the construction of barracks for ten thousand pilgrims, secured adequate food and medical supplies, added fifty beds to the Zadonsk city hospital, and dispatched a doctor from the provincial capital. In order to ensure safe passage of Tikhon's relics during the ceremonies, all trade around the monastery square was moved and a fence erected to keep the area clear for liturgical processions. Police reinforcements from the capital, along with detachments from the Voronezh fire brigade, were on hand to guarantee order and safety. Monks living in the Zadonsk Monastery joined the effort and vacated their cells, local residents opened their homes to visiting pilgrims, and still others organized the construction of 120 wooden dormitories and raised tents on open squares. Through their efficient preparations, local officials demonstrated that Voronezh province was worthy of such a national event and that Zadonsk was an attractive destination for future pilgrims.[29]

The hustle and bustle to prepare for the event occasioned both avaricious and charitable behavior and gave rise to numerous wondrous works. One story tells of innkeepers who sought to increase their profits by raising nightly rates, while another tells of local merchants who fixed the price of kvas and agreed to sell water (which was otherwise free). The very next day a fire broke out in a neighborhood surrounding the monastery that destroyed tens of wooden homes and all of the inns except that of an innkeeper who refused to agree to price fixing. One of the homes saved from the fire belonged to a pious woman of little means who planned to distribute food to impoverished pilgrims. Of greater symbolic importance, however, was the story of the protection of the Zadonsk Monastery, which was also threatened by the raging fire until its wonderworking Vladimir Mother of God icon was carried around the premises and placed in front of the relics of Archbishop Tikhon.[30]

Anticipation of the canonization mounted for several weeks as many pilgrims—mostly peasants—arrived after having spent three days walking to Zadonsk from the shrine of St. Mitrofan in Voronezh. According to one eyewitness, the combined pilgrimage to Voronezh and Zadonsk was already an established tradition by which "all of the pilgrims *(bogomol'tsy)* who came . . . to revere the relics of St. Mitrofan already considered it a sacred obligation to visit [Tikhon] in order to take their prayers to his grave."[31] Another eyewitness emphasized the unwavering determination of commoners "who came on foot . . . set up . . . outside the monastery wall, on the monastery square, nearby streets, anywhere they were able to lay their head for the night. . . . Cripples of all types, the weak, blind, possessed, and all sorts of lame people were brought and came in great numbers in expectation of heavenly assistance through prayers and appeals to the saint."[32] Nikolai Ivanovich Subbotin, a professor at the Moscow Theological Academy and the invited guest of Bishop Sergei of Kursk (later Metropolitan of Moscow), who had been dispatched to the canonization by the Holy Synod, offered an elite perspective of the same events as he enjoyed all the conveniences that were available, including "a lovely little house . . . prepared for us. . . . From our window the entire monastery and all that was going on there could be seen."[33] As the event neared, the mood in Zadonsk was one of great expectation.[34]

During the three-day event, more than three hundred invited dignitaries, including Grand Prince Nikolai Nikolaevich; the chief procurator of the Holy Synod, Alexander Petrovich Tolstoy; representatives of the senate and Ministry of Internal Affairs; lesser military and civilian officials; distinguished merchants from Voronezh province; Metropolitan Isidor of Novgorod and St. Petersburg (a member of the Holy Synod); Bishop Feofan of Tambov; Bishop Sergii of Kursk; numerous abbots; and hundreds of clergymen. Surrounding these representatives of imperial officialdom were three hundred thousand pilgrims, most arriving on foot from all over Russia and as far away as Mt. Athos. Between 8 and 15 August 1861 more than seven thousand people confessed, and more than twenty thousand received the Eucharist.[35]

Throughout the canonization ceremonies, the divine and national significance of Tikhon's sanctity emphasized Russia's seminal transition away from the darkness of serfdom to a bright future promised by modernization.[36] Metropolitan Isidor of Novgorod and St. Petersburg created his own symbolic unity that portrayed the shrine as an embodiment of Orthodoxy, autocracy, and nationality, the nationalist formula created in 1833 by Tsar Nicholas I's education minister, Count Sergei Uvarov.[37] Archbishop Iosif of Voronezh, who had pressured the Synod on the matter of canonization, was portrayed as sympathetic to the "voice of the people who had long considered Tikhon a saint."[38] Another observer interpreted the outpouring of pilgrims to be an expression of national Orthodox harmony between the various social estates and "another sign of God's pleasure with Russia," which would provide a source of national strength and greatness in the future.[39] Although declarations of national unity were not new, what distinguished the canonization pronouncements was their appeal to popular piety through a much-loved provincial holy man to justify the new direction that Russia was taking.

In portraying officialdom as receptive to the religious sentiment of the people, organizers drew attention to the common points between elite Orthodoxy and more narrowly focused local interests. By bowing to the wishes of Petersburg officials, local authorities were not simply duped into following more sophisticated political and religious leaders, but eagerly identified their backwater province with the prestige of the empire through its nationally recognized local hero. By cleaning up the city, building hospitals and lodging, and ensuring order and propriety, provincial officials were determined to prove that their Voronezh was capable and worthy of a national event. The glory of the empire was brought—for a brief time—to this provincial capital, and its residents, who attended the ceremonies, could not have failed to notice.[40]

The Shrine of St. Tikhon and Pilgrimage Experience

As a sacred place offering direct contact with the divine, the Zadonsk Monastery was transformed by the canonization into a popular and significant national shrine (see fig. 7). Year after year Voronezh bishops noted that as many as forty thousand pilgrims trekked to Zadonsk on 13 August, and as many as five thousand visited during the first week of Great Lent.[41] Miracles continued to be attributed to St. Tikhon for many years, although a decrease in their number after 1861 suggests a decline in the saint's efficacy, a shift in pilgrims' interest to other holy places, or the diminishing role of wondrous works in shrine experience and stories about it (either because wondrous works became commonplace with the increase in pilgrimage or because they were no longer considered exceptional or critical to spirituality).[42] Official accounts imprecisely noted at least one hundred cures during the canonization ceremonies for St. Tikhon, but unofficial published accounts reported only thirty-eight specific cases.[43] Stories of cures were, naturally, of a very personal nature as deformed, ailing, and possessed sinners were drawn by choice or force to the saint. The case of Tat'iana Grigorievna Kamianaia, a peasant from Voronezh province, illustrates the effect of St. Tikhon as he worked through spiritual wanderers for whom ordinary believers had a great deal of respect. Tat'iana's story began long before 1861 when her family was visited by an unknown pilgrim *(strannik)* on his way to the Zadonsk shrine. At the time, Tat'iana was a ten-year-old girl who suffered from a variety of physical ailments that left her in a semicomatose state. Even though the stranger did not invite her to join him, he advised her parents to pray to certain saints and to request a special liturgy for her health. As she later recalled, the stranger left a deep impression on her.

> [A]fter the pilgrim left, when my mother had done everything that he ordered, I began to regain consciousness and to remember everything that was said to me. . . . I began to learn prayers. And the spasms in my arms began to weaken from that terrible illness which, after some time began to go away and little by little my arms began to improve and to come alive . . . after a little while I could work a bit. My legs and waist began to go back to normal [and I stopped having] convulsions. . . . [Then] I began to learn how to crawl.[44]

A few years later Tat'iana's uncle and another villager took her on a pilgrimage to the Zadonsk Monastery during Pentecost, but full spiritual and physical renewal came only in 1861 when she determined to accompany her father and younger sister to the canonization.

The lessons to be learned in these stories were no doubt clear to those who heard them. Through perseverance, faith, and appeal to the Zadonsk holy man, ailments could be cured, wishes fulfilled, and normal life restored. Occasionally, as in the story of Anastasiia Evdokimova Il'ina, individuals living nontraditional lives were portrayed as in need of a spiritual cure that, by implication, would restore their natural function in society. Anastasiia was a bitter and withdrawn twenty-three-year-old state peasant from neighboring Tambov province who had renounced all earthly things, shirked her domestic duties, and remained on friendly terms only with her 1½-year-old son. Little by little Anastasiia began to suffer from depression, insomnia, and lack of appetite, and finally she lost her faith in God. The sudden death of her young son drove Anastasiia mad, and all attempts by her family to ease her suffering failed. Anastasiia's life took a turn for the better when she saw herself in a dream standing before the relics of Tikhon. Upon awaking, Anastasiia accompanied her mother on a journey to Zadonsk and at Tikhon's shrine at once began to feel better. Full health was restored to Anastasiia, however, only on a subsequent visit to the shrine during the canonization ceremonies.[45]

Fig. 7—Shrine of St. Tikhon of Zadonsk, 1902

Other stories emphasized hierophantic power in action and the extreme physical and spiritual transformation a pilgrimage could effect. When Matfei Dmitriev Poliakov, a thirty-year-old peasant from Tambov province, heard about Tikhon's canonization, he set out for Zadonsk in hope of a cure for his progressive rheumatism. "On the first day, with great effort, I walked more than four miles. On the second and third days, already feeling somewhat weakened from the illness, I was able to walk up to nineteen miles, and, nearing Zadonsk, with prayers to the saint, the sores on my body [from rheumatism] withered and I became completely well."[46] A few years later a secretary from the city of Voronezh, having suffered for nine years from debilitating and untreatable rheumatism, decided to visit the relics of Saints Tikhon and Mitrofan as a double intervention. Confined to a bed, she immediately felt better when she kissed the relics of Tikhon and, with the help of her servant, stood up.[47]

As the flow of pilgrims to the Zadonsk shrine continued unabated, certain shrine-related practices emerged, such as receiving the Eucharist at the shrine, especially during the first week of Lent, when up to five thousand pilgrims usually communed.[48] Local officials were always wary of large gatherings of people, and eventually they came to suspect the intentions of pilgrims as petty theft and pickpocketing increased during well-attended services. But for most observers of these occasions, the outpouring of spirituality by the faithful peasantry was a local expression of national traits. A Zadonsk schoolteacher, writing at the end of the nineteenth century, put it this way:

> If there is still a living, pure, just, and redemptive faith, then it lives mostly in the simple Russian people and burns brightly with a genuine light in their innocent hearts. . . .
>
> In this simple and unwavering bulwark lies the living faith as the basis of the life of the all-Russian state, preserving the originality, nationality, power, praise, and honor of our dear fatherland.[49]

Even if we dismiss this description for its hyperbole, popular spirituality was an indisputable aspect of pilgrimage to the shrines of Saints Mitrofan and Tikhon, as was the assimilation of national ideals into local identity after 1861. As pilgrimage became an important manifestation of popular piety, shrines became symbols of the highly localized Russian identity in which provincial residents could acknowledge common traits that distinguished them from other European nationals. At the same time their primary loyalty was not to the empire, but to the very plots of earth that provided fields of sustenance, spheres of activity, and chambers for eternal repose. As a new provincial identity emerged in post-emancipation Russia, it was aided by the hallmarks of modernization—education, popular literacy, and physical mobility—that were guaranteed by an increasingly remote bureaucratic autocracy. This new identity was clearly visible in Zadonsk already during the small-scale centenary celebration of Tikhon's death in 1883 when the official program and descriptions of the festive events made no mention of his national significance, but instead hailed him as a local hero.[50]

The Jubilee of St. Tikhon

The fiftieth anniversary of Tikhon's canonization marks the completion of the Zadonsk holy man's transition from nation symbol to local hero. The provincial orientation of Russian identity was expressed by the official organizer of the jubilee, the Voronezh Church Historical and Archeological Committee. Through its extensive publishing program, in its erection of memorials to St. Tikhon, and in its public appeal to the residents of the province, the committee portrayed the celebration as a *local* event honoring a *local* hero, whose Russian traits were deeply rooted in, if not derived from, his ministry in Voronezh.[51] Invited guests represented secular and religious provincial officialdom, district representatives of the various social estates, school teachers, and citizens of distinguished piety.[52] Despite its provincial focus, the jubilee was noted from afar in national religious periodicals, as well as in a special service performed in the Cathedral of Saints Peter and Paul in St. Petersburg and in congratulatory telegrams sent by Bishops Evlogii of Kholmsk, Metrofan of Elets, Mitrofan of Ekaterinburg, and Evgenii of Murom, and other lesser clergymen. But most important were the numerous editions of the life of St. Tikhon produced by the influential Moscow publisher of popular fare I. D. Sytin, who marked the occasion by issuing twenty thousand copies of *The Life of St. Tikhon of Zadonsk and the Venerable Trifon.*[53]

References to the nation made by local priests and pilgrims demonstrated another important development in Russian identity, the replacement of the tsar with a pride in the uniqueness of the Russian people.[54] Clerical and secular elites reminded their audiences of the symbolic importance of St. Tikhon as a unifying force for all the people, while speeches and poems written in honor of the anniversary, such as the lines penned by the psalmist Ivan Prozorovskii in the epigraph to this chapter, expressed the spiritual distinctiveness that unified all Russian Orthodox believers.[55] Archbishop Arsenii of Novgorod, who attended the jubilee, eloquently described this sentiment as a unifying motion that gathered people along the way. Leading a group of pilgrims on the three-day journey from the Annunciation Mitrofanov Monastery in Voronezh to Zadonsk, Archbishop Arsenii was met along the way by joyous communities who "came out onto the street from the stores and forgot their business; people stopped their domestic work, and one thing became most important: the ceremonial procession of this great crowd of people."[56]

When the procession led by Archbishop Arsenii stopped in Riadnoe village so that pilgrims could regain their strength with tea, water, and snacks, everyone enjoyed the beautiful weather, fresh air, tranquility, and voices of the choir. Pilgrims were so spiritually aroused that nobody was hungry or thirsty when they stopped for the night, and few were able to sleep. The next morning, shortly after five o'clock, they set off for the next village, Kon'-Kolodez', where the village elder and distinguished residents greeted them in festive clothes and offered them lunch. In the next village they were met with the traditional greeting of hospitality, bread and salt, as well as food and vodka. Despite the rain on their second night, not a complaint was uttered. As the procession approached Zadonsk on the third day, thousands of people lined the road, singing the Easter hymn. That evening, during a memorial vesper service in honor of the parents and relatives of St.

Tikhon, as well as Catherine the Great (who reigned when Tikhon served as bishop of Voronezh), the commotion produced by anxious believers pushing their way closer to the relics threatened to spoil the solemnity of the event when other believers became irritated by the disturbance. On the streets and squares near the monastery, the buzz of a "human wall" of people could be heard as they alternately glanced at the monastery and dashed into shops, booths, and pubs for souvenirs, food, and drink.[57]

A special correspondent for the *Voronezh Telegraph* offered one of the few depictions of mundane aspects of this religious event that were also part of pilgrimage experience. As the procession led by Archbishop Arsenii of Novgorod made its way from Voronezh to Zadonsk, the author observed tardy pilgrims rushing to catch up with the group, heard complaints about pickpockets, and overheard conversations about the best viewing places in Zadonsk. A colorful encounter between the correspondent and a peasant man working at the zemstvo medical station opened specially for the occasion (in the same village, Riadnoe, that Archbishop Arsenii described) suggests the variety of experience that was entirely washed out of more official and religious accounts. Arriving in the village by bicycle, the author was met by a young peasant man who emerged from his hut to offer tea or boiled water.

> [Peasant:] "Off t'Zadonsk?"
>
> "Yes, Zadonsk."
>
> "Yeah . . . Many peopl've 'lready walked and ridden there."
>
> "And how many would you say? Approximately how many have been here at your point?"
>
> "Who knows—y' couldn't count 'em all! One day y' give out eight barrels of water—the next ten. Turns out when the procession arrived from Voronezh, all four wells we have here in Riadnoe, figure, we scraped the ground, hit sand. There wasn't enough water."
>
> "How much did you give out that day?"
>
> "Well, how much: seventy-two buckets boiled and a hundred buckets of cold water . . . 'round two hundred buckets were drunk."[58]

As the procession neared Zadonsk, both sides of the road were filled with sellers doing a brisk business in fruit. Near the Zadonsk Monastery, pilgrims filled religious shops, which were stocked with icons of St. Tikhon, ringlets inscribed with his image, and medals made for the occasion. Yet, despite the author's interest in the profane moments of pilgrimage experience, he reiterated the commonly used image of unity and harmony that whitewashed distinctions based on class, wealth, or politics: "The sea of human heads! Village pilgrims mixed with city dwellers blocked all of Bol'shaia Moskovskaia Street [the main thoroughfare of Voronezh], stopping horse-drawn trams, automobiles, and cabs."[59]

Misled by the unchanging Orthodox liturgical practice and possibly swept up in the religious sentiment of the occasion, observers failed to note the differences between the canonization and the jubilee, or just how much rural society had changed since 1861, and thus perpetuated the myth of eternal and unchanging piety.[60] Chief among the changes was literacy, which left no aspect of society or culture untouched as the written word became an unavoidable presence in everyday life. In Zadonsk and in the capital of Voronezh, public readings were organized by local officials, clergymen, and religious brotherhoods that addressed large, attentive crowds about the negative effects on the Orthodox way of life that were caused by industrialization, revolutionary activity, and the religious toleration edict of 1905. As a justification of their concerns, one needed only to look at the security measures taken in Zadonsk, which recalled the revolutionary unrest of 1905–1907 and the need to ensure that the event would not be used by political activists as a venue for propagation. Criminal activity was an added concern, and local officials were searching constantly for gangs of petty thieves who now traveled the shrine circuit in search of new victims.[61]

Valid though these concerns were, they overshadowed widespread expressions of support for Orthodox Christianity and St. Tikhon as the smallest and remotest communities organized their own celebrations with a sense of pride and connection to a greater family of believers.[62] One such village was the community of Iasenovko, whose clergy marked the occasion by performing holiday vespers in festive robes and by singing the Akathist hymn before a flower-draped icon of St. Tikhon. During the liturgy on 13 August, the parish priest delivered a sermon about St. Tikhon and honored the request of parishioners to end the service with a procession with the holy icon. A local student from the Zadonsk clerical school carried the icon as the procession moved to the village square for a prayer service and the singing of "Many Years" to the imperial family, the Holy Synod, and the sitting archbishop, Anastasii. Later that afternoon the parish priest delivered a speech about St. Tikhon, which was followed by a special collection for a lamp to be placed at the shrine in Zadonsk.[63] If allowance is made for the much smaller size and fewer resources available to the village, the celebrations of Iasenovko and Zadonsk were quite alike. Local pride, combined with spiritual devotion to the saint and any possible benefits that might be received by showing him favor, were clearly present in both, but by purchasing a lamp for the shrine of St. Tikhon the Iasenovko community expressed its solidarity with the larger community of Orthodox believers who lived and worshiped beyond the boundaries of the village.

Pilgrimage and Modern Russian Orthodox Identity

The growth in pilgrimage among the Russian peasantry in the last half century of tsarist rule was encouraged by a deep folk belief in a world enchanted by benevolent and malevolent forces engaged in an endless battle involving ordinary mortals. The rigors of the daily struggle to negotiate a moderate path closer to good than evil were mimicked in the difficulties of religious travel, which required physical suffering as a prerequisite for spiritual renewal. Even with the construction of better highways and railroads, the most popular shrines, such as the Zadonsk and Sarov monasteries (in Nizhnii Novgorod), often remained at least half a day away by coach from the nearest coach stop or train station. But each shrine had its own significance, and the Zadonsk Birthgiver of God Monastery owed its importance to both Tikhon of Zadonsk and the synodal officials, who transformed his canonization into a model for future attempts to present a modern version of national identity that affirmed by divine approval the new paths taken by the empire. Eager to demonstrate the harmony of an increasingly disunited people, religious and secular leaders admired devout pilgrims, who, often traveling in groups, represented the strongest counterexample of the squalid and debauched life to be found in lower-working-class districts of any large city. The model seldom worked as well as it did during the Zadonsk celebrations in 1861, and by the time of the infamous canonization of Serafim of Sarov in 1903, the imperial household's attempt to insert its own favorite holy man into the framework of the empire pointed to the insurmountable chasm between the monarchy and its people.

The juxtaposition of traditional and modern paradigms is common in the creation of modern national identity. What distinguished Russia from its European cousins was the failure to create a sense of nation, while forging a strong cultural identity that was both difficult to separate from Orthodox ethos and deeply rooted in local experience. As an event, the canonization of St. Tikhon was unique, but the Zadonsk shrine was one of hundreds like it in Russia that attracted regular groups of devoted members of the Orthodox faith as pilgrimage became more common in the late nineteenth century. Living in the ambiguous space between "the culture of our fathers" and the rapidly changing present, Russian pilgrims were engaging in what Benedict Anderson has called "the most touching and grandiose journeys of the imagination" away from the routines of ordinary life toward the uncertainties of a modern future.[64]

CHAPTER SIX

The Modernizing Village—
Rituals, Reading, and Revolution

It is my deep conviction that at the present moment the cinemas and

theaters are more attractive to the public than religious services. The satanic

temptation of young people is greater than religious motivation.

—**Voronezh priest, 1915**

*O*ne of the hallmarks of the modern era is the secularization of the public sphere as the nonreligious functions of organized religion are subsumed by specialized government institutions.[1] In countries like tsarist Russia, where a monopolistic state church enjoyed legal protection, the political and cultural authority of Orthodox Christianity slowly weakened in the last half of the nineteenth century; at the same time devotion to localized religious practice deepened among rank-and-file members of the faith. Although the Russian Orthodox Church was not yet irrelevant as a bureaucratic administrative structure, beginning with the great reforms in the 1860s and culminating with the Bolshevik edict establishing the separation of church and state in January 1918, it simply could not compete in the field of its most important nonreligious endeavors in primary schooling and popular culture. Despite the appeal of secular schools and culture, Orthodox peasants remained loyal to their faith, even after the 1905 edict on religious toleration delivered a sharp psychological blow to church leaders, who were left struggling to define the new role of Orthodoxy in revolutionary Russia. In Voronezh province, where important pockets of Old Believers and sectarians could have become centers of large disaffection from Orthodoxy, a consistently high percentage of the Orthodox population fulfilled the basic requirements of annual communion and confession, baptized its children and buried its dead in the faith, or refused to leave the church after 1905.[2]

What then lay at the root of church leaders' trepidation about the demise of Orthodoxy? Was it the gradual empowerment—through literacy and knowledge—of the peasantry, or was it a reaction to the secularization of society and culture that implied a marginalized, superfluous role for the church? As the village faithful turned to religious activism, the Orthodox episcopate interpreted their behavior in terms of dissent and feared the consequences of an independent, literate, and rational peasantry who followed the provincial newspapers, consumed popular literature, and, most alarming for religious conservatives, read and interpreted the Russian-language Bible, which finally appeared in 1876, four years after the first translation of Karl Marx's *Capital* became available in the land of the tsars.

Literacy, Cultural Enlightenment, and Social Change

More than anything else in post-emancipation Russia, literacy helped to shatter illusions about age-old village traditions, raised hopes about the opportunities offered by modernization, and, from the state's point of view, would create a civic awareness rooted in the principles of Orthodoxy and autocracy.[3] These patriotic goals were born out of educated Russians' stereotypes of peasant "cultural impoverishment," a conveniently imprecise idea that led conservatives and liberals alike to stake the future of the empire on an enlightened, economically productive, and self-sufficient peasant citizenry. In the process of creating a capable and trustworthy folk, a bitter competition for limited resources pitted educators who believed that instruction ought to have a strong religious basis against supporters of a secular curriculum in which faith was treated, if at all, as one of many important cultural phenomena. Between 1864 and 1884, secular village primary schools outnumbered their religious counterparts and had acquired twenty years of experience and broad peasant support by the time the Holy Synod attempted to establish a parish school system virtually out of air. In Voronezh tremendous initial gains were made by parish schools; between 1894 and 1904 they outpaced the efforts of the zemstvos, the peasant communes, and the Ministry of Education and claimed nearly 39 percent of all village pupils in the province. This rapid growth, however, masked the church's difficult financial circumstances, and most parishes lacked sufficient resources, trained teachers, or permanent quarters for their schools. The demise of the parish school system was all but certain when, in 1907, the Ministry of Education introduced new regulations that linked school funding to rigid standards of quality. Few parish schools could meet these standards, and their number declined rapidly. But, by then, they had educated a significant portion of peasant children in Voronezh and contributed to the doubling of literacy rates between 1894 and 1914.[4]

Among the achievements of primary schooling, religious or secular, was an overall "civilizing process" that transformed the way schooled peasants thought and behaved. In the words of one zemstvo teacher, the literate peasant is "more developed than the illiterate peasant, speaks more correctly, is not as superstitious . . . , looks more skeptically at prejudices, is more intelligent about religion, goes to church more frequently, and in general is more religious than the illiterate peasant."[5] Schooling also left its mark on the reading tastes of peasants, who were avid consumers of religious and moral literature. In 1894 a study conducted in the Nizhnedevitsk district revealed the traditional predilections of peasants who had completed primary education.[6] Fifty-seven percent of those questioned claimed to read often; nearly two-thirds of them listed "religious or moral books" as the type of works they preferred most; and nearly one-third claimed that "stories or tales," especially if historical, were their favorites.[7] A less detailed study conducted in 1909 and 1910 by the Voronezh Provincial Primary School Education Society reiterated the "civilizing effects" of literacy without revealing what peasants were reading. It is safe to assume, however, that the literary tastes of peasants in Voronezh followed the general trends described by Jeffrey Brooks, that is, religious topics continued to hold sway, while stories of adventure, success, and exotica were becoming the standard fare of newly literate peasants. Among the most popular religious publications were illustrated pamphlets *(listki),* or what one priest called the "journal for the people," which excerpted from standard collections of saints' lives *(Chetii-Minei)* and *Tales from the Life of St. Tikhon of Zadonsk.*[8] Like their secular counterparts, many religious stories were about adventure (arduous travel to a sacred place, a struggle against a spiritual enemy or temptation), exotica (a faraway sacred place, a spiritual eccentric), success (victory over dark forces), and fame (sainthood).

Religious publications for the peasantry were widely available for sale at local bookshops and local fairs and by traveling salesmen or could be read at village libraries and in reading rooms.[9] The beneficial influence of local libraries, many of them with lending privileges, was noted by Bishop Serafim of Voronezh already in 1868, when 679 out of 866 churches in the diocese made their collections of books, periodicals, and pamphlets available to the public. Some village parish libraries maintained impressive holdings that ranged from several hundred to nearly one thousand titles. Altogether, nearly sixty-seven thousand published items could be found in Voronezh church libraries; many of these were sermon collections, spiritual and moral writings, and dogmatic treatises, but more than 10 percent were of a secular nature.[10] Parish libraries did more than broaden the intellectual horizons of villagers; they also narrowed the gap between peasants and other social groups with whom they shared an interest in reading.

Church and secular leaders agreed that libraries and reading rooms were suitable arenas for informal edificatory contacts between educated Russians and commoners.[11] Yet, despite their support for libraries and reading rooms as venues of cultural enlightenment for the masses, church and secular authorities were unprepared for peasants' interest in low- and middlebrow literature, or their attraction to the "harmful" literature of religious sectarians and revolutionary publicists, and urged believers to work harder to fill their parish libraries with Orthodox religio-moral works.[12] When this tack failed, repression and eradication through imprisonment and exile were the best means of silencing the purveyors of antireligious and antigovernment ideas, whom religious and secular authorities labeled enemies of the church *(vragi tserkvi)* and plotters against the state *(kramol'niki)*.[13] In short, religious and secular officials in Voronezh believed that literacy threatened to complete what the emancipation had begun in terms of legal and social reform: the radical restructuring of patriarchal village life and its chief cultural adhesive, Orthodox Christianity.

While Orthodox leaders were apprehensive about sectarian and revolutionary publications, they also hesitated to allow free access to the Bible. One year after the emancipation had offered the prospects of personal and economic freedom, the publication of the first modern Russian translation of the New Testament offered every literate believer the possibility to read and interpret the basic text of Christianity. Very quickly, under the auspices of the Society for the Dissemination of Holy Scripture in Russia (est. 1863) and other groups, such as the British and Foreign Bible Society, an extensive colportage system emerged and eventually distributed nearly 1 million Bibles annually by 1900. Church officials reacted defensively because they feared that the Holy Scriptures in the hands of ordinary and uneducated believers could lead to personal interpretation, individual thought, and challenges to ecclesiastical authority. Unable to control supply or demand, bishops and leading clergymen concentrated their efforts on scriptural education lest, in their simple-mindedness, peasant believers misconstrue the true meaning of the Bible.[14]

As the main distribution system for the Scriptures, colportage quickly came under the shadow of sectarianism, and church leaders expressed their concern about the enthusiastic involvement of foreign, mostly Protestant, missionaries in spreading the written word of God.[15] The active promotion of the written word by non-Orthodox religious groups coincided with a softening of public attitudes toward Old Belief and sectarianism in the mid-1860s, the most noteworthy turning point being the bicentennial observation of the church schism of 1666–1667. Subdued in tone and devoid of extremist interpretations, the anniversary commemoration signaled a new intellectual curiosity about religious dissidents and their often antimodernist tendencies.[16] Old Belief began to look more benign when set alongside religious groups whose identities were grounded in the written word and revolutionary imagery.[17] As one of the best-known groups who fell under this category, the followers of writer-turned-religious-renegade Leo Tolstoy based their activities on the Boguchar estate of his chief supporter and propagator, Vladimir Grigor'evich Chertkov.[18] Religious and secular authorities tolerated

Chertkov until he threw his support behind Tolstoy's defense of the eccentric sect of the Spirit Wrestlers *(dukhobory),* whose conscientious objection eventually forced them to emigrate to Canada.[19] What bedeviled church leaders about Chertkov and the followers of Tolstoy was their authoritative teachings against the Orthodox faith and the tsarist social order. The Tolstoyans were not alone: The New Israelites were alleged to be against the government; the Adventists were accused of anarchism; the Spirit Wrestlers were purported to be adherents of Tolstoy's ideas and socialism; Shtundists were known for their social democratic tendencies; and, during World War I, Baptists were among the worst public enemies because of their passivist beliefs.[20] In Voronezh a consensus of official opinion on these groups was hard to come by, but the edict on religious toleration clearly emboldened other religious groups, such as the New Israelites, whose leader, Vasilii Semenovich Lubkov, a native of Bobrov city, came up from underground to register legally.[21]

Well-educated Russians were also blamed for their indifference to religious teachings, which struck a chord among some newly literate peasants unsatisfied with the traditionalism and conservatism offered by the church. As Archbishop Anastasii repeatedly complained, the same disciples of enlightenment in the village, the "third element" of zemstvo professionals, were "trying to destroy the people mentally and morally" at the very moment "when a thirst for knowledge and love for reading is beginning to take shape." In Anastasii's opinion, the best defense against these pernicious ideas was the construction of more parish libraries that could be stocked with "a good selection of books . . . for reading at home, good books that can provide healthy food for the soul and occupy free time with a useful activity," and the expansion of public readings of religio-moral texts. By selecting libraries and public readings as venues for the guidance of believers along the Orthodox path, Archbishop Anastasii acknowledged the popular ferment for religious knowledge and direct access to the teachings of the faith that had inspired new interactive lectures that were organized by ordinary parish clergymen.[22] As they acquired a deeper knowledge of the faith from the written word, peasants actively sought to understand the relevance of Orthodox teachings in a changing world. Although viewing this interest as a positive development, church leaders were unable to control peasants' use of religious knowledge, especially after they departed their villages for work in towns and cities.[23]

New Mores at the End of an Era

Most critiques of the Russian peasantry at the end of the nineteenth century argued that alcohol and urban culture contributed to the rise in disrespect for elders, theft, sexual offenses, alcoholism, gambling, foppery, and antireligiosity. Supporting the fears of educated Russians about the breakdown of the village moral code was the new science of statistics, a convenient tool for counting everything from crop yields to offenses against the faith. Although statistical calculations enable us to outline the types and tempo of deviations from patriarchal norms, they reveal nothing about the reasons behind breaches of tradition or what followed in its stead.[24] Social and cultural change in the village was precipitated by two related phenomena, literacy and migration, the chief metaphors for the city and its promises of a bright future to young peasants facing the pressures of land shortages, cramped living spaces, poverty, and boredom. Among the lures of late-nineteenth-century urban life were an array of consumer products unavailable in the countryside, social mobility, and revolutionary ideas. By the beginning of the twentieth century, a distinctly modern urban youth culture had taken shape that posed real and symbolic challenges to the hierarchies of Russian society.[25] Rather than offer a detailed account of changing mores in the last decades of the old regime, I will provide an overview of an assortment of issues that preoccupied the clergy and laity of the Voronezh countryside in order to illustrate the central relevance of religion in everyday village life.[26]

ALCOHOLISM

At the beginning of the twentieth century, tsarist reformers, critics, and medical professionals distinguished between three main categories of drinking: merrymaking on and around personal, village, and parish holidays; symbolic use to seal an agreement or reciprocate a favor; and dependency that had long-term consequences for agricultural productivity and morality. A dazzling array of statistics offered proof of the debilitating effects of alcohol on the peasantry and became *de rigueur* in discussions of peasant and lower-urban-class social ills, but the most harmful of all were the new drinking customs that migrant workers brought with them when they returned home for the holidays.[27] One prominent psychiatrist, writing in 1897, was moved to label alcoholism the "disease of our century."[28] Speaking at a special session on alcoholism at the Ninth Congress of the Pirogov Society of Russian Physicians in 1904, Professor G. V. Khlopin declared that "Russia has the sad privilege of being first in Europe in the incidence of death from alcoholism," yet made little effort in reducing consumption.[29] In its resolutions, the session called for an end to the state liquor monopoly, but also framed alcoholism in the broader context of civil liberties that would allow for the free dissemination of information on the detriments of excessive and addictive alcohol use.[30]

For all of the negative imagery about alcoholism, it was impossible for most Russians, peasant or otherwise, to conceive of dry religious festivals, for a feast without drink was no fun at all.[31] It is no wonder that the bishops and governors of Voronezh called for a general ban on the sale of alcohol on Sundays and holidays in the hope of bringing the people to their senses and to the church.[32] Short of prohibition, a synodal decree of 1889 forbade the sale of hard liquor within ninety-three yards of churches, monasteries, prayer houses, and chapels, but alcohol-producing enterprises were exempt from this regulation provided that they did not interfere with worship services.[33] The effect of such decrees was negligible, and the parish clergy complained of its helplessness in the battle against excessive merry-making at the end of the agricultural season and during holidays. The bleak situation led one priest to conclude in 1901 that the people were only interested in the proverbial "bread and circus."[34] Others warned that the greatest threat facing the clergy was a general skepticism toward things religious by those who lived by the slogan "eat, drink, and be merry, for tomorrow you die, and all that will remain of you will be at the grave."[35]

More was at stake than peasant morality, and the endless succession of village feast days was held up by church and secular officials as a drain on the economy. Between 1867 and 1909, as part of the general reformation of post-emancipation society, bishops and provincial officials increasingly framed their moral indignation of peasant religious festivals in terms of lost agricultural and industrial productivity. For many officials, the antidote to frequent drunkenness was a reduction in days off of work.[36] In 1907, a special commission of the state council drew up a new list of national holidays that came to a mere sixty-three, including Sundays, the twelve main feasts of the Orthodox calendar, and the days honoring the imperial family. Two years later, however, the commission acknowledged the failure of its efforts and added seven more holidays.[37] Such a number was unrealistic, and while the state council formulated its policy and the Synod debated definitions, district administrators throughout Voronezh province introduced their own regulations.[38] Similarly intricate lists drawn up by the other district capital administrations demonstrate how abstract regulations at the national level were adjusted to local needs and moral standards whose constant evolution could not wait for the latest directive from St. Petersburg while alcoholism rose and productivity dropped.

SEXUALITY AND FAMILY LIFE

Following the customary prudishness of elite society in late-tsarist Russia, in which matters of sex were discussed with scientific clinicism, Voronezh church leaders and clergymen limited their public statements on sexuality to traditional gender relations that glorified masculine and feminine virtues, harmonious relations between family members, and fraternal love between the extended family of believers.[39] These Christian values were the basis of teachings on family life in the primary-school system, which depicted the patriarchal social order as sacred. A proper religio-social upbringing started early and at home, rather than at an older age and in school, as parents taught their children to be kind members of the community, good housekeepers, and useful contributors to society who truly loved to work.[40] At greatest risk of sliding into a life of immorality were young people who had left the village for the factory, fallen out of parental control, and, brandishing their new independence, refused to respect their elders. The result was a growing peasant tolerance for openly illicit relations between the sexes, especially among the younger generation, a rise in marital separations (with or without the church's approval), and the disintegration of the family through harmful household divisions.[41]

Statistical information about marriage provides little insight on sexual mores because of the near universal custom of early matrimony among peasants and because the church strictly limited the number of divorces it granted. Recent social research on the village suggests, however, that despite the high rate of marriage and virtual absence of divorce, important shifts in sexuality were taking place, which are evident in illegitimacy rates. Between 1864 and 1904 the number of babies born out of wedlock in rural and urban areas of Voronezh province followed the same trends as elsewhere in the empire and declined by nearly 50 percent. But between 1904 and 1914 rural illegitimacy rose by an astonishing 47 percent, which perhaps reflected the growing popularity of seasonal migration, as well as the general social and political disorganization after 1905.[42] Just as the cases discussed in chapter 4 revealed that believers saw no contradiction between being upstanding members of the Orthodox faith at the same time they staked out their priest's home or bathhouse and peeked into his windows to witness his lewd behavior, a growing number of peasants who baptized their children also engaged in premarital sex.[43]

INSULTS, FIGHTING, FOPPERY, AND HOOLIGANISM

The rise in impolite or uncouth behavior that took the form of insults, disrespect for elders, insubordination, swearing, quarrelsomeness, and fighting drew the attention of educated Russians.[44] None of these breaches of social norms were new, but by the beginning of the twentieth century they were taken to be direct threats to the stability of the community as the young challenged the right of their parents to make important decisions about their future, as women began to fight for what they considered was their due, and as peasants of all ages and backgrounds began to question civil and religious authorities. A fascinating challenge to traditional village propriety resulted from the foppery that accompanied the introduction of factory-made cloth and clothing, or what Jeffrey Burds has called a "revolution in village fashion" fueled by envy as peasants became attracted to the allure of urban products that went far beyond clothing.[45] The attention paid to one's appearance as part of the daily routine startled some clergymen, who observed the extent of village poverty around them as they struggled to instill a sense of Christian modesty, restraint, and prudence. As usual, one vice seemed to burn a path to others: foppery was related to vanity, which was a result of leisure, which led to immoral behavior and a culture of insults, which resulted in a general village chaos.[46]

Many religious and secular authorities considered the urban culture that seeped into village life to be immoral, thus threatening the entire post-emancipation social system. Beginning in 1905, moral rectitude and revolutionary activity were posed as mutual opposites, a point not lost upon peasants attracted to new ideas of rebellious political change. A story related by Fr. N. Generozov leaves no doubt about the link between renunciation of the faith, the embrace of revolutionary propaganda, and the premature death of its main character, I. Khakhalev, a resident of Biriuch district. Khakhalev was a devout man who fulfilled his religious obligations like most other villagers, until his personal transformation occurred during a short stay in jail for having participated in the 1905 agrarian disorders. During his incarceration, he fell under the sway of a fellow inmate who spoke against religion. Khakhalev's demise was a slow process, which ended six years later during a trip to a village bazaar. After having drunk his fill, he decided to visit the local church, where he annoyed surrounding worshipers with his improper demeanor and appearance. One worshiper's stern reprimand prompted Khakhlev to respond with curses against the church and the people around him. On the following day he went to work as usual but, despite being in good health and only thirty-five years old, he fell mysteriously ill, suffered horribly throughout the night, and succumbed to an unknown ailment without making a final confession or asking forgiveness from those whom he had insulted in church the previous Sunday. Generozov concluded that Khakhalev had been struck down for his crime against the faith, which was caused by his new propensity for antireligious teachings and drink. His death surprised everyone, particularly those who witnessed his blasphemy, and readers were warned that his behavior in church had led to his death two days later.[47] Even those peasants who were unconvinced by this obvious moral story and its unabashed pedanticism could not ignore the sudden and unexpected death of Khakhalev or his final hours of agony which, according to superstition, would have been proof of his evilness.

The stories about individuals like Khakhalev misrepresented everyday peasant life which, far from saintly, continued to be filled with a considerable amount of cursing, quarrelsomeness, and fighting that provided continuity, rather than contradiction, between the converging worlds of the past, present, and future. Troubled local officials, unable to escape their stereotyped notions of the rural folk, instead reacted with fear and harshness to these uncouth behaviors, which they took to be the reasons for and contributors to rising crime, social disorder, and religious disaffection.

Hooliganism presented local authorities with an entirely new problem that was as much a factor of generational tension as a cultural clash between urban and rural Russia. A wide variety of breaches of the prevailing social order fell under the rubric of "hooliganism," but behind the official notion lay a belief that village youth in particular had been infected and that special measures had to be taken in the schools and through the provincial legal system.[48] In an extraordinary session dedicated to contemporary social evils, the Voronezh diocesan clerical assembly of 1913 (which included church elders) made twenty proposals of how to counter hooliganism, most of which depended on education, extraliturgical preaching, the opening of libraries, the creation of sobriety societies, limitations on bazaars, greater surveillance of bootlegging, the use of township courts, and, only in the most extreme cases, administrative banishment. The effects of post-emancipation reforms were as evident in this list as the church's inability to offer more than hope and prayers (proposal 3 of the assembly) that hooliganism would fade away soon.[49]

ATTACKS ON CHURCH LANDS

Beginning in 1905, at the same time that hooliganism threatened urban and rural sensibilities, attacks on church land and property—the illegal use, harvesting, and destruction of arable lands, meadows, woods, water sources, and crops that belonged to the parish clergy or monasteries—occurred with greater frequency. Disputes over landownership, user rights, and usufruct drew out the worst in the clergy and laity as each defended its own interpretation of proprietorship. Peasants understood proprietorship to be a matter of oral agreement that was reconfirmed through use, while landowners and clergymen depended on written documents. At the center of most land conflicts was the law requiring parishes to provide 89 arable acres for use by the clergy, a thorny issue for both priests and believers.[49] When peasants considered this land to be "on loan" rather than an outright transfer to the parish church or its clerics, when clergymen failed in their duties, or when a village became part of another parish, peasants usually sought to reclaim what they considered to be rightfully their own.

Such was the case when 134 peasants from Boguchar district were arrested in 1906 for illegally cutting down the grass in a meadow belonging to the parish church. Proclaiming their innocence, this group of peasants argued that in 1833 their "grandfathers" had merely rented, and not transferred permanently, 170 acres of meadow and 81 acres of arable land in order to save for a new church. From the start the peasants spoke of these large tracts as "church land" while continuing to think of it as belonging to the commune. After the church was built, the clergymen assigned to the parish began to use the land and eventually appropriated it. The clerics went so far as to register the tracts as parish property by informing the local land captain. Once the peasant commune learned what had transpired, they sought to reclaim the land by using its produce. In the end, the Ostrogozhsk circuit court decided that the 134 peasants ought to be freed, but that the land indeed belonged to the church.[51] This group of peasants always maintained that it was acting legally—even though this is not how the case was framed by the civil authorities—and argued that the integrity of their property rights had been violated. With the written word on their side, the clergymen of this parish were able to dismiss the peasants' oral tradition as inferior and manipulative.

A similar case in Mokrets village demonstrates the social tensions underlying cultural difference. When the Mokrets village commune decided in 1907 to plow 16 acres of land that the clergy claimed as its own, they were charged with illegal use of church fields. In building their defense, villagers argued that their fathers had indeed given nearly 19 acres to the Dmitrievskaia clergy in 1852 as part of their contribution to clerical land (the remainder was given by other villages that belonged to the same parish). Some time later, when a redrawing of parish boundaries placed Mokrets in another congregation, the commune appealed to the Dmitrievskaia clergy and to the local land captain to have the plot returned to them so that it could be transferred to the church they now belonged to. The Dmitrievskaia clergy and land captain refused to comply and told Mokrets villagers to take their plea to the circuit court. Protesting that the necessary documentation existed in the parish registry and that such a court case was prohibitively expensive, Mokrets believers, feeling that they were victims of trickery, decided to plow the land instead. In the end, the Voronezh police sided with the Dmitrievskaia clergy and allowed it to keep the land.[52]

Peasants were not always innocent defenders of what they perceived as their trampled rights, but the similarity between land disputes in communities scattered around the diocese suggests that peasants felt they were disadvantaged in a system that weighted the sociocultural norms of the literate over oral tradition. The turning point in post-emancipation land disputes came in 1905, when revolutionary violence and social unrest made the parish clergy a new target of peasant frustration, which helps to explain why the church suddenly felt itself under siege in a very physical way.

CINEMA AND OTHER FORMS OF POPULAR ENTERTAINMENT

A lack of power and influence characterized the church's criticism of the cinema and other popular entertainments, especially the spread of provincial theater, People's Houses, and cinemas. Writing in the popular clerical journal that he edited, *Troitskoe slovo*, just as World War I was about to begin in August 1914, Archbishop Nikon of Vologda saw little good in these new "distractions" and blamed provincial secular authorities for allowing a People's House to be built, with public funds, near the Sergiev Trinity Lavra, one of the most sacred national shrines, which symbolized the victory of medieval Muscovite princes over the Russian lands and their stalwart resistance to the Mongols. Alternatively referring to the People's House by its proper name, *narodnyi dom*, as well as incorrectly as a theater, club, and place of entertainment, Archbishop Nikon described its activities as "satanic," supported by "Yid newspapers" *(zhidovskie gazety),* and with no public value.

With these harsh words, Nikon expressed a keen awareness of the waning influence of the church in social and cultural matters after 1905. Nikon underscored this loss of status in his description of the decade-long effort by local authorities to open the People's House. The first attempt in 1904 was initiated by the provincial committee for popular sobriety without the knowledge of the *lavra*. According to the proposal, public funds were to be set aside for the construction of a People's House in the environs of the *lavra* in order to serve the high volume of pilgrims and their families who were in need of entertainment that the monastery could not provide. Monks from the *lavra* lobbied hard to prevent the People's House from being constructed and fired off a response, written by Archbishop Nikon, to Grand Prince Sergei Aleksandrovich, Metropolitan Vladimir of Moscow, Minister of the Interior V. K. Plehve, and Chief Procurator of the Holy Synod K. P. Pobedonostsev. This apparently led to a Ministry of Finance circular forbidding People's Houses to be built in areas heavily frequented by pilgrims. The events of the following decade forced a more secular approach to public entertainment, and provincial authorities eventually permitted the house to be opened *with* funding from the public coffers.[53]

Whether we agree or disagree with Archbishop Nikon's criticism of the People's House, since the 1860s popular entertainment had become a contested ground for elites attempting to bring acceptable culture and uplifting moral literature to the people. Unlike their cultural cousins, seasonal carnivals and periodic fairs, which offered time and space for peasants to release social tensions and to momentarily reverse the inequities of Russian society, theatrical performances for the people had the broader aim of enculturation by bringing literature and political awakening to the people by introducing themes and situations in ways unfamiliar to traditional peasant entertainment. An urban-rural link was also established when productions in factories were closed down by the police, forcing the troupes of amateur actors to move on to nearby villages.[54] The arrival of the People's House via England and Germany in the 1880s combined elements of the peasant carnival and traveling theatrical productions by offering a physical structure and regular programs for what Richard Stites has termed "culture as social prophylaxis by the intelligentsia, factory owners, government agencies, and charities."[55] But the People's House was not just about entertainment, and often it had a library and tearoom for more serious uses of leisure time.

The advent of cinema raised new problems for elites concerned about the potential influence of a new medium, whose stunning popularity was unmatched in Russian history. Just as they had looked down upon middle- and lowbrow literature, elite Russians reacted with disdain for the "vulgar" and "erotic" cinematic tastes of the masses. But the problem was more alarming because of cinema's overnight success and the depth of its penetration into mass culture. Unlike the gradual and more limited growth of popular literature, by 1912, only four years after the first Russian feature film was made, the cinema was reaching all segments of the population, literate and illiterate, urban and rural, poor, rich, and middling, or nearly all residents of the empire. Production and distribution methods were primitive, theaters were safety hazards or ad hoc assemblages, and yet, despite these potential obstacles, in 1911 nearly 100 films were domestically produced and shown in as many as fifteen hundred permanent cinemas that served 108 million viewers.[56]

Drawing from recognizable themes in the *lubok,* folk tales, and popular literature, the cinema created what Richard Stites has called "a vast archipelago of democratized space and an unprecedented revelation of the power of the cultural marketplace."[57] Movies also presented audiences with juxtapositions of different social categories that aggravated peasants' resentment of the excessive luxury and immorality of the upper classes as they flocked to see films in which the poor served the rich in an uncomfortable and unamiable coexistence. Church leaders quickly realized their powerlessness in the face of the new "electrotheater" and, had the revolution of 1917 not abruptly discredited the public presence of religion, they might have developed a more effective response that could have used the cinema to probe important religious issues or to teach believers about the faith. Instead, a revanchist stance was assumed that began with a formal prohibition of cinematic representations of the church and its rituals and ended with a condemnation of the cinema as another in a long series of temptations to lure the innocent people away from worship. In the moving words of one elderly parish priest, the cinema was the worst challenge he had faced during his many years of service. "Not long ago I became convinced that, although during the past two years the young people, particularly teenagers of school age . . . might be in church, they rarely stay until the end of the service, especially if it is a vesper service. . . . The very exploiters of the cinema try to kindle the passion for pictures by showing them on the eve of holidays and Sundays (for students who are let out on the night before holidays), thus deadening the conscience and killing religious feeling."[58] These sentiments were echoed in diocesan clerical assemblies throughout the empire: cinematographers were labeled the great dupers of the people whose body of work was more powerful than books because it appealed to everyone regardless of the ability to read. The risqué content of the most popular movies cast in an alluring light a variety of socially irresponsible subjects such as illicit love, free-spirited women, excessive drinking, and unfathomable luxury, all things that had implicit subversive qualities.[59] The vandalism of 1917–1918 seems to bear out the warnings of this elderly priest, who cannot have welcomed the new Bolshevik use of cinema.

Religious Relevance on the Eve of Revolution

With changes affecting all aspects of village life, what were peasants looking for and was there a place for religion? Like many of their contemporaries, peasants were seeking a way out of the miserable past filled with servitude, drudgery, and poverty, but they were not interested in destroying the cultural base from which they would create a new world. Often they merely sought a spiritual leader who could provide guidance to a better life. The story of Krasnorechenskoe village poignantly illustrates this desire. Left without a priest, Krasnorechenskoe residents waited patiently for another to be assigned to their backwater parish. That individual was Fr. Mikhail Kosyrev, who happened upon the village during his travels in the province in 1911. Shocked by the dilapidated condition of the church, a "small, dark, dirty building with a rickety bell tower" without a priest to look after it, Fr. Kosyrev found himself well treated, installed in the home of a local peasant, and served a bevy of snacks by his hosts. As he enjoyed the refreshments with the parish elder, one by one curious neighbors began to trickle in to size up the stranger. This being the eve of the Exaltation of the Cross, one of the twelve high holy days of the Orthodox Church, several peasants, along with the parish elder, asked Fr. Kosyrev to stay overnight so he could perform a special liturgy in honor of the holiday. The kindly priest agreed, and before long the small church was overflowing with villagers, including many sectarians, who attended the service and listened to his sermon with great interest. Afterward an exhausted Fr. Kosyrev returned to his lodgings, only to find a crowd of people requesting special prayers, beseeching him to be their priest, and begging him to deliver their request to the archbishop.

Upon his return to the city of Voronezh, Fr. Kosyrev met with Archbishop Anastasii and delivered their request, to which the elderly prelate willingly gave his approval, calling the priest the "guardian angel" of the parish. When Fr. Kosyrev moved to the village, he discovered that the parish elder was given to drink and filled his home with noisy drunkards who spent their time singing boisterously and uttering obscenities. This led Fr. Kosyrev to the conclusion that under the influence of the parish elder many peasants had led a dissolute life, while those who sought spiritual uplift were forced to turn elsewhere, namely to Baptists and the Milk Drinkers sect, which were active in the area. To stem the tide of conversion, between the middle of January and the beginning of November 1911, Fr. Kosyrev organized thirty-four extraliturgical religious discussions, each lasting an average of six hours. Almost immediately drunkenness, revelry, and gambling abated. The peasants themselves praised their new priest as "an angel who has flown to our village," and soon they began to condemn public revelry. They also demanded more religious discussions, opened a temperance society with nearly four hundred members, and, in August 1912, the village assembly voted to close the local state wine shop. Attendance at Sunday, holiday, and daily liturgies began to match that of Easter, and after each service the faithful lingered in Christian fellowship until the psalmist, weary from the long service, told them to go home. Fr. Kosyrev showed signs of exhaustion by the end of the year and expressed concern when peasants pleaded with him to continue his sermons for up to two hours.

After Sunday liturgy, more preaching in the form of extraliturgical discussions sometimes ran until ten o'clock in the evening with listeners flocking from neighboring villages to hear this rural wonder orator. When Kosyrev forbade local Baptists and members of the Milk Drinkers sect to participate in these discussions, they branded him as the devil and the Antichrist, a further indication of Fr. Kosyrev's success. Fortunately for the residents of Krasnorechenskoe, a "guardian angel" had alighted on their troubled community, although Fr. Kosyrev and the many other parish clergymen like him claimed to be only fulfilling their calling.[60]

As the church authorities noted with alarm after 1905, the misguided religiosity that Fr. Kosyrev stumbled upon in Krasnorechenskoe could be found in parishes with their own priest. One anonymous clergyman called on his brethren to lead the peasantry in their natural search for "truth" and away from the material and moral bankruptcy of the village.[61] This call for leadership barely masked church leaders' suspicions about the uncontrollable effects of the spread of literacy and consequences of a peasantry capable of thinking critically about organized religion. As they learned to read and write and developed new cultural tastes, most peasants remained, however, strongly attached to the religious belief and practice that operated within the framework of parish life, upon whose renewal they pinned their hopes of a brighter future.

CHAPTER SEVEN

Failed Visions of Reform at the End of an Era

I looked for many years

At Tikhon in the coffin

And for too many years I looked

And saw no doll at all.

But now I look at it [the doll] *in awe.*

—Anonymous ditty, Voronezh, 1919

*A*t the beginning of the twentieth century, the most serious challenges to the authority of the church came from the clergy and laity, whose mounting opposition to synodal administration aimed at no less than a devolution of episcopal power. Within the episcopate, a consensus was emerging that staked the future of the Russian Orthodox Church on the three principles of a restored patriarchate, a church independent from the unpopular autocratic regime, and a revitalized parish life.[1] The restoration of the patriarchate depended, however, on the will of the tsar, who, according to custom, possessed sole power to convoke a national church council authorized to elect a patriarch and institute wide-ranging reforms. The crucial turning point in the struggle for church autonomy from the state was the issuance of the manifesto of 17 April 1905, which introduced the edict on religious tolerance and promised a broad range of civil liberties that virtually abolished state censorship. With the end of its religious monopoly and the introduction of a free press, the Orthodox Church suddenly found itself publicly attacked not only by long-standing critics of state religion, but also from the grass-roots base the episcopate had long depended upon: rank-and-file parish clergymen and ordinary believers.[2]

Notwithstanding the tumultuous consequences of the manifesto and the widespread revolutionary unrest, by the end of 1905 there were reasons for bishops and parish clergymen to be hopeful about church reform. In July of that year, the chief procurator of the Holy Synod sent a questionnaire to diocesan bishops that inquired about the current state of Orthodox Christianity. Most questions were about dissatisfaction with church administration and parish life that religious leaders believed had caused the recent provocations against the faith. When diocesan clerical assemblies around the country convened to respond to the synodal questionnaire, they expressed almost unanimous support for a national church council that would have the authority to enact reform and restore the patriarchate; they also agreed that a reorganization of the church hierarchy was inseparable from the transformation of the parish into a self-administered unit with expanded control over nonliturgical aspects of local religious life. In his response to the findings of the Synod's questionnaire, Tsar Nicholas II sympathized with the calls for reform and promised to convoke a church council as soon as the revolutionary furor had settled down.[3] Such a time never came, and soon after the tsar's abdication in March 1917, the episcopate received permission from the provisional government to convene the first national church council in over two centuries. In the twelve intervening years, between Tsar Nicholas II's promise and the first session of the council, heated exchanges in the religious and secular press raised three basic questions that needed to be addressed if reform were to succeed: How did the church and ordinary believers define the parish? How did clergymen and believers apply this definition to everyday religious practice? And how could parish clergymen and peasants transform grass-roots Orthodoxy to make it more responsive to local needs?[4]

Revolt of the Clergy

No other topics had the potential of uniting the clergy than improvements in professional life and parish reform, or renewal (obnovlenie) as it was often called. Discussion related to professional issues increasingly preoccupied district and province-wide clerical assemblies and congresses, and, beginning in 1905, state salaries and pensions for clergymen eclipsed all other topics at these meetings as participants worked out alternative plans to abolish the traditional sources of income, emoluments and cultivation of the land. The only consensus reached in thousands of hours of debate was that an improvement in the economic condition of the clergy would only be realized after the parish had been transformed into a self-administrative unit managed by a board of parishioners who would have the right to buy, sell, and protect church property.[5]

The other main venue for disseminating ideas about reform was the Voronezh Diocesan Gazette, which introduced a clergy-friendly tone after the diocesan congress of 1907 demanded the resignation of the editor and the transformation of the unofficial part of the newspaper into a forum for clerical debate about professional issues and parish life.[6] Although the editor refused to resign, he eventually conceded changes in content and format. From 1910 until June 1917, the *Gazette* became an organ of the parish clergy, who penned short articles and published the works of parishioners (including a small number of peasants).[7] The final victory in the clergy's struggle to gain control over the newspaper came in June 1917, when a new editorial board consisting of ordained and lay members dissolved the *Voronezh Diocesan Gazette* and replaced it with the *Herald of Diocesan Unity (Vestnik eparkhial'nogo edineniia;* later, *Voronezhskii vestnik eparkhial'nogo edineniia),* whose title suggested a new harmony between the clergy and laity. Faced with high prices, material shortages, and a new regime that was hostile toward the church, the new publication paled next to its predecessor in both size and content, taking a philosophical approach to contemporary concerns about the relationship between church and state following the abdication of the tsar, and the social and political role of the clergy throughout Russian history.

The crowning moment in the clergy's attempt to reform parish life was the first diocesan clergy-laity assembly at the end of April and beginning of May 1917, which called for an independent community of believers who would administer church property and finances, as well as select its ordained personnel.[8] According to this proposal, the priest would remain the symbolic leader of the parish, but its administration would be handed over to the laity; diocesan administration would be taken up by a new council of six clerics and seven laypersons and would have parallel institutions at the district level; and the *Gazette* would be reorganized and edited by representatives of both the clergy and laity.[9] In addition to these proposed changes in diocesan church life, the assembly expressed qualified support for the mother church, but also noted critically that its association with the discredited tsarist regime had alienated the people. To restore the honor of the church, the assembly proposed that its new guiding principles be freedom, equality, and brotherhood.[10] Unfortunately, this was the first and last time that the Voronezh clergy and laity cooperated at the diocesan level before parting ways during their next meeting at the end of June and beginning of July 1917.

The dramatic and articulate calls for change by a parish clergy that had been the subject of mostly negative stereotyping throughout the post-emancipation period should have come as no surprise given the explosive atmosphere of the post-emancipation Voronezh clerical seminary where they had received their training. Beginning in the 1870s, seminary disorders were signal proof that the synodal reform of clerical education in the previous decade had failed to diminish the scholasticism of the curriculum or to eliminate the draconian regime of school life.[11] As seminarians continued to face oppressive administrators and wretched dormitory conditions, they searched for ways to improve their lot. United in their misery, these future clergymen proved to be exceedingly open to revolutionary ideas and violent measures, which led seminary administrators to respond with house arrests and expulsions. Year by year, students became more impetuous, provocative, and threatening. Although seminary officials worked with civil authorities to root out the most egregious troublemakers, no amount of force succeeded in quashing mounting student rebellion. Beginning in 1905, instruction became all but impossible as classes were regularly cancelled and academic years cut short in response to student activism.[12]

Eventually many seminarians were ordained, and some of them became active in spreading revolutionary propaganda at the same time they diligently served the religious needs of their parishioners. The case of Fr. Ivan Meretskii, the parish priest of Ivan Stoliariov, demonstrates the complex situation faced by church and secular authorities when a clergyman became involved in revolutionary activity. Variously labeled by his opponents as "antigovernment," "liberal," or "populist," Fr. Meretskii was respected by his flock as a well-read man of God, whose sermons were meaningful because they touched on everyday problems. The esteem in which Fr. Meretskii was held worried local secular authorities, who, in 1906, arrested him, along with his wife, for organizing a special meeting of the village assembly at which the community decided to replace the sitting communal administration, elected a new elder who was more amenable to their goals, seized the property and official seal of the ousted elder, and refused to honor its redemption payments. Additional charges against Fr. Meretskii and his wife were the incitement of insubordination to local authorities and the establishment of a credit society to support revolutionary activities. While in prison, Fr. Meretskii shared a cell with Ivan Stoliarov, who had been detained on unrelated charges of revolutionary activity. Stoliarov described Fr. Meretskii as a tireless servant of the people, a seeker of justice, and a man devoted to the true teachings of the faith even when they opposed the dictates of church superiors. Because Fr. Meretskii had cultivated warm relations with his parishioners and had earned their trust as a spiritual and secular leader in the community, his parishioners put up a spirited defense of local religious traditions that put them at odds with diocesan authorities.[13]

By 1917 the majority of Voronezh clergymen could claim, like Fr. Meretskii, to have participated in, supported, or witnessed the disorders and subversion of authority that increasingly disrupted late tsarist seminary life, and were prepared to fight for radical improvements in the parish system by which they made their living.

Peasants Demand Reform

Unlike the clergy, peasants had neither a newspaper nor regional assemblies that could serve as fora to discuss parish reform. Most of what is known about peasant notions of Orthodox Church institutions is based on their expressions of hostility or frustration toward the clergy. Information about these utterances and acts have survived in statements made during official investigations of complaints made or offenses committed by peasant believers.[14] Just as the clergy drew on old models when it attempted to adjust to contemporary circumstances, peasants constructed their notions of reformed parish life on the foundation of what already existed. Despite the many changes in traditional village life in the decade leading up to 1905, there is very little direct evidence that peasants in Voronezh veered from their definition of the parish community as having physical and spiritual components or that the new religious and civil freedoms of 1905 diminished their interest in religious belief and practice. What had changed was the peasants' willingness to express in increasingly forceful ways their strong dislike for the prevailing church and parish system.[15]

Complaints and appeals to the diocesan administration or Holy Synod, as well as attacks on symbols of Orthodoxy, were the result of three sources of conflict that had deep roots extending back to the early–nineteenth century. The first concerned religio-moral violations of community norms that were committed by members of the parish clergy. A certain amount of flexibility and tolerance of alcoholism, licentious behavior, and rudeness—none of which were strangers to the village—was demonstrated in these cases, provided that certain religious needs of the peasants were fulfilled. More than half of the complaints against the clergy was for insobriety and sexual impropriety, both of which often interfered with the performance of basic liturgical services, although a small number of cases comprised physical abuse, theft, and insults. The picture that emerges from peasant petitions is a set of expectations of parish life that included enormous patience with egregious behavior, as demonstrated by the parish that tolerated its priest's immorality until he fell asleep at the altar table, or the parishioners that accused their priest of numerous repeated offenses, including adultery and making errors during liturgical services.[16]

The next source of confrontation was contradictory understandings of the terms under which the community provided land to the clergy. These cases had long histories that dated back several generations, and the basic story was always the same: many decades before the conflict came to a head, the peasants' forefathers established a new parish and apportioned communal land for use by the parish priest. More often than not, peasant communities considered this newly designated "church land" to be a loan in perpetuity, and not an outright transfer of ownership. Many decades later, the rightful ownership of the land became the center of disputes between peasants who wanted the land to revert to the commune and priests who claimed that they were the rightful owners of the plot they tilled.[17] Frustrated and offended by their priests' affront to village norms, the parish elders usually organized attacks on clerical lands with the full support of the peasant commune. In their attempts to reacquire disputed lands from their parish clergyman, peasants were not attacking religion, as contemporary authorities often claimed, but instead were affirming the parish system at the same time they pressed their demand to control the material realm of their religious community.

The final points of tension between clergy and laity concerned the appointment and dismissal of members of the clergy and special religious services in honor of occasions that were significant to the community. In their desire to restore the elective principle in clerical assignments, peasants reserved their greatest anger for members of the clergy who openly spoke against democratic selection. A typical example was that of the Bol'shaia Usman' parish. Between 1877 and 1907 the priest of Bol'shaia Usman', Fr. Georgii Alekseev, had fulfilled his duties as a faithful servant of the church without incident, but on the night before Easter in 1907 a group of parishioners threatened to kill him if he performed the Easter vespers and proceeded to burn down his house. Unflinching in the face of disaster, Fr. Alekseev performed the service, which provoked angry parishioners to burn the home of the parish schoolteacher and the school itself. What had led to this outburst of violence against a seemingly dedicated clergyman with thirty years of service to a community whose members he had baptized, married, and buried? On the eve of the revolutionary events of 1905, Fr. Alekseev had spoken vigorously against clerical selection by the people, claiming that peasants were not prepared for such important decisions.[18]

These cases offer a glimpse into the ways peasants understood the parish and religiosity in the last decade of tsarist rule and demonstrate how far villagers were willing to go in order to take control of many aspects of their religious life. It is not difficult to imagine that a peasant community would enact its own surveillance of an unpopular cleric by slowly, even methodically, gathering evidence and waiting until the appropriate moment to file a complaint with the diocese. Certainly this is one of the reasons why so many of the cases involving clerical impropriety or liturgical errors included long lists of examples gathered over a period of many years and, sometimes, decades. Likewise, it is easy to understand why land-hungry peasants attempted to reclaim allotments they believed were rightly theirs, and not the property of the clergy.

Speculation about peasant notions of the parish comes to an end in 1917, when parishioners openly challenged the existing system of church administration. Distinctions between sacred and secular, religious and revolutionary, were ambiguous. When deputies of the Voronezh Council of Workers, Soldiers, and Peasants arrested Archbishop Tikhon IV on 9 June 1917 and charged him with counterrevolutionary activity, the event that precipitated his arrest was his decision to remove a certain priest and psalmist against the wishes of the parishioners.[19] Tikhon's arrest was followed by a diocesewide outbreak of violence by peasants who sought to prevent the transfer of their parish clergymen or to replace their unwanted clergy with candidates of their own. So common were these arbitrary acts that the newly created clergy-laity diocesan assembly established guidelines for parish communities wishing to dismiss and appoint clergymen. Following the recommendations of a Holy Synod decree on 13 April 1917, which established temporary regulations for parishes that were to remain effective until a national church council was convened, the assembly gave parish councils the right to choose their own clerics when a vacancy arose due to death, transfer, or removal from the priesthood.[20] Afterward parishoners, under the supervision of the district clerical superintendent or a special representative of the bishop, were to interview finalists and to vote on a winner. In the event that a finalist could not be selected or was not approved by the bishop, parishioners were allowed to begin a new search. Once a decision was made, a written contract was to be sent to the diocesan assembly for approval.

While the opinion of the clergy-laity diocesan assembly appears to have been widely supported, dissenters took a more conservative position. In a petition to the reinstated Archbishop Tikhon at the beginning of September 1917, a group of parishioners and priests from Zhuravka, Konstantinovka, Grushovka, and Demianova villages criticized the temporary regulations on parishes as unnecessary conciliations to the abnormal revolutionary "psychology of the moment" that was wreaking havoc on ordinary religious life. The complainants were unconvinced of the parishioners' ability to select clergymen, which "in practice ends up in the mass expulsion of the clergy under the influence of a small group of agitators without a trial or investigation. . . . In view of the political immaturity of the dark parish masses, the situation of the clergy, especially the parish clergy, is so difficult that it . . . turns them into martyrs of the elective principle."[21] Moreover, "the elective principle is put into the hands of villagers who are led by people of the dark past, people of an unchristian spirit who completely are given over to the mob violence of the ignorant crowd and malicious people." The only way to prevent arbitrary treatment of the clergy was for the newly reinstated elective principle to be rescinded.

In the meetings of the diocesan assembly, peasants expressed their opinions through their own representatives. When a session at the end of June rejected more radical ideas such as direct voting by all Voronezh residents for positions in the diocesan assembly and the participation of women in the assembly, a large and more liberally oriented group of dissatisfied lay members retaliated by accusing the majority of participants of counterrevolutionary activity. For several months this group of lay people and supporters of the traditional diocesan assembly filed a series of charges and countercharges to the Voronezh Soviet of Workers, Soldiers, and Peasants, and thus politicized religious reform. In a communication to the diocesan assembly one month later, Archbishop Tikhon hoped to quell the brewing storm by urging both sides to remember that decisions of the diocesan assembly could be enforced only with the approval of a national church council, but his words went unheeded.

Although Tikhon did not approve of the divisiveness of believers and the pretentiousness of the diocesan assembly, he recognized that institution as a legitimate forum for discussion, debate, and recommendation. What disturbed him more was the peasantry's widespread disregard for church authority as they took matters into their own hands when they disagreed with diocesan or synodal decrees, thus questioning the very foundation of the church as institution. In making accusations of counterrevolutionary activity, the opposition faction chose to fight against the majority, who were ostensibly fellow believers, and ensured that its voice of reform would never be heard in the assembly. Local Bolshevik authorities wasted little time in labeling the action of the minority faction "revolutionary" and "antireligious."[22]

Revolution, Democracy, and Grass-Roots Orthodoxy

As peasants eased into the solemn and somber mood of Great Lent at the beginning of March 1917, they were confronted by the abdication of the tsar and the stark reality that suddenly Russians no longer lived in an autocracy. Exceptional events require exceptional actions, and despite the prohibitions on festivity during Lent, peasants throughout Voronezh province joined in the official and unofficial jubilation about the overthrow of the Romanovs. In their euphoria, Voronezh believers, like their Orthodox counterparts throughout the empire, spontaneously tore down imperial symbols from public buildings, removed the generic crowns on or above the royal doors in their church, attacked and drove out of the village defenders of the old regime, and offered prayers of thanksgiving to God, whose status as supreme spiritual guardian of Russia remained intact despite the revolutionary uncertainty. Just as they, their parents, and their grandparents had done upon the death of one tsar and installment of a successor, peasants quickly proclaimed their loyalty to the new government in St. Petersburg. But instead of mourning the demise of Nicholas II, they released a torrent of criticism of the autocratic regime and uncharacteristically agreed with church leaders on the excision of prayers for the royal family from all religious services.[23] In an act of tactical sensitivity to the needs of ordinary believers, Orthodox leaders echoed popular sentiment and cast the church as no less a victim of the autocracy than the peasantry, but also declared a victory for the reformist goals of the moderate and liberal episcopate, who had long waited to liberate the faith from state tutelage.[24]

With a unanimity that had been less and less frequent in the years before 1917, the elite of Voronezh portrayed Nicholas's abdication as the national liberation of Russia from an oppressive monarchy that had prevented the country and its people from reaching their great potential. As the leading article in the *Voronezh Telegraph* proclaimed, in one historic act "the border between what *was* and what *should be*" had been crossed, and the only thing that stood in the way of *Svobodnaia Rossiia* (Free Russia) was the war against Germany. Carefully shifting with the political winds in St. Petersburg, the Voronezh governor, M. Ershov, urged residents throughout the province to remain steadfast in their support for a military victory in Europe, which would be attained only through loyalty to the new government. As for things divine, Ershov was careful to underscore God's continued protection of Mother Russia and her inhabitants.[25] During the Easter celebrations in April 1917, churches were packed with believers, and prayers of thanksgiving were offered to God for having delivered the people from their darkness and for providing stability under the provisional government.

Throughout the spring and autumn of 1917, as the new Russia without a tsar became the status quo, believers went about their religious observations following age-old traditions. On the annual feast days of St. Tikhon and St. Mitrofan in August, the usual crowds of more than five thousand people trekked to the shrines in Voronezh and Zadonsk. Elsewhere parishes appealed, as they always had, to wonderworking objects for special protection. At the end of August 1917, the Sicilian icon of the Mother of God was carried in a procession from the Divnogorsk Monastery in Korotoiak to the city of Ostrogozhsk. Despite inclement weather, the two-day event drew large crowds that filled the hotels and left throngs of attendees in the streets, unable to find a room to sleep. At the end of November the memorial service commemorating the anniversary of St. Mitrofan's death was performed amid a large crowd of believers, who had gathered at the Annunciation Mitrofanov Monastery. By this time, the Orthodox faithful of Voronezh appear to have reconciled themselves, at least temporarily, to Archbishop Tikhon, who was free from imprisonment and felt confident enough to deliver a sermon about the newly revived patriarchate.[26]

Among the many heralds of the revolution, newspapers were the most important sources of information for villagers. Before 1917, with the exception of the short-lived Constitutional Democrat *Voronezhskoe slovo* (Voronezh Word), the Bolshevik *Golos truda* (Voice of Labor), and the pro-church *Voronezhskii krai* (Voronezh Region), most newspapers in Voronezh had been published in the provincial capital by well-educated writers, journalists, clergymen, teachers, and businessmen of moderate and liberal political persuasions. By late spring of 1917 every district capital touted a politically oriented daily or weekly that served as news and propaganda pipelines to the people. Peasant-run newspapers appeared a year later, in 1918, and were characterized by their skepticism about or hostility toward the church and the liberal bourgeoisie, who had published the old standards, the *Voronezh Telegraph* and *Don*. Typical of the new journalistic tone was the lead article in the first issue of *Proletarii*, which appeared at the end of April 1918. The Orthodox episcopate and clergy were squarely blamed for having duped the simple rural folk, who were in the greatest need of truth and clarity, into believing that the tsar was "God's anointed one" and for having falsely raised hopes about life in this and the next world. Comparing the open activities of the tsarist police and the subliminal messages of the clergy, the anonymous author concluded that "the difference between them is that the police stood at train stations and walked the streets, whereas the clergy stood in the churches and schools.

Together they supported 'our autocratic and great sovereign,' while the people thirsted for light, knowledge, and truth. Instead the church gives them only darkness and deception."[27]

A much stronger line against the Orthodox Church was taken by other newspapers, whose journalists attacked the heart of village life, popular piety. In 1919 the propaganda organ of the Voronezh Provincial Executive Committee depicted the clergy as part of a monarchist threat for reportedly continuing to celebrate the personal feast days of the imperial family without ever referring to the church's proscriptions against prayers for the monarchy, which had been in force for nearly two years. Additional evidence of the unreliability of the Orthodox Church was its refusal to recognize the calendric changes introduced by the Bolsheviks, which the editors considered to be "a protest against the new order, as well as outright stupidity."[28] Charges like these abounded in the press of 1918 and 1919, but they should be read as both genuine criticism of clerical disapproval of Bolsheviks religious policy and as an indirect criticism of the peasantry, the very people who were supposed to be a main pillar of the revolution. But just as tsarist officials had reluctantly conceded in 1905 that peasant loyalty could not be automatically counted on, Bolshevik authorities were forced to admit that the peasantry could not be expected to support wholeheartedly the new government or to renounce its faith.

To win over the peasantry, Bolshevik publicists borrowed unabashedly from religious imagery. In an article that appeared in the newspaper of the Ostrogozhsk District Executive Committee at the beginning of January 1919, the word for Christmas, *rozhdestvo*, was used to argue that the nativity of Bolshevik-style socialism was the logical historical successor to Christianity.[29] In April 1919, in a letter from Fr. Mitrofan Smirnov, which was published on the front page of the newspaper, the priest criticized his fellow brethren for having supported the old regime and for continuing to deceive the people with superstitious teachings about the uncorrupted remains of St. Mitrofan and St. Tikhon. A week later, a letter from the peasant Trofim Bondarev elaborated Fr. Smirnov's criticism and warned that rumors about the Bolsheviks' replacing the relics of the beloved saints with false ones obscured the fact that the uncorrupted remains were not authentic.[30] As local believers were reeling from the desecration of their beloved shrines in Voronezh and Zadonsk in January and February 1919, *Sovetskaia gazeta* (the organ of the Zadonsk District Executive Committee) unabashedly plagiarized the Gospels in its condemnation of the collection of fees and donations at holy places as "religion for profit" and held up Christ as "the first great teacher of socialism," who had chased the money-changers from the temple.[31]

As attacks on religion increased in 1918 and 1919, believers fiercely defended their faith and its significant places and symbols—just as they and their ancestors had done in the past whenever authorities threatened to confiscate them—through the manipulation of old and new images and language to achieve their goals.[32] Quite often believers' initial tacit response to the desecration of their beloved churches, shrines, and holy objects was a continuation of their customary resignation to the political status quo, which was based on a deep distrust of tsarist authority and a strong sense of self-preservation. Local Bolshevik officials often interpreted silent inaction as a sign of peasant disillusion with organized religion, but it did not take long before believers awoke from their stupor and defended their sacred places with passive resistance or violence.

The Bolshevik ceremonies staged at the beginning of 1919 to reveal the "truth" about St. Tikhon and St. Mitrofan provoked all of these reactions in a newly created cultural space for religion that, despite its secular and antireligious tone, was not unlike that of the prerevolutionary shrine experience that had gathered large numbers of believers to the sacred homes of their beloved saints. The actual sequence of events in these ceremonies also resembled the canonization of the two Voronezh saints, which had begun with investigators examining the relics. After a private examination of the relics of St. Tikhon of Zadonsk, a public ceremony was staged on 27 January 1919 in which local officials, the abbot of the monastery housing the relics, monks, nuns, and medical and scientific experts served as chief witnesses while hundreds and possibly thousands of onlookers watched with intense curiosity (no doubt because many of them hoped for a last look at their beloved saint). Then the shrine was unsealed and the allegedly false remains displayed. The contents of the sarcophagus were photographed and filmed.

> Removing the last piece of cloth covering the body, they saw a layer of wadding about 4.4 cm wide that covered an empty skull. It appeared to be an ordinary human being of dull color. . . .
>
> The skin, subcutaneous membranes, muscles, cranial hair, beard, and whiskers were all completely missing.
>
> When they removed the shoes, flesh-colored cardboard was revealed, which had the shape of an instep sewn with white thread.
>
> Inside the cardboard, instead of relics, wadding was discovered.[33]

Afterward the public was allowed to view the opened relics close up to witness for themselves the alleged deception of church authorities. A documentary film, which was quickly made and widely used by antireligious propagators throughout the early 1920s, allowed those who could not make the journey to Voronezh to participate vicariously in the event.[34]

As the shrine of St. Tikhon was being desacralized in Zadonsk, tensions between believers and revolutionary authorities mounted at the Ascension Mitrofanov Monastery in Voronezh, the resting place of St. Mitrofan. On 24 January 1919, with the monastery full of pilgrims, an armed guard sent by local authorities placed a seal on the door of the Archangel Church at the shrine of the first bishop of Voronezh and friend of Peter the Great. When a devout woman rushed forward and tore down the seal, the crowds threw themselves at the guard, and he and his small entourage narrowly escaped. News of the incident and rumors that local Bolsheviks wanted to move Mitrofan's remains to a city museum prompted an outburst of support for the shrine, and large crowds of believers surrounded the monastery to protect it from desecration. A contingency of believers appealed to Archbishop Tikhon to call a meeting of the clergy and laity of Voronezh city in order to discuss measures to protect the monastery and its holy objects. Tikhon complied, and on the evening of 24 January a large group of believers formed a voluntary round-the-clock security detachment to protect their beloved shrine.

At the same time, resident monks began to stage their own protest in the form of nearly continuous services and religious processions, using one of the other sacred objects of the monastery, the Smolensk Mother of God icon, which had been included on the diocesan list of specially revered icons in 1900. The swelling crowds at the monastery were not limited to Orthodox believers but included a small faction of antireligious propagators, and violent confrontations soon broke out between the two groups. Two days later, on 26 January, two cross processions set out, one from the nearby Alekseev Monastery, the other from the Trinity City Cathedral, with plans to meet at the Ascension Mitrofanov Monastery. While thousands of people lined the street to observe the two processions, shots were fired from a nearby rooftop, seriously wounding one man. Despite this, the crowd remained steadfast in its desire to see the processions, and the service continued until several members of the Red Guard arrived and began to fire shots into the air. Several bullets missed their heavenly target and hit a woman and a girl in the head. Chaos broke out as people ran for cover, while the choir and clergy remained in place. After a short while, calm was restored and the liturgy resumed. At four o'clock in the afternoon two armored cars appeared at the monastery gates and fired shots into it under the pretext that the White Guard was using it as a refuge. Several people at the monastery were arrested. At midnight on the following day, twelve soldiers, most of them drunk, searched the residence of Archbishop Tikhon for weapons, but only found a gold watch, sugar, and a typewriter, which they confiscated. A member of the Red Guard was placed at the monastery, and Tikhon gave up his attempt to protect the holy site. A few days later, the relics were desecrated.[35]

Despite their ultimate defeat, for the first time in more than two hundred years, local communities of believers took charge of most aspects of practicing their faith. This fortuitous independence was fraught with difficulties as peasants clumsily negotiated their way through the cacophony of the new political and social discourse that had come to dominate public life in the first years following the abdication of Nicholas II.

Bittersweet Victory

Voronezh peasants were not exceptional in defending themselves against revolutionary assaults on their sacred places and believing in the continued efficacy of their beloved saints. Six months after the relics of St. Mitrofan were unsealed, a member of the Voronezh Russian Communist Party reported that "malicious and provocative rumors were spreading among the dark population about the uncorrupted remains" that attributed many healings to the relics.[36] One month later, when the shrine of St. Pitirim was opened in neighboring Tambov province, officials observed that the "cult of relics was still not liquidated" because believers had not yet had a chance to examine them; the viewing period was extended another three months. In the following year the relics of St. Serafim of Sarov were opened to reveal a skeleton with stuffing, yet nearby peasants refused to let this shatter their faith and petitioned the provincial executive committee for permission to use the relics in a procession of the cross.[37]

Many other believers remained unconvinced that they had been deceived by the Orthodox episcopate and continued to express their faith in the *idea* of the sacred by physically defending relics and holding ad hoc prayer services with or without a clergyman. Loyalty to the faith proved to revolutionary leaders that the masses were unprepared for the great task of dethroning religion, and if they could not be convinced through rational argumentation and secular education, they needed to be disabused by force of their ignorance, which was now described as an epidemic of "psychosis" that particularly affected women.[38] But women were not the only ones to express their devotion to relics. Throughout the post-emancipation period, the outpouring of faithful at shrines and public celebrations had created a semireligious public sphere whose rituals included images of a modern empire as viewed through the prism of local identity. The huge number of peasants who organized and turned out for these events expressed its tacit approval of the messages conveyed by religious and political elites and proved more adept at manipulating symbols of the faith and empire than most educated observers have been willing to admit at the time or since. In the following humorous exchange, which was reported in the Zadonsk *Sovetskaia gazeta* a few days after the unsealing of St. Tikhon's relics, the nanny employed by the author, along with her friend, demonstrated typical peasant suspicion of political authority, this time of the Bolsheviks' attempt to reveal the "truth" about the saints.

> "Our Voronezh province has blundered. *The so-called saints turned out to be false,*" the old nanny exclaimed to her friend.
>
> "What of it, Nanny!" replied the friend. "Saints are supposed to go up to heaven."
>
> The nanny protested: "Rubbish, dearie! **If Tikhon had been a saint**, do you think he would have allowed such mockery? Well, in Kiev—there are many true relics and saints, but **ours are false**."[39]

As we learn more about the nanny—she is a seventy-year-old woman who took the job six years earlier to be closer to the shrine—and the exchange (her remarks modify a popular joke about the "alleged forgery" of St. Mitrofan), we realize that in spite of the women's sarcastic interpretation of the unsealing ceremonies their comments represent an enduring popular belief in relics. Other popular jokes referred to the "doll" found in the shrine, as well as voiced dissatisfaction with local authorities' deception of the local population. Popular humor and criticism of "deceptive" church authorities were often expressions of frustration with revolutionary activities rather than proof, as claimed in the local press, that antireligious sentiment was finally prevailing over superstition.[40]

In the end, believers lost their battle to preserve their beloved shrines and churches, which rapidly fell victim to the new ideology of exaggeration that contorted the importance of Orthodoxy among peasants at the very time they finally won control over their religious life. In many ways, this victory was a logical outcome of the attempts at parish reform between 1905 and 1917, when both the clergy and laity of the Voronezh diocese had considered the existing system of church administration to be inadequate and begun to place their hopes in parish reform. Without always stating it, both groups envisioned a decentralized and debureaucratized Orthodox faith whose support would come from the grass-roots level—a conglomeration of independent parishes that would have the priest as its local figurehead, who would derive his authority from a parish council selected by the laity. The intransigence of Archbishop Anastasii between 1905 and his death in 1913 further aggravated bitter relations between the clergy and laity and the episcopate. Anastasii's age—he was seventy-seven years old in 1905—and his identification with the Orthodox hierarchy might help to explain his inability to grasp the challenges facing the church, but his views were also shared by many senior Voronezh clergymen, diocesan administrators, and lay religious leaders of the day. Although in his scheme the parish clergy was superior to its parishioners, Anastasii never concealed his contempt for its failure to serve as exemplars of the faith. This breach of responsibility had, in Anastasii's mind, contributed to the widespread ignorance among the peasantry of even the most basic teachings of Orthodoxy and the alienation between *batiushki* and their flocks, shortcomings that enabled emerging non-Orthodox religious and cultural elites to successfully disseminate indifference and hostility to Orthodoxy and religion.[41]

Despite their shared vision of church reform, believers and parish clergymen were unable to bridge the gap that separated them and thus to present a united front against external threats not only to Orthodox Christianity, but to religious belief altogether. The parish clergy failed to abandon old frameworks when it attempted to react to new circumstances, as can be seen in its use of the diocesan newspaper as the main forum to discuss reform and in its support of change through a higher national church body. With such an understanding of reform, the majority of clergymen was not able to act upon peasant opinion until the middle of 1917, when there seemed to be no choice but to listen or face the ire of the masses.[42] Peasants were certainly motivated by the new circumstances of 1905, but they, too, used old frameworks to find answers to their discontent with parish life. Petitions, physical or verbal violence, and self-justice all were well-developed strategies to make themselves heard. When the opportunity finally came to participate in a diocesan clergy-laity assembly in 1917, only a minority of peasants chose to exclude itself and to create an opposition group. Far away in Moscow, a national church council was finally convened and turned out to be what Catherine Evtuhov has called both the crowning moment for the debates of the turn of the century and "one of the most significant and grandiose 'nonevents' of 1917–[1918]."[43] The council's dual concerns with the medieval Russian notion of conciliarity *(sobornost')* and an improvement in the church's responsiveness to the demands of post-tsarist Russian society followed the de facto restoration of parish independence.[44]

The consequences of the precipitous decline in the public authority of religion were devastating for communal identity and peasant understandings of history. The everyday life of the parish as a community of believers was quickly stripped of its cultural and social status as church buildings came under increasing attack, especially with the confiscation of church property during the famine of 1921 and 1922, which marked the turning point in the physical removal of state religion from public life. Spiritually, believers were forced to restrict their expressions of faith to the private sphere, and eventually religiosity became a clandestine activity that was subject to ridicule and repression. At the deeper level of social practice, religious celebrations of the late imperial period served as models for Bolshevik mass spectacles. During the summer of 1918 Voronezh enacted the first secular mass festival in Bolshevik Russia when it staged a reenactment of the taking of Azov.[45] The theme of the spectacle referred to the earlier greatness of Voronezh, without whose shipbuilding skills the southern fleet would not have been victorious under Peter the Great. Azov also alluded to the presence of the great tsar in Voronezh and implicitly linked this southern region to a critical moment in Russian history. Although St. Mitrofan was not mentioned in the official program and the spectacle took place half a year before the desecration of the Ascension Mitrofanov Monastery, most people in attendance would have known that St. Mitrofan was the confessor and confidant of the tsar. Given the ubiquitous presence of Peter the Great in village origin stories, many participants of the Azov commemoration would have felt a local association with the event. Moreover, few in attendance would have missed the parallels between the drama, entertainment, and tourist aspects of the elaborate mise-en-scène in 1918 and traditional religious pilgrimage. At the very time that Orthodoxy was being excised from the public sphere, the triple function of religious celebration remained in force as participants looked to the past for explanations of the present that helped them to imagine the future. Just as St. Tikhon had served as a bridge between enserfed and liberated Russia, organizers of the 1918 celebration of Voronezh's contributions to the modern navy linked glorious feats of yesteryear with traditional peasant dreams of freedom and justice, this time without Orthodoxy and autocracy.

Religion without a Tsar or a Church

*I*n the first years of the Bolshevik regime, antireligious activists concentrated their energies on destroying Orthodox Christianity on two levels. Their more urgent task was to dismantle the church as an administrative structure that possessed ready lines of communication and loyal personnel willing to stir opposition to the new regime among the millions of Orthodox Christians living in Russia. With astonishing speed, the church crumbled under the pressure of official sanctions and popular protests that stripped the episcopate of its authority, material resources, and independence.[1] As sacred places were desecrated, as Orthodoxy was lampooned in popular culture, and as the clergy was attacked physically, ordinary believers in Voronezh and elsewhere often looked the other way as they seized the opportunity to free themselves from the tentacles of church bureaucracy to enact their own style of parish reform, which centered around the liturgy and community of parishioners. The paradox of the believer who supported revolution confounded antireligious activists throughout the 1920s; having mastered the texts of revolution and being thoroughly schooled in the worldview of late-tsarist educated Russians, they searched for the best method of weeding religion out of the peasant brain and realized that their training had not prepared them for the more difficult task of negotiating the contradictions and complexities of village reality. When one enthusiastic educator complained in early 1919 that the October Revolution had failed to destroy the lifestyle and mentality of the old village, he wrote with the well-honed arrogance of Russian elites, who understood popular piety as a soft layer of superstition that could be wiped away with a few lessons in rational thinking.[2]

Historians sympathetic to the regime diminished the importance of Orthodoxy among Russian peasants by depicting village religious practice as nothing more than a collection of static cultural "survivals" from archaic peasant times. Faced with a dynamic set of religious practices that were intricately woven into the fabric of rural life, Bolshevik activists employed forceful tactics—the desecration of holy people and sacred objects and the ostracism, arrest, and execution of clergymen. To their credit, peasants resisted as best they could by attending religious services, staging processions with their beloved icons, streaming to shrines before and after local authorities revealed their saints to be frauds, providing shelter and sustenance to officially ostracized clerics, and using their newly acquired literacy to send petitions to local and central authorities in the hope that, one day soon, the barbarous attacks on their world would be declared egregious misinterpretations of central directives.[3]

The attacks on religion in the 1920s represented another chapter in the failure of educated elites to comprehend the nature of peasant piety and its pivotal role in the transition from traditional to modern life. Ever since Catherine the Great's experiment with the Enlightenment, reform-minded Russians had shed blood, sweat, and tears to save their country brethren from cyclical poverty born of ignorance. Until 1917, intellectuals looked condescendingly upon peasant belief, resigned themselves to its central role in village life, and hoped to lessen its importance, rather than root it out altogether. The results were usually disappointing because peasants stubbornly held on to their traditions, although they proved to be flexible in their combination of old and new. Traditions and customs passed on through the generations were facilely shaped to new lifestyles, social settings, and political realities. Armed with reading skills, literate peasants were attracted to the burgeoning genre of religious pamphlets, which educated them about new and favorite holy people and sacred places. This knowledge was duly transmitted to illiterate members of the community, who set out on pilgrimages by foot, carriage, or train in such great numbers that one could speak of a nation in constant procession to hierophantic centers scattered throughout the land. What pilgrims sought in these religious journeys was not only spiritual uplift, but also relief from the hardships of everyday life as they visited new places and took in the breathtaking magnificence of the Russian countryside.[4] Along the way, they communed with fellow religious travelers in a temporary gathering of the greater family of believers, a liminal experience that became part of individual autobiographies ready to be woven into village histories (see fig. 8).

Harmonic moments in pilgrimage were, of course, exceptional, and religious life in the parish community was not immune from ordinary village tensions and quarrelsomeness. Increasingly aware of church bureaucratic procedure, peasants adopted the petition as a means of defending their local religious life and thus etched themselves into the narrative of Russian history with the meager paper trail they left in the chanceries of the diocesan administration and Holy Synod. In these pleas from the heart, a clear sense of parish identity and loyalty to the faith shone through lucid enumerations of offenses committed by parish clergymen. The odds were against villagers, who seldom won in the game of literary dispute and social

Fig. 8—"Return of the Pilgrim," 1914

prejudice as they filed petition after petition about the most prosaic element of religious life—church lands. Beginning in 1905, questions about the use of church lands became inseparable from peasants' vigorous demands for greater administrative authority over parish life and a devolution of episcopal power.

Church leaders were unaccustomed to brash peasant assaults on episcopal authority and, besieged by creeping secularization and self-conscious about their institutional subordination to the state, they failed to address villagers' genuine religious concerns. Instead, the episcopate constructed elaborate arguments that portrayed the church as a victim of the autocracy. As the losses of the World War I spurred social upheavals that pushed the empire of the tsars toward its apocalyptic conclusion, church leaders threw caution to the wind and began to dream about the end of autocracy as the only means of surviving the rising revolutionary tide against religion. By the time of Nicholas II's abdication, the Orthodox faithful had broken into competing interest groups unwilling or unable to recognize that, regardless of their status or rank, they sought to improve the practice and administration of a common religion. The absence of unity among the masses of Orthodox Christians in Russia served the Bolshevik antireligious campaigns well, so that eventually they succeeded in bringing down the church and many trappings of the faith, thus transforming religious practice into an underground activity.

The expiration of the post-emancipation period in March 1917 was as much a proof of the bankruptcy of the tsarist imperial identity, as it was a demonstration of certain of its strengths that would be appreciated by Soviet ideologues over the next two decades. Since 1861 history and historical interpretations involving religious images had steadily reminded both literate and illiterate Russians of the basic cultural elements that bound them together as members of the empire and as inheritors and creators of its central narratives. What emerged was a flexible image of identities constructed on cultural bases (ethnicity, religion, locality) that tolerated difference and pointed to an overarching symbolic structure. The result was a variety of Russian identities that, for long stretches of time, allowed for a sense of unity even during moments of crisis and fragmentation. Not quite a civil society, yet with enough civility to permit coexistence between bitter enemies, late-imperial Russia forged ahead until the diverse masses and educated elite could no longer tolerate the fantasies of the autocracy.[5]

Appendix

Table 1—Days associated with belief in Voronezh Province villages[a]

January

25 December–5 January Yuletide

1	St. Basil the Great
6	Epiphany of the Lord
7	St. John the Baptist
11	Mikhail Klopskii the Holy Fool
16	Veneration of the Chains of St. Peter
22	St. Timothy
30	SS. Basil the Great, Gregory the Theologian, and John Chrysostom

February

2	Presentation of the Lord in the Temple
3	Symeon, Receiver of the Lord, and Anna the Prophet
8	St. Theodore Stratelates
12	St. Alexis, metropolitan of Moscow
17	St. Theodore the Recruit
NFD[b] *(3–7 days)*	Shrovetide
NFD	Forgiveness Sunday (last day before Great Lent)

March

1	St. Eudocia
6	Icon of Our Lady of Chenstokhovskii
9	Aleksi, Man of God
9	Forty Martyrs
25	Annunciation to the Mother of God

NFD, running into April (48 days, including Palm Sunday) Great Lent and Holy Week

April

NFD (40 days) Easter to Ascension of the Lord

NFD (second Tuesday after Easter) Radonitsa

NFD (midpoint between Easter and Pentecost) Feast of the Tabernacles
NFD   Ascension of the Lord
23   St. George the Martyr

May

NFD (seven or eight weeks after Easter and lasting up to ten days) Rusalka Week
NFD (2 days) Pentecost
9   Translation of the relics of St. Nicholas

June

1–28   Fast of SS. Peter and Paul
24   Nativity of St. John the Baptist (midsummer)
29   SS. Peter and Paul

July

20   Prophet Elias
24   SS. Boris and Gleb

August

1–14   Fast of the Dormition of the Mother of God
6   Transfiguration of the Lord
7   St. Mitrofan of Voronezh
13   St. Tikhon of Voronezh
15   Dormition of the Mother of God
18   SS. Florus and Laurus
29   Beheading of St. John the Baptist

September

1   St. Symeon the Stylite
4   Icon of Our Lady of the Burning Bush
5   SS. Zacharias and Elizabeth, parents of St. John the Baptist
6   Miracle of Archangel Michael
8   Nativity of the Mother of God
9   Joachim and Anna, parents of the Mother of God
12   Martyr Autonomus
13   Restoration of the Church of the Resurrection of Christ in Jerusalem[c]
14   Exaltation of the Cross
15   Martyr Necetas
17   Martyrs Vera, Nadezhda, and Liubov' and their mother, Sophia[d]
21   St. Dimitrii, metropolitan of Rostov
23   Conception of St. John the Baptist

25	St. Sergei of Radonezh
26	St. John the Theologian

October

1	Intercession of the Mother of God
2	St. Andrei the Holy Fool
5	SS. Peter, Alexius, Jonah, and Philip, metropolitans of Moscow and All Russia[e]
6	St. Thomas
9	St. James, Son of Alphaeos Chersun, or Ephesus, Icon of the Mother of God
15	St. Efim
17	St. Dmitrii Saturday
18	St. Luke the Evangelist
19	St. Ioann of Ryl'sk
21	St. Hilarion the Great
22	Wonderworking Icon of the Kazan Mother of God
23	St. James, Brother of the Lord[f]
24	Icon of the All-Holy Birthgiver of God of the Joy of All Suffering
26	St. Demetrios of Thessaloniki
28	Paraskeva-Piatnitsa St. Dimitrii, metropolitan of Rostov
29	St. Avraam the Wonderworker, archimandrite of Rostov

November

1	SS. Cosmas and Damian
3	Renewal of the Church of St. George in Lydia
8	Synaxis of Archangel Michael and other Incorporeal Forces
14 November–24 December (40 days)	St. Philip's Fast
15	Martyrs Gouria, Shamuna, and Habib
21	Presentation of the Mother of God in the Temple
23	St. Mitrofan of Voronezh
24	St. Catherine
27	Remembrance of the Sign and Miracle of the Icon of Our Lady of Novgorod
30	St. Andrew, the First Called

December

4	St. John of Damascus
6	St. Nicholas the Wonderworker
9	Conception of the Mother of God
15	Stefan the Confessor, archbishop of Surozh
25	Nativity of Christ
25 December–5 January	Yuletide
26	Synaxis of the Mother of God
27	St. Stephen

Weekly observances

    Sundays, Wednesdays, and Fridays[g]   56 days

Total number of days associated with belief (approx.)   291 days

---

Sources:

    VEV, supplement to the unofficial part (1884–1886); and Stoliarov, *Zapiski russkogo krest'ianina,* 72–73, 82.

Notes:

    [a] The following list is a compilation of holidays celebrated by peasants throughout Voronezh Province. In addition to the most widely observed holidays, I have included a representative number of feasts celebrated in only one village, such as the day of the Holy Martyr Autonomus (12 September).

    [b] NFD = Non-fixed dates.

    [c] Although this holiday was mostly celebrated on 13 September, in some parishes it was also commemorated during the first or second week of Easter.

    [d] This day honored Faith, Hope, Love, and Wisdom.

    [e] Each of these holy men was also honored individually on 21 December (Peter), 12 February (Alexius), 15 June (Jonah), and 9 January (Philip).

    [f] St. James, Brother of the Lord, and St. James, Son of Alpheus, are believed to be one and the same individual.

    [g] Wednesdays and Fridays were fast days. To avoid double counting, this number takes into account overlapping holidays and fast days, e.g., Sundays, Wednesdays, and Fridays that coincided with ordinary fast and feast days are counted only once.

Table 2—Specially revered objects in Voronezh Province, 1900

Item	Location	Special Significance
1–3 Three icons of the Mother of God	Alekseevskii Akatov Monastery, city of Voronezh	
4 Icon of the Smolensk Mother of God	Annunciation Mitrofanov Monastery, city of Voronezh	Popular wonderworking icon, frequently on loan.
5 Icon of the Hodegetria Mother of God	Veil Monastery, city of Voronezh	
6 Icon of the Sorrowful Mother of God	Bogoslovskaia Church, city of Voronezh	
7 Icon of the Sretensk Vladimir Mother of God	Birthgiver of God Monastery, city of Zadonsk	Wonderworking copy of the Vladimir icon in the Sretensk monastery. Original icon played a role in the defeat of Tamerlane and has since been associated with Russian invincibility.
8 Icon of the Maria of the Unexpected Abundance Mother of God	Belogorskii Voskresenskii Monastery, Ostrogozhsk District	
9 Icon of the Savior	Cemetery Church, city of Ostrogozhsk	
10 Icon of the Sicilian Mother of God	Divnogorsk Dormition Monastery, Korotoiak District	Popular wonderworking icon, frequently on loan.
11 Icon of John the Baptist	Dontesk Monastery of the Forerunner of Christ, Boguchar District	
12 Icon of the Niametskaia Mother of God	Mikhailovka Village, Boguchar District	
13 Icon of St. Nicholas the Wonderworker	Dormition Monastery, Valuisk District	Monastery founded by Tsar Michael in 1613 on the site where this icon spontaneously appeared.

Item	*Location*	*Special Significance*
14 Icon of the Vladimir Mother of God	Vladimir Cathedral, city of Valuiki	
15–16 Icon of the Savior and icon of the Bogoliub-skaia Mother of God	Dormition Lysogorskii Monastery, Novokhopersk District	
17 Icon of the Tikhvin Mother of God	Userd, Biriuch District	Popular wonderworking icon, frequently on loan.

Sources:

"Zhurnaly zasedanii soveta Voronezhskogo Tserkovnogo-Istoriko-arkheologicheskogo Komiteta obshchikh sobranii komiteta," *VS* 1 (1902): 13–14; and *Pravoslavnye Russkie obiteli,* 480–93.

Note:

I have been unable to locate the list drawn up by Voronezh officials in response to the synodal directive of 1893 that requested bishops to enumerate revered icons in the diocese. Consequently, this list is based primarily on the findings of the Voronezh Church Historical and Archeological Committee.

Table 3—Parish churches and clergy in Voronezh Province,
1870–1914

Year	Churches (% change)	Priests (% change)	Deacons (% change)	Psalmists (% change)	Total parish clergy (% change)
1870	827	1,108	574	2,000	3,682
1878[a]	807 (-2.4)	1,082 (-2.4)	480 (-16.4)	1,587 (-20.7)	3,149 (-14.5)
1890	876 (+8.6)	1,066 (-1.5)	421 (-12.3)	1,306 (-17.7)	2,793 (-11.3)
1900	914 (+4.3)	1,159 (+8.7)	463 (+10.0)	1,185 (-9.3)	2,807 (+0.5)
1910	966 (+5.7)	1,207 (+4.1)	232 (-50.0)	1,216 (+2.6)	2,655 (-5.4)
1914	984 (+1.9)	1,223 (+1.3)	274 (+18.1)	1,234 (+1.5)	2,731 (+2.9)
1870–1914	+19.0	+10.4	-52.3	-38.3	-25.8

Sources:
   VOOSS (1871), pril., 15, 18–19; ibid. (1878), pril., 15, 18–19; ibid. (1890–1891), pril., 130–31, 134; VEV, no. 17, of. pt. (1901): 322–23; ibid., no. 18, of. pt. (1901): 340–43; VOOSS (1910), pril., 6, 22; and ibid. (1914), pril., 6, 24.

Note:
   These figures include only parish churches with assigned clergy and regular religious services, that is, churches that were most likely to have peasant parishioners. For this reason, they exclude private houses of worship, cathedral churches without regular parishes, monastery churches that did not regularly serve peasants, and all other peripheral houses of worship that were part of the parish (i.e., cemetery churches, prayer houses, chapels).

[a] Figures for 1880 were not available.

Table 4—Average number of peasants to parish churches and clergymen in Voronezh Province, 1870–1914

Year	Churches (% change)	Priests (% change)	Deacons (% change)	Psalmists (% change)	All parish clergy (% change)
1870	2,124	1,586	3,061	878	477
1878–1880[a]	2,300 (+8.3)	1,715 (+8.1)	3,866 (+26.3)	1,169 (+33.1)	589 (+23.5)
1888[b]	2,225 (-3.3)	1,833 (+6.9)	4,844 (+25.3)	1,425 (+22.0)	688 (+16.8)
1901[c]	2,303 (+3.5)	1,756 (-4.2)	4,536 (-6.4)	1,772 (+24.4)	739 (+7.4)
1910	2,342 (+1.7)	1,875 (+6.8)	9,753 (+115.0)	1,861 (+5.0)	852 (+15.3)
1914	2,708 (+15.6)	2,178 (+16.2)	9,723 (-0.3)	2,159 (+16.0)	976 (+14.6)
1870–1914	+27.5	+37.3	+217.6	+146.0	+104.6

Sources:

IVO (1871), pril., 15, 18–19; ibid. (1878), pril., 15, 18–19; RGIA, f. 796, op. 151, d. 285a, ll. 43–44; ibid., op. 442, ed. khr. 868 (1880 g.), ll. 7, 12 ob.; ibid., op. 162, ed. khr. 2327 (1880 g.), ll. 29 ob.–30; *VEV*, no. 17, of. pt. (1901): 322–23; ibid., no. 18, of. pt. (1901): 340–43; RGIA, f. 796, op. 182, ed. khr. 4604, ll. 109–11; ibid., op. 442, ed. khr. 1888 (1901 g.), ll. 10, 14 ob.; *VOOSS* (1910), pril., 6, 22; RGIA, f. 796, op. 440, ed. khr. 55, ll. 109–19; *VOOSS* (1914), pril., 6, 24; and RGIA, f. 796, op. 440, ed. khr. 55, ll. 83–84.

[a] Figures for churches, priests, deacons, and psalmists are based on 1878 data; figures for peasants are based on 1880 data.

[b] Data for the number of Orthodox peasants in Voronezh in 1890 were not available.

[c] Data for the number of Orthodox peasants in Voronezh in 1900 were not available.

Glossary

antimension   A blessed cloth or piece of wood that covered the altar table and upon which the holy gifts and Eucharist were placed during the liturgy.

batiushka   Literally, "little father," an endearing term for older males and honorary title conferred by peasants on their priests. Depending on the context, it could evoke a sense of endearment or refer to the social and patriarchal authority of the clergy over the laity.

blagochinnyi   District clerical superintendent responsible for the oversight of up to two dozen parishes.

bogomolets (m.), bogomol'ka (f.)   Pilgrim, derived from the words for god *(bog)* and prayer *(mol)*. Emphasizes spiritual activity.

bogomol'e   Pilgrimage.

bozhnitsa   Icon shelf in the sacred corner of the peasant cottage.

bratstvo   Religious brotherhood, a type of adult religious education for people of all backgrounds created by clergymen and lay people. It provided public instruction on religio-moral topics through popular religious pamphlets and preaching outside the framework of the liturgy. The first brotherhoods date from the 1870s; a decree of the Holy Synod in 1885 ordered brotherhoods to be established in all communities.

cherti   Frolicking, mischievous devils.

derevenskie monashki   Peasant lay nuns, also known as *chernitsy, chernichki, keleinitsy,* and *spasennitsy,* different ways of referring to the black clothing they donned, their ad hoc monastic communities, and their focus on attaining salvation.

domovoi   House spirit who protected the welfare of the extended family; from the Russian word for house, *dom.*

dvoeverie   Literally, "dual faith." Term used by educated Russians to emphasize tension between what they viewed as pure forms of institutional Orthodoxy and peasant religious practice.

eparkhial'noe upravlenie   Diocesan administrative board that oversaw day-to-day operations of the diocese, made clerical appointments, and settled parish disputes.

filippovki   St. Philip's fast, lasting forty days before Christmas.

glaz   Much dreaded evil eye.

gornyi   Hill spirit, who could be malevolent or benevolent; from the Russian word for hill, *gora*.

iurodivye   Holy fools.

khlysty   Flagellants. Name given to the followers of the Khlystovshchina sect.

koldun (m.), koldun'ia (f.)   Sorcerers, who usually worked outside the framework of Orthodoxy.

krasnyi ugol   Sacred corner of the peasant cottage where holy objects were stored and where family rituals were performed.

leshii   Mischievous forest spirit, who played pranks on innocent peasants; from the Russian word for forest, *les*.

lzheucheniia   Literally, "false teachings." Term applied to followers of the Old Belief and various sectarian groups.

molokane   Literally, "Milk Drinkers." Known for their practice of drinking milk during Orthodox fast periods.

odnodvortsy   Small landowners of peasant or petty-service origin who employed little or no dependent labor to farm their freestanding estates.

palomnik (m.), palomnitsa (f.) Pilgrim, from the Russian word for palm, associated with movement.

palomnichestvo   Pilgrimage.

Paskha   Easter.

perezhitki   Literally, "survivals." Term used by educated Russians to refer to a wide range of popular religious beliefs and practices. Mostly used pejoratively.

podvizhniki   Religious itinerants.

pover'e   Ethnographic jargon used to describe folk piety.

prikhod   Parish, the basic physical and spiritual community of Orthodox believers.

prikhodskaia obshchina   Parish commune, encompassing believers, clergymen, the church proper, and worship.

prikhodskii skhod   Parish assembly, which met annually and gave a vote only to adult males, but allowed adult females to voice their opinions.

prikhodskoe popechitel'stvo   Official name of the parish council, introduced by the reform of 1864.

rusal'ka   Water nymph associated with powers of fertility and known for her siren-like beauty, who appeared just before Pentecost. She threatened to seduce and drown young men.

strannik (m.), stranitsa (f.)   Religious itinerant, pilgrim, foreigner, stranger. Spiritual and physical wanderer on the outside or margins of ordinary social life.

strannichestvo   Pilgrimage.

starovertsy, staroobriady   Literally, "Old Believers," "Old Ritualists." Also known as Schismatics *(raskol'niki).*

svetlaia sed'mitsa   The first week of Easter, traditionally called "Bright Week."

sviashchennosluzhiteli   Ordained parish clergymen (priests and deacons).

sviatki   Christmastide, lasting from 25 December until 6 January.

tserkovno-prikhodskaia obshchina   Official name given to the parish commune in 1905 in the Holy Synod's attempt to revitalize parish life.

tserkovnosluzhiteli   Unordained ancillary members of the parish clergy (psalmists, readers, elders, wardens, sacristans, bakers of the communion bread)

vedom (m.), ved'ma (f.)   Witches, who usually worked outside the framework of Orthodoxy.

Velikii Post   Great Lent, lasting forty days before Easter.

verovanie   Ethnographic jargon used to describe institutional Orthodoxy.

vnebogosluzhebnye besedy   Extraliturgical preaching that became a standard appendage to worship by the end of the nineteenth century.

vodianoi   Spirit who ruled over the underwater kingdom, from the Russian word for water, *voda.*

vybornoe nachalo   Elective principle that gave parishioners a voice in the selection of their clergymen. The elective principle was at the center of a fierce debate by clerics after 1905 and was the long-standing aim of parishioners hoping to assert their control over local religious life.

zemstvo   District and provincial organs established by the statute of 1864, which brought state services within a day's journey of most villages in the thirty-four provinces of European Russia. Nine more were opened in 1911 and 1912.

znakhar' (m.), znakharka (f.)   Healers, who usually worked within the framework of Orthodoxy.

Abbreviations

AREM	Arkhiv Rossiiskogo etnograficheskogo muzeia
ARGO	Arkhiv Russkogo geograficheskogo obshchestva
EO	*Etnograficheskoe obozrenie*
GAVO	Gosudarstvennyi arkhiv Voronezhskoi oblasti
IVO	*Izvlecheniia iz vsepoddanneishego otcheta ober-prokurora sviateishego sinoda po vedomstvu pravoslavnogo ispovedaniia*
OSVE	*Otchet sostoianii Voronezhskoi eparkhii*
PBE	*Pravoslavnaia bogoslovskaia entsiklopediia*
PKVG	*Pamiatnaia knizhka Voronezhskoi gubernii*
PPBES	*Polnyi pravoslavnyi bogoslovskii entsiklopedicheskii slovar'*
RGIA	Rossiiskii gosudarstvennyi istoricheskii arkhiv
RH	*Russian History/Histoire Russe*
RR	*Russian Review*
SE	*Sovetskaia etnografiia*
SR	*Slavic Review*
TL	*Troitskie listki*
TVUAK	*Trudy Voronezhskoi Uchenoi Arkhivnoi Komissii*
VEV	*Voronezhskie eparkhial'nye vedomosti*
VGV	*Voronezhskie gubernskie vedomosti*
VOOSS	*Vsepodaneishii otchet Ober-Prokurora Sviateishego Sinoda*
VS	*Voronezhskaia starina*
VT	*Voronezhskii telegraf*
VVTsE	*Voronezhskii vestnik tserkovnogo edineniia*
ZS	*Zhivaia starina*

Notes

Introduction: Orthodoxy, Russianness, and Local Identity

1. For a contemporary account of St. Tikhon's canonization, see *Proslavlenie sviatitelia Tikhona, obretenie i otkrytie sviatykh moshchei ego* (St. Petersburg: Tip. Departamenta udelov, 1862).

2. Although it is unlikely that the peasantry knew about Tikhon's many publications, they are considered to be among the most important treatises on spirituality written in the post-Petrine era. For an introduction to St. Tikhon's life and works, see (Maslov), Skhiarkhimandrit Ioann, *Sviatitel' Tikhon Zadonskii i ego uchenie o spasenii* (Moscow: Izdatel'skii otdel Moskovskogo Patriarkhata, "Mir Obshchestva"), 1993.

3. According to Miroslav Hroch, the absorption of elite symbolism by the masses is the last of three stages of national identity formation, which begins with a small elite group of patriotic intellectuals and proceeds to the urban bourgeoisie. See *Social Preconditions of National Revival in Europe: A Comparative Analysis of the Social Composition of Patriotic Groups among the Smaller European Nations* (Cambridge: Cambridge University Press, 1985). On the integration of scattered communities into illusively seamless grand politicocultural entities, see Benedict Anderson, *Imagined Communities: Reflections on the Origin and Spread of Nationalism,* rev. ed. (London: Verso, 1991); Eric Hobsbawm and Terence Ranger, eds. *The Invention of Tradition* (Cambridge: Cambridge University Press, Canto, 1992); and John Breuilly, *Nationalism and the State* (Chicago: University of Chicago Press, 1994).

4. As folk images of national and imperial identity encountered educated representations, urban elites acknowledged that their images of Russianness owed a great debt to peasant traditions. For a discussion of how elements of folk culture provide the archetypes for modern national symbols, see Ernest Gellner, *Nations and Nationalism,* New Perspectives on the Past, ed. R. I. Moore (Oxford: Basil Blackwell, 1983), 56–58; and Anthony Smith, *Theories of Nationalism* (London: Duckworth, 1971), 21–22. On the use of the peasant image by educated Russians, see Cathy A. Frierson, *Peasant Icons: Representations of Rural People in Late-Nineteenth-Century Russia* (New York: Oxford University Press, 1993). At times, the multiplicity of visions of the nation that emerged after 1861 challenged the idea of a unified Russia.

5. The role of newspapers and popular literature in the development of national identity is discussed in Benedict Anderson, *Imagined Communities;* Jeffrey Brooks, *When Russia Learned to Read: Literacy and Popular Literature, 1861–1917* (Princeton: Princeton University Press, 1985); and Louise McReynolds, *The News Under Russia's Old Regime: The Development of a Mass-Circulation Press* (Princeton: Princeton University Press, 1991).

6. The classic discussion of the links between the "little tradition" to the "great tradition" can be found in Robert Redfield, *The Little Community: Peasant Society and Culture* (Chicago: University of Chicago Press, 1960). William Christian has

described this relationship in terms of the interaction of local communities of believers and the Church Universal. See *Local Religion in Sixteenth-Century Spain* (Princeton: Princeton University Press, 1981).

7. See the classic works of Eric Hobsbawm, *Primitive Rebels: Studies in Archaic Forms of Social Movement in the Nineteenth and Twentieth Centuries* (New York: Norton, 1959); James C. Scott, *The Moral Economy of the Peasant: Rebellion and Subsistence in Southeast Asia* (New Haven, CT: Yale University Press, 1976); and Daniel Field, *Rebels in the Name of the Tsar* (Boston: Unwin Hyman, 1989).

8. The basic text on this period is John Shelton Curtiss, *Church and State in Russia: The Last Years of the Empire, 1900–1917* (New York: Columbia University Press, 1940). See also the recent review of literature in Gregory L. Freeze, "Church Politics in Late Imperial Russia: Crisis and Radicalization of the Clergy," in *Russia under the Last Tsar: Opposition and Subversion, 1894–1917*, ed. Anna Geifman (Oxford: Basil Blackwell, 1999), 269–97.

9. A discussion of the secularization theories that influenced attitudes toward peasant religion inside Russia and beyond can be found in Bryan Wilson, *Religion in Secular Society* (New York: Penguin Books, 1969); David Martin, *A General Theory of Secularization* (New York: Harper and Row, 1978); and Karel Dobbelaere, "Secularization: A Multi-Dimensional Concept," *Current Sociology* 29 (1981). For an elaboration of how these theories influenced studies of peasant religion in Russia, see Chris J. Chulos, "The End of Cultural 'Survivals' *(perezhitki)*: Remembering and Forgetting Russian Peasant Religious Traditions," *Studia Slavica Finlandensia* 17 (2000): 190–207.

10. Among recent reconsiderations, see N. A. Minenko, *Kul'tura russkikh krest'ian zaural'ia XVIII-pervaia polovina XIX v.* (Moscow: Nauka, 1991); Chris J. Chulos, "Myths of the Pious or Pagan Peasant in Post-Emancipation Central Russia (Voronezh Province)," *RH* 22, no. 2 (1995): 181–216; Laura Engelstein, "Paradigms, Pathologies, and Other Clues to Russian Spiritual Culture: Some Post-Soviet Thoughts," *SR* 57, no. 4 (1998): 864–77; and Simon Dixon, "How Holy Was Holy Russia? Rediscovering Russian Religion," in *Reinterpreting Russia*, ed. Geoffrey Hosking and Robert Service (London: Edward Arnold, 1999), 21–39.

11. Two excellent reevaluations of *dvoeverie* and *perezhitki* can be found in M. M. Gromyko, S. V. Kuznetsov, and A. V. Buganov, "Pravoslavie v russkoi narodnoi kul'ture: napravlenie issledovanii," *EO*, no. 6 (1993): 60–84; and Eve Levin, "*Dvoeverie* and Popular Religion," in *Seeking God: The Recovery of Religious Identity in Orthodox Russia, Ukraine, and Georgia*, ed. Stephen K. Batalden (DeKalb: Northern Illinois Press, 1993), 31–52. For a comparative perspective on folk piety that did not conform to theological dogma, see Keith Thomas, *Religion and the Decline of Magic: Studies in Popular Beliefs in Sixteenth- and Seventeenth-Century England* (New York: Scribner, 1971); and James Obelkevich, ed., *Religion and the People, 800–1700*, Shelby Cullom Davis Center for Historical Studies, Princeton University (Chapel Hill: University of North Carolina Press, 1979).

12. Similar approaches have been taken by Vera Shevzov, "Popular Orthodoxy in Late Imperial Rural Russia" (Ph.D. diss., Yale University, 1994); and Nadieszda Kizenko, *A Prodigal Saint: Father John of Kronstadt and the Russian People* (University Park: Pennsylvania State University Press, 2000).

13. I. Taradin, *"Zolotoe Dno": Ekonimika, istoriia, kul'tura i by volosti tsentral'nochernozemnoi oblasti* (Voronezh: Izd. Voronezhskogo kraevedcheskogo obshchestva, 1928), 3–4. For general introductions to the history of Voronezh, see E. G. Shuliakovskii, ed., *Ocherki istorii Voronezhskogo kraia s drevneishikh vremen do velikoi oktiabr'skoi sotsialisticheskoi revoliutsii*, 2 vols. (Voronezh: Izd-vo. Voronezhskogo univer-

siteta, 1961–1967); and *Iz istorii voronezhskogo kraia: Sbornik statei,* 7 vols. (Voronezh: Izd-vo Voronezhskogo universiteta, 1961–1977; Voronezh: Regional'nyi tsentr "Uchebnaia literatura," 1998).

14. St. Mitrofan met Tsar Peter during one of his visits to Voronezh to supervise the construction of the Russian navy. The details of their friendship can be found in *Sviatitel' i chudotvorets Mitrofan, pervyi episkop Voronezhskii,* 2d ed. (Moscow: I. D. Sytin, 1901), 37–40.

15. F. A. Shcherbina, "Semeinye razdely u krest'ian Voronezhskoi gubernii," part 2, *PKVG* (1897): 55–67.

16. Although in the early days of Voronezh's history there were significant differences between Ukrainian and Russian peasants, by the nineteenth century, ethnic distinction was less a factor than regional economic differentiation. For a typical comment on this, see G. Tkachev, "Etnograficheskie ocherki Bogucharskogo uezda," *PKVG* (1865–1866): 219–20.

17. These songs were published in 1914 as *Kontserty M. E. Piatnitskogo s krest'ianami* (Moscow: 1914).

18. Linëva was one of the most important promoters of folk songs abroad with concerts in the United States and England. These performances generated enough interest for her collection *Velikorusskie pesni v narodnoi garmonizatsii* (St. Petersburg: Imperatorskaia Akademiia Nauk, 1904–1909) to be published in an English-language abridgement: *The Peasant Songs of Great Russia as They Are in the Folk's Harmonization* (St. Petersburg: Imperial Academy of Sciences, 1905).

19. On the multiple components of identity, see Alfred J. Rieber, "The Sedimentary Society," in *Between Tsar and People: Educated Society and the Quest for Public Identity in Late Imperial Russia,* ed. Edith W. Clowes, Samuel D. Kassow, and James L. West (Princeton: Princeton University Press, 1991), 344–66.

1: Varieties of Piety

1. The cultural clashes that broke out between these groups were usually instigated by new peasants, most of whom returned temporarily to the village at the end of a work contract, or at the completion of schooling in a faraway location. The consequences of this encounter between village and urban intellectual worlds will be discussed in chapter 6.

2. Ivan Stoliarov, *Zapiski russkogo krest'ianina,* Récit d'un paysan russe, with a preface by Basile Kerblay and with notes by Valérie Stoliaroff, with the assistance of Alexis Berelowitch, Cultures et sociétés de l'est, no. 6 (Paris: Institut d'études slaves, 1986). Although Stoliarov made no explicit statement about his faith, his sympathetic portrayal of village Orthodoxy and clergymen suggests that he may have remained a believer throughout his life.

3. The nuns who gave Stoliarov's mother the complete set of the series were visiting from Moscow's famous Novodevichii Monastery. From these pamphlets Ivan developed an appetite for knowledge about the world beyond Karachun's borders. Between 1884 and 1917, more than one thousand individual pamphlets in the series were published by the venerable Trinity-Sergiev Monastery outside of Moscow. According to the Holy Synod of the Russian Orthodox Church, *Troitskie listki* was "to provide common Russian people with edifying reading and thus promote their religious and moral education and enlightenment." *IVO* (St. Petersburg: Sinodal'naia tip., 1884), 84–86.

4. From 1905 until it was closed down by the tsarist authorities in 1907, the Peasant Union supported the abolition of private landowning without compensation (including church, monastery, court, and princely lands) and a constitutional assembly by general election. The Union equivocated on the monarchy. When the party reemerged in March 1917, it favored socialized landholding, but opposed the seizure of privately owned land. It also favored the provisional government's prowar policy and was disbanded soon after the Bolsheviks came to power. In both periods of its existence, the Union was popular throughout European Russia.

5. For a less spectacular example of personal transformation, see the autobiography of peasant-turned-revolutionary Semën Kanatchikov, *A Radical Worker in Tsarist Russia: The Autobiography of Semën Kanatchikov*, ed. Reginald E. Zelnik (Stanford, CA: Stanford University Press, 1986).

6. Folk representations of Paradise are discussed in Stephen Lessing Baehr, *The Paradise Myth in Eighteenth-Century Russia: Utopian Patterns in Early Secular Russian Literature and Culture* (Stanford, CA: Stanford University Press, 1991), 14–16. Similar ideas about Paradise were known throughout the world. See Mircea Eliade, *Images and Symbols: Studies in Religious Symbolism*, trans. Philip Mairet (Princeton: Princeton University Press, 1991), 39; and Christian, *Local Religion*, chap. 5. Mircea Eliade's description of the mythical center of the earth is described in *The Myth of the Eternal Return, or Cosmos and History*, trans. Willard R. Trask, Bollingen Series, no. 46 (Princeton: Princeton University Press, 1954; Princeton/Bollingen Paperbacks, 1991).

7. Moshe Lewin, *The Making of the Soviet System: Essays in the Social History of Interwar Russia* (New York: Parthenon Books, 1985), 63–64, 71.

8. For a general discussion of these beliefs, see A. A. Lebedeva, "Znachenie poiasa i polotentsa v russkikh semeino-bytovykh obychaiakh i obriadakh XIX-XX vv.," in *Russkie: Semeinyi i obshchestvennyi byt*, ed. M. M. Gromyko and T. A. Litova (Moscow: Nauka, 1989), 229–47; I. A. Kremleva, "Ob evoliutsii nekotorykh arkhaichnykh obychaev u russkikh," in *Russkie*, ed. Gromyko and Litova, 248–64; and Tsekhanskaia, "Ikona v russkom dome."

9. [Iakovlev], "Poslovitsy, pogovorki, krylatye slova, primety i pover'ia, sobrannyi v slobode Sagunakh Ostrogozhskogo uezda," *ZS*, vyp. 1–2 (1905): 151, 164–165, 167, 170; A. I. Selivanov, "Etnograficheskie ocherki Voronezhskoi gubernii," in *Voronezhskii iubileinyi sbornik v pamiat' trekhsotletiia g. Voronezha* (Voronezh: Tip.-lit. Gubernskogo Pravleniia, 1886), 2:102, 108, 109, 114; and A. S., "Ocherki poverii, obriadov, primet i gadanii v Voronezhskoi gubernii," *Voronezhskii literaturnyi sbornik* 1 (1861): 376–77.

10. Ibid., 377–79; and Polikarpov, "Bytovye cherty iz zhizni krest'ian sela Istobnogo, Nizhnedevitskogo uezda, Voron. Gub.," *PKVG*, otd. 3 (1906): 26.

11. [Iakovlev], "Poslovitsy, pogovorki, krylatye slova," 149; and Selivanov, "Etnograficheskie ocherki," 103.

12. F. A. Shcherbina, comp., *Svodnyi sbornik po 12 uezdam Voronezhskoi gubernii: Statisticheskie materialy podvornoi perepisi po gubernii i obzor materialov, sposobov po sobiraniiu ikh i priemov po razrabotke* (Voronezh: Tip. Isaeva, 1897), 133.

13. Shcherbina required his team to be trained in statistics and mathematics, to be familiar with peasant life and customs, and to be well versed in local dialect, slang, and expressions. See ibid., 190–98.

14. Ibid, 133.

15. T. Oleinikov, "Iz putevykh vpechatlenii," *VEV*, no. 27, unof. pt. (1915): 736.

16. RGIA, f. 796, op. 442, ed. khr. 2757 (OSVE) (1916), l. 20–20 ob.

17. Vera Shevzov uses the term "pilgrimage in reverse" to describe the movement of special icons between communities. See Shevzov, "Popular Orthodoxy," 412. My usage of "reversed pilgrimage" is broader and includes the movement of objects and people that believers considered to be holy but that were not always recognized as such by official Orthodoxy.

18. Biographies of spiritual wanderers and holy fools were published in the provincial newspapers and as separate pamphlets in *Troitskie listki*. A circular narrative structure gave shape to these stories, which began when a devout believer renounced his or her expected roles in life, refused to fulfill obligations to society, withdrew from family and community to wander the countryside and minister to the peasantry, and returned home, or at least stopped roaming, to live in isolation or in a small ad hoc monastic community that ministered to the local population. Along the way, these exceptional individuals visited holy places, performed wondrous deeds, and inspired others. Aside from their lessons about spirituality, these tales underscored the possibility, despite the social rigidities of the village, to choose a different path to salvation. The spiritually motivated Orthodox Christians discussed in this section are a more diverse group than Vera Shevzov's "self-willed Orthodox Christians," who would not include holy fools or religious wanderers. See Shevzov, "Popular Orthodoxy," chap. 6.

19. "Sezenovskii podvizhnik," *TL*, no. 54 (1901); and *Pravoslavnye russkie obiteli (Polnoe illiustrirovannoe opisanie vsekh pravoslavnykh russkikh monastyrei v Rossiiskoi imperii i na Afone)* (St. Petersburg: P. P. Soikina, 1910), s.v. "Sezenovskii Ioanno-Kazanskii monastyr'." Most of the spiritual wanderers and holy fools featured in *Troitskie listki* and other religious and secular publications were uncanonized exemplars of selfless devotion to the faith.

20. The names peasants gave to lay nuns—*chernitsy, chernichki, keleinitsy, spasennitsy*—referred to the black clothing donned by these women, their penchant for living in ad hoc communities that recalled nunneries, and their striving for salvation through the religious life. Lay nunnery has been little studied. Brief introductions to the phenomenon can be found in: L. A. Tul'tseva, "Chernichki," *Nauka i religiia*, no. 11 (1970): 80–82; M. M. Gromyko, *Mir russkoi derevni* (Moscow: Molodaia gvardiia, 1991), 120–21; Brenda Meehan-Waters, "To Save Oneself: Russian Peasant Women and the Development of Women's Religious Communities in Prerevolutionary Russia," in *Russian Peasant Women*, ed. Beatrice Farnsworth and Lynne Viola (New York: Oxford University Press, 1992), 121–33; Brenda Meehan, "Popular Piety, Local Initiative, and the Founding of Women's Religious Communities in Russia, 1764–1907," in *Seeking God*, ed. Batalden (DeKalb: Northern Illinois University Press, 1993), 83–105; and Rose L. Glickman, "'Unusual Circumstances' in the Peasant Village," *RH* 23, nos. 1–4 (1996): 225–26.

21. In 1893 Archbishop Anastasii reported two informal women's communities, where 116 women resided. RGIA, f. 796, op. 172, ed. khr. 1749, OSVE (1893), l. 16. Most lay nuns sharing the same residence probably lived in groups of two, three, or four, the number of rooms in a typical peasant cottage. But unlike the typical peasant dwelling, whose cramped space was put to practical use, the homes of lay nuns directed their attention to the spiritual life through large sacred images, which usually covered two entire walls. Below the icons lay a psalter and several notebooks of handwritten hymns. The remaining two walls contained pictures depicting religious history, liturgical practice, or acts of piety. The other distinguishing characteristic of lay nun cottages was the constant burning of incense as a means of deterring unclean

forces. The healing power of this incense was revered by local residents, who mixed particles of it with water to make a curative. No statistics exist about the number of small communities of lay nuns.

22. As a form of female spirituality, lay nunnery can be seen as an expression of independence and living proof that peasants tolerated alternative lifestyles that were beneficial to village life. Refusing to accept traditional roles as daughters, wives, mothers, and companions to the household head (bol'shukha), these women enjoyed freedom otherwise unknown to peasant women. Communal tolerance was, however, not matched by the church. Before the emancipation, official pronouncements about lay nuns were cautious, but as the Holy Synod sought to crack down on nonstandard practice in the late 1860s, lay nunnery became associated with sectarianism. None of the works cited in note 20 commented on the sympathetic position of the church earlier in the nineteenth century, or the periodic shifts in its attitudes toward lay nunnery. Regional differences may explain this omission. The accusation of sectarianism was anachronistic and seems to have applied to an earlier generation of lay nuns that was alleged to belong to the local Flagellant sect. For example, see Georgii Lebedev, "Chernichki v Alferovke," *VGV,* no. 88, unof. pt. (1869): 376.

23. Christine D. Worobec, *Possessed: Women, Witches, and Demons in Imperial Russia* (DeKalb: Northern Illinois University Press, 2001), 64.

24. Although the belief in sorcery and witchcraft was predominantly a rural phenomenon in late-tsarist Russia, the appeal of herbal treatments cut across the rural-urban divide. As the authors of a popular, though very dense, manual on medicinal herbs acknowledged in the early 1890s, "[W]e *involuntarily* bow down before the Blessed One—Our Almighty God, who created everything so that practically no plant is without its use and service to man." V. Goretskii and V. Vil'k, comps., *Russkii narodnyi lechebnyi travnik i tsvetnik,* 2d ed. (Moscow: Tip. V. V. Chicherina, 1892–93).

25. There were many other types of people with special powers living in the village, such as fortunetellers (m. *gadal'shchik,* f. *gadalka*). The words used to refer to them varied tremendously. For example, in certain contexts, *babka* referred to witches, but also connoted "married woman" and "granny." The aim of this section is to explain why sorcerers, witches, and healers were important in peasant society and why peasants used their services without considering themselves to be in violation of Orthodox teachings. For a general introduction to the topic in Russia and Europe, see respectively Worobec, *Possessed;* and Robin Briggs, *Witches and Neighbors: The Social and Cultural Context of European Witchcraft* (New York: Penguin Books, 1998). Although medical professionals expressed their skepticism about witchcraft and homeopathic treatments, church officials condoned the work of herbal healers, who were usually in good standing with Orthodox Christianity, regularly attended worship services, and took part in sacramental life. Prominent churchmen even recommended their own folk treatments and implored the parish clergy to use them in battling common peasant ailments. For example, see "Domashnaia aptechka prikhodskogo sviashchennika," *VEV,* no. 22, unof. pt. (1887): 910–15. The practice of witchcraft and sorcery was, however, roundly rejected by religious authorities because of its association with Satan and his demonic minions.

26. Selivanov, "Etnograficheskie ocherki," 90. On the variety of fevers and their personification, see *Slavianskaia mifologiia: Entsiklopedicheskii slovar'* (Moscow: Ellis Lak, 1995), s.v. *"likhoradki."*

27. Such combinations were widespread among the Russian peasantry. For examples, see ibid., "Lechebnye zagovory" (medicinal charms).

28. [Iakovlev], "Poslovitsy, pogovorki, krylatye slova," 152.

29. The contentious, envious, and jealous reality of village life meant, however, that peasant women in the late–nineteenth century were careful to nurture their reputations as exalted earth mothers, chaste homemakers, and vessels of tradition in order to avoid being labeled a dreaded virago, wild temptress, or transmitter of ignorant "wives tales." The precarious position of women could be compared to the extremely popular Mother of God, a compassionate, yet compromised, figure in the Orthodox pantheon, who was eternally subordinated to the authority and significance of her own son. The Mother of God symbolized the liminal position of all women in late-imperial Russia, elevated or denigrated, as imperfect counterimages of the men who so dominated society. The symbolism and popularity of the Orthodox Mother of God was matched in rural Catholic Europe by the ubiquitous "Our Lady."

30. This paragraph draws from the vast literature about feminine myths and the role of peasant women in late-imperial Russia, but especially: Joanna Hubbs, *Mother Russia: The Feminine Myth in Russian Culture* (Bloomington: Indiana University Press, 1988); Farnsworth and Viola, eds., *Russian Peasant Women;* Christine D. Worobec, *Peasant Russia: Family and Community in the Post-Emancipation Period* (Princeton: Princeton University Press, 1991; DeKalb: Northern Illinois University Press, 1995); Barbara Alpern Engel, *Between the Fields and the City: Women, Work, and Family in Russia, 1861–1914* (Cambridge: Cambridge University Press, 1995); and Elena Hellberg-Hirn, "Mother Russia: Soil and Soul," in *Soil and Soul: The Symbolic World of Russianness* (Aldershot, England: Ashgate, 1998), 111–35.

31. Chulos, "Pious or Pagan."

32. RGIA, f. 796, op. 442, ed. khr. 1384, OSVE (1892), l. 10 ob. Archbishop Anastasii, like his predecessors, was incapable of reconciling peasant religiosity with his understanding of Orthodoxy. His successor, Archbishop Tikhon, echoed these sentiments in his first report for 1913, the only year of his tenure unmarked by war or revolution. See ibid., ed. khr. 2572, OSVE (1913), l. 13 ob.

33. Throughout modern Russian history, the terms "Orthodox Christian," "Old Belief," and "sectarian" have been subjected to definitional shifts, often quite subtle, which reflected the power relationships between the institutional church and actual belief and practice. Although Old Believers were not technically deemed to be heretics in the late-tsarist period, defenders of Orthodoxy nevertheless often referred to them as sectarians. Not included among heretics are the followers of other main branches of Christianity, Judaism, and Islam, which, following Russian cultural and ethnic prejudice, the Orthodox Church lumped together as "members of other faiths" *(inovertsy)* and "foreigners" *(inorodtsy)*. For different approaches to the categories of Orthodoxy and heterodoxy, see Nadieszda Kizenko, "Ioann of Kronstadt and the Reception of Sanctity, 1850–1988," *RR* 57, no. 3 (1998): 325–44; Roy R. Robson, *Old Believers in Modern Russia* (DeKalb: Northern Illinois University Press, 1995), xi–xii; Eugene Clay, "The Theological Origins of the Christ-Faith *(Khristovshchina),*" *RH* 15, no. 1 (1988): 21–41; Engelstein, "Rebels of the Soul"; idem, *Castration and the Heavenly Kingdom: A Russian Folk Tale* (Ithaca, NY: Cornell University Press, 1999), esp. 11–12; and John W. Slocum, "Who, and When, Were the *Inorodtsy?* The Evolution of the Category of 'Aliens' in Imperial Russia," *RR* 57, no. 2 (1998): 173–90.

34. Baptized members of the faith who no longer considered themselves to be

religious were formally categorized as apostates. On the adaptation of revolutionary language in the countryside, see Orlando Figes, "The Russian Revolution of 1917 and Its Language in the Village," *RR* 56, no. 3 (July 1997): 323–45.

35. Certain distinctions were made, however, between Orthodox Christians in good standing (i.e., those who confessed and communed annually) and those who had fallen away from the flock or had been excommunicated. Vera Shevzov has recently proposed a solution to the problem of counting peasant believers: self-definition should determine how peasants "identified with the Orthodox Church and viewed themselves as Orthodox Christians, and who, at the same time, were considered as part of 'the flock' by representatives of the institutional church." Not only does she tacitly accept the church's line by construing "popular religion" to be essentially Orthodox, but she fails to address the silence of the majority of believers who never made unmediated statements about its religious affiliation declarations about its faith. Shevzov, "Popular Orthodoxy," 14–17. The problematics of counting has been little discussed. A variety of issues about membership was raised before the Bolsheviks came to power and more recently. See I. V. Preobrazhenskii, comp., *Otechestvennaia tserkov' po statisticheskim dannym s 1840–41 po 1890–91 gg.* (St. Petersburg: Tip. E. Arngol'da, 1897), 43; I. Kirillov, "Statistika staroobriadchestva: Tsifrovye dannye," *Staroobriadcheskaia mysl'* 3 (1913): 249–62; Clay, "Theological Origins," 21; N. D. Zol'nikova, *Sibirskaia prikhodskaia obshchina v XVIII veke* (Novosibirsk: Nauka, Sibirskoe otdelenie, 1990), 5; and Robson, *Old Belief,* 19–24.

36. On the same in the Vologda diocese, see Shevzov, "Popular Orthodoxy," 156–57. One leading Orthodox cleric expressed the irony of the love-hate relationship with Old Believers, admitting that "it would be much easier for the Orthodox Church to defeat the lack of belief and indifference [prevalent in Orthodox parishes] if the faithful would form sects, because at the present they lack the spiritual enthusiasm that is part of every sect." See P. Nikol'skii, "1 ianvaria 1901 goda," *VEV,* no. 1, unof. pt. (1901): 4.

37. AREM, f. 7, op. 1, d. 1486, Saratov Province, l. 21; Chris J. Chulos, "Orthodoxy and Nationality Among Peasants in Late Nineteenth-Century Russia," *Idäntutkimus/Finnish Journal of East European Studies* 1 (1995): 48–56; and idem, "'A Place without Taverns': Village Space in the Afterlife" in *Beyond the Limits: The Concept of Space in Russian History and Culture,* ed. Jeremy Smith, Studia Historica, no. 62 (Helsinki: Finnish Historical Society, 1999), 193–94.

38. AREM, f. 7, op. 1, d. 540, Kaluga Province, l. 3.

39. The 1906 renovation included the installation of a new iconostasis. "Materialy po istorii staroobriadchestva," *Tserkov'* 48 (1908): 1647. This Old Believer parish was established in the late–eighteenth century.

40. Petr Petrov, "K voprosu o bor'be s raskolom i sektantstvom. (Zametka sel'skogo pastyria)," *VEV,* no. 9, unof. pt (1890): 425–31; T. Tozhdestvenskii, "Otkrytoe pis'mo 11–e (Nekotorye itogi po delam missii, o missionerskom fonde i okruzhnykh missionerakh)," *VEV,* no. 1, unof. pt. (1901): 12–21; and "Narodno-Missionerskie kursy v Valuiskom Uspenskom Nikolaevskom monastyre," *VEV,* no. 16, of. pt. (1916): 223–26. Missionary activities in European Russia generally were not aimed at Jews, Muslims, Catholics, or Protestants.

41. RGIA, f. 796, op. 176, ed. khr. 2139, l. 5.

42. Followers of Mokshin were also required to abstain from meat and wine and to help the poor. This section is based on G. Nedotovskii, "Vasilii Fedorov Mokshin: Epizod iz istorii sektantstva v Voronezhskoi gubernii," *TVUAK,* vyp. 1 (1902): 79–92; RGIA, f. 796, op. 442, ed. khr. 1068, OSVE (1885), l. 16; A. I. Klibanov, *Istoriia*

religioznogo sektantstva v Rossiia (60-e gody XIX v.–1917 g.) (Moscow: Nauka, 1965), 60, 62; and J. Eugene Clay, "Russian Israel," *Communal Societies* 18 (1998): 81–91.

43. RGIA, f. 796, op. 442, ed. khr. 2202, OSVE (1907), l. 20. Archbishop Anastasii substantiated neither of his claims, although peasant youths were increasingly interested in urban culture.

44. Singing by the faithful, not a part of traditional Orthodox liturgical life, was an innovation of the late–nineteenth century. See Shevzov, "Popular Orthodoxy," 142, 151.

45. For examples, see AREM, f. 7, op. 1, d. 484, Kaluga Province, l. 1; and ibid., d. 551, Kaluga Province, l. 6.

46. Ibid., l. 7; and ibid., op. 1, d. 484, l. 2. Conversion might also put an end to years of ridicule and ostracism, something that made the Orthodox faith especially appealing to Old Believer boys and girls. Out of paternal respect, Old Believers who found Orthodox spouses waited until their parents died before joining the Orthodox Church. Revanchism among this group was low.

47. The sources remain silent about the sudden rise in hostility between Orthodox believers and sectarians at the end of the nineteenth century. Although it is tempting to believe that sectarians were emboldened by the relaxation of religious oppression, the cases I read suggest that this was only one of a variety of factors that was related to social and cultural changes in village life at the end of the nineteenth century. For an interesting example of peasants making charges of heresy and heterodoxy to express their envy of peasants who went to work in factories, see Jeffrey Burds, *Peasant Dreams and Market Politics: Labor Migration and the Russian Village, 1861–1905* (Pittsburgh: University of Pittsburgh Press, 1998), 186–218.

48. GAVO, f. I-6, op. 1, ed. khr. 560 (1903). Unfortunately, no information was given about the reasons for the confrontation or the subsequent fate of these Flagellants. They may have reconciled themselves to their neighbors by returning to the Orthodox faith—at least ostensibly—or by better obscuring their meetings.

49. RGIA, f. 796, op. 442, ed. khr. 1551, OSVE (1895), l. 55 ob. Distinctions must be made, and Faith Wigzell has suggested that, in urban culture, superstition was associated more with fun and entertainment than conviction. See her *Reading Russian Fortunes: Print Culture, Gender and Divination in Russia from 1765* (Cambridge: Cambridge University Press, 1998).

50. RGIA, f. 796, op. 442, ed. khr. 1551, OSVE (1895), l. 52

51. Ibid., ed. khr. 2139, OSVE (1906), ll. 26–27; ibid., ed. khr. 2325, OSVE (1909), ll. 60, 63; and ibid., ed. khr. 2693, OSVE (1915), ll. 17 ob.–18.

52. Eugene Clay has referred to this as an emphasis on "charismatic over institutional authority, prayer over sacraments, and ascetic feats over an ordered sacerdotal system." See his "Theological Origins," 40.

2: Telling Time

1. For example, see N. Maksheev, *Krest'ianskii i sel'sko-khoziastvennyi kalendar' 1901* (Moscow: 1901). Church holidays continued to be included in secular calendars well into the 1920s. See *Krest'ianskii kalendar' na 1925 g. S ob'iasneniiami prazdnikov i poleznymi sovetami dlia sel'skikh khoziaev* (Kazan': Izd-vo Krasnaia Tatariia i Novaia derevnia, 1925), which also included an annotated list of the main Christian holidays (15–20).

2. Mircea Eliade has described the repetitious performance of rituals connecting sacred life and mundane reality as "a continual present" when time is regenerated to produce a sense of eternal return (to a new birth after death or to a renewal of social order or bonds). See Eliade, *Myth of the Eternal Return*, 86; and Eliade, *Images and Symbols*, chap. 2. In his work on the British calendar, Ronald Hutton has looked to nature for symbols of timelessness and mortality. See Ronald Hutton, *The Stations of the Sun: A History of the Ritual Year in Britain* (Oxford: Oxford University Press, 1996).

3. T. A. Bernshtam has discussed the role of ritual in the formation of a shared identity in *Molodezh' v obriadovoi zhizni russkoi obshchiny XIX - nachala XX v.: Polovozrastnoi aspekt traditsionnoi kul'tury* (Leningrad: Nauka, 1988); and *Molodost' v simvolizme perekhodnykh obriadov vostochnykh slavian: Uchenie i opyt Tserkvi v narodnom khristianstve* (St. Petersburg: Peterburgskoe Vostokovedenie, 2000).

4. The slow introduction of modern medicine to the village was reflected in high infant mortality rates and periodic epidemics. Almost until the end of the tsarist period, mortality in the first five years of life ranged between 40 and 50 percent. See A. G. Rashin, *Naselenie Rossii za 100 let (1811–1913): Statisticheskie ocherki* (Moscow: Gosudarstvennoe statisticheskoe izd-vo, 1956), 192–297.

5. Worobec, *Peasant Russia*, 135–36; and Engel, *Between the Fields and the City*, chap. 2.

6. The most important holy days of the year consisted of the twelve major feasts. Eight of the major feasts honored Christ (Epiphany, Presentation in the Temple, Palm Sunday, Ascension, Pentecost, Transfiguration, Exaltation of the Cross, Nativity), and the remaining four honored his mother (Annunciation, Dormition, her own Nativity, and Presentation of the Mother of God in the Temple).

7. Christian, *Local Religion*, 174.

8. Leonid Heretz's calculation that "about 180" days "or half the year" were devoted to fasts suggests that Voronezh believers were not unusual in designating so many days as religious. See his "Practice and Significance of Fasting in Russian Peasant Culture at the Turn of the Century," in *Food in Russian History and Culture*, ed. Musya Glants and Joyce Toomre (Bloomington: Indiana University Press, 1997), 69. See also Minenko, *Kul'tura russkikh krest'ian*, 190–95; and T. A. Voronina, "Problemy etnograficheskogo izucheniia russkogo pravoslavnogo posta," *EO*, no. 4 (1997): 85–95.

9. Stoliarov, *Zapiski russkogo krest'ianina*, 75–76. The great student of the peasantry, S. V. Maksimov, found that Yuletide included the longer period from St. Nicholas Day (6 December) to Epiphany (6 January), but none of my sources for Voronezh corroborate this. See his general description in S. V. Maksimov, *Nechistaia, nevedomaia i krestnaia sila*, Etnograficheskoe biuro kniazia V. N. Tenisheva (St. Petersburg: R. Golike i A. Vil'borg, 1903); reprint, St. Petersburg: "POLISET," 1994), 240–61.

10. As elsewhere in Europe, the Russian Yuletide carnival provided a legitimate forum for the release of social pressures, which was critical to pre- and early-modern societies. The other main carnival was *maslenitsa*, which lasted the entire week preceding Easter. For an introduction to European carnival customs and their meanings, see Edward Muir, *Ritual in Early Modern Europe* (Cambridge: Cambridge University Press, 1997), chap. 3.

11. Tkachev, "Etnograficheskie ocherki," 182–84; Nikonov, "O blagochestivykh obychaiakh," 355–56; A. Fon-Kremer, "Obychai pover'ia i predrassudki krest'ian sela Verkhotishanki," *PKVG* (1870–1871): 276; Ioann Snesarev, "Obyknoveniia malorossian Voronezhskoi gubernii, Biriuchenskogo uezda," manuscript held in Biblioteka Voronezhskogo gosudarstvennogo universiteta, 254, 262, 295; and

V. Kutepov, "Sloboda Meniailova," *VGV*, no. 66, unof. pt. (1886): 3. A general introduction to holiday and ritual songs can be found in S. G. Lazutin's introduction to *Voprosy poetiki literatury i fol'klora* (Voronezh: Izd. Voronezhskogo universiteta, 1977). Appeals to the forces of nature in the middle of winter and memorials for the deceased went hand in hand as essential activities in agrarian societies, for whom success and failure depended on a proper relationship between the living and the dead, the seen and unseen.

12. Any number of divination games were played during the New Year's holiday. Some of them are still played today, although they are no longer believed to foretell the future. According to one popular game, a group of girls went to the woodshed and brought out a log. A long piece of wood revealed that the future groom would be tall, while a stump suggested a husband of smaller physical stature. See G. Iakovlev, "Poslovitsy, pogovorki, krylatye slova, primety i pover'ia, sobranny v slobode Sagunakh Ostrogozhskogo uezda," *ZS* vyp. 4, otd. 2 (1906): 165.

13. Although the water was normally preserved for up to a year, peasants refused to believe that it could be spoiled, saying: "Epiphany water does not get old (of course, only if it is kept in a clean vessel)." See [Iakovlev], "Poslovitsy, pogovorki, krylatye slova," 149.

14. Tkachev, "Etnograficheskie ocherki," 182–84; Nikonov, "O blagochestivykh obychaiakh," 355–56; Fon-Kremer, "Obychai," 276, 286; Snesarev, "Obyknoveniia malorossian," 262, 295; and *VVTsE*, no. 4 (11 January 1918): 3; and Kutepov, "Sloboda Meniailova," *VGV*, no. 66, unof. pt. (1886): 3. For a description of similar Epiphany customs elsewhere in Russia, see Maksimov, *Nechistaia, nevedomaia i krestnaia sila*, 277–82.

15. GAVO, f. I-6, op. 1, ed. khr. 1717 (1910–1911), l. 3.

16. Usually falling in the last half of February, Shrovetide did not mark the end of winter as much as it anticipated the onset of the spring plowing season. Popular belief held that the seasonal shift from winter to spring fell on either 2 February, the day of the Presentation of the Lord in the Temple, or 1 March, the feast of St. Eudocia, when the heavy sheets of snow and ice usually began to thaw. See Maksimov, *Nechistaia, nevedomaia i krestnaia sila*, 283, 291–92.

17. *Maslenitsa* is occasionally translated literally as "butter" *(maslo)* week, which is an indirect reference to the church's prohibition of meat consumption during the final week before Great Lent, which is also known as Cheese Week *(syrnaia nedelia)*.

18. Ivan Stoliarov described how a girl's fate could be sealed during such a ride. See Stoliarov, *Zapiski russkogo krest'ianina*, 80. As Stoliarov noted, Yuletide divination games were not forgotten during *maslenitsa* but instead could focus a young man's or woman's attention on the presaged beloved.

19. Tkachev, "Etnograficheskie ocherki," 219–20.

20. Stoliarov, *Zapiski russkogo krest'ianina*, 86.

21. Fon-Kremer, "Obychai pover'ia," 279.

22. Snesarev, "Obyknoveniia malorossian," 294–95; and Stoliarov, *Zapiski russkogo krest'ianina*, 87–88.

23. As an integral and integrated part of village life, the cemetery offered a communal gathering point not unlike that of the church and market square where social interaction was as important as religious or economic pursuits. Contrast this with French village cemeteries in the nineteenth century which, after a law of 1804, were gradually moved beyond village boundaries for hygienic and cosmetic purposes. See Thomas A. Kselman, *Death and the Afterlife in Modern France* (Princeton: Princeton University Press, 1993), 176–80.

24. S., "Ocherki poverii," 377–79; N. P. Grinkova, "Obriad 'vozhdenie rusalki' v sele V. Vereika Voronezhskoi oblasti," *SE,* no. 1 (1947): 178–79; and T. A. Kriukova, "'Vozhdenie rusalki' v sele Os'kine Voronezhskoi oblasti," *SE,* no. 1 (1947): 185–92. See also Maksimov, *Nechistaia, nevedomaia i krestnaia sila,* 379–82.

25. Peasants commonly used the word *edok* when speaking of a nonperforming member of the family, usually a child or adult unable to work. The word derives from the verb to eat, *est'.*

26. A general introduction of peasant birth customs can be found in D. K. Zelenin, *Vostochnoslavianskaia etnografiia* (Berlin and Leipzig, 1927; Moscow: Nauka, 1991), 319–22.

27. S., "Ocherki poverii," 389.

28. Early baptism minimized the anguish felt by parents who lost their newborns since, according to some variants of popular belief, stillborn babies and infants who died before being baptized, along with their mothers, would be condemned to hell. See N. N., "Vnimaniiu dukhovenstva (narodnye sueveria)," *VEV,* no. 42, unof. pt. (1915): 1215–16.

29. The parents' absence from the baptism is explained by church and popular belief that mothers were unclean for forty days after birth. The father's association with the mother also made him a vehicle of unclean forces.

30. "Poslovitsy, pogovorki, krylatye slova," 154; Selivanov, "Etnograficheskie ocherki," 74; Kutepov, "Sloboda Meniailova," *VGV,* no. 67, unof. pt. (1886): 3; and ARGO, raz. 9, op. 1, d. 55, l. 2 ob.

31. Polikarpov, "Bytovye cherty," 22. A family of daughters was doomed because without a male heir it would cease to exist upon the death of the household head. In rare cases, a daughter's husband could be adopted by her parents, thus producing a surrogate heir.

32. Iakovlev, "Poslovitsy, pogovorki, krylatye slova," 167.

33. The eves of Wednesdays, Fridays, and Sundays were also forbidden times for weddings. On marriage restrictions, see Tkachev, "Etnograficheskie ocherki," 185; Polikarpov, "Bytovye cherty," 14; and Aleksei Putintsev, "Talagaiskaia svad'ba," *PKVG* (1913): 103.

34. Although individual choice in spousal selection was slowly becoming more acceptable by the beginning of the twentieth century, boys and their families continued to be agents in the process (initiating contact and making proposals) while girls and their families assumed the role of passive recipients (responding to offers of marriage). See Barbara Alpern Engel, "Peasant Morality and Pre-marital Relations in Late Nineteenth-Century Russia," *Journal of Social History* 23, no. 4 (1990): 703–9.

35. The norms of patriarchal society, and not Orthodox Christianity alone, favored parental decision making. Although the documentary sources concentrate on the cruelty of forced marriages, little was written about spousal selection that respected the younger generation's wishes.

36. For further discussion on the role of peasant marriage in village society, see especially Worobec, *Peasant Russia,* chaps. 4–5. Worobec's conclusions are convincing despite their dependence on Gromyko's romanticized notion of peasant life. See M. M. Gromyko, *Traditsionnye normy povedeniia i formy obshcheniia russkikh krest'ian XIX v.* (Moscow: Nauka, 1986), which Worobec used, and her more recent *Mir russkoi derevni.* See also Zelenin's summary of wedding customs in European Russia and his useful bibliography in *Vostochnoslavianskaia etnografiia,* 332–45, 358–59.

37. Gromyko, *Traditsionnye normy*, 161–266; and Bernshtam, *Molodezh' v obriadovoi zhizni*. For an example of Voronezh church support for these events, see RGIA, f. 796, op. 442, ed. khr. 2510, OSVE (1912), l. 23. As Christine Worobec has pointed out, this social encouragement contributed to lower marriage ages in Russia vis-à-vis Western Europe (*Peasant Russia*, 125–27).

38. Polikarpov, "Bytovye cherty," 11.

39. ARGO, raz. 9, op. 1, d. 55, ll. 2 ob.–3; Snesarev, "Obyknoveniia malorossiian," 262; Kutepov, "Sloboda Meniailova," *VGV*, no. 67, unof. pt. (1886): 3; Polikarpov, "Bytovye cherty," 10–12; Putintsev, "Talagaiskaia svad'ba," 98–102; and GAVO, f. 1138, op. 1, d. 10, ll. 1–3.

40. ARGO, raz. 9, op. 1, d. 55, l. 3–3 ob; Snesarev, "Obyknoveniia malorossiian," 262, 270–71; Polikarpov, "Bytovye cherty," 12–13; Putintsev, "Talagaiskaia svad'ba," 102–5; and GAVO, f. 1138, op. 1, d. 10, l. 3. On wedding lamentations, see T. A. Bernshtam, "Svadebnyi plach v obriadovoi kul'ture vostochnykh slavian (XIX-nachalo XX v.)," in *Russkii sever: Problemy etnokul'turnoi istorii, etnografii, fol'kloristiki*, ed. T. A. Bernshtam and K. D. Chistov (Leningrad: Izd. Nauka, 1986), 82–100.

41. Taradin, *"Zolotoe dno,"* 195.

42. Tkachev, "Etnograficheskie ocherki," 189; Kutepov, "Sloboda Meniailova," *VGV*, no. 67, unof. pt. (1886): 3; Polikarpov, "Bytovye cherty," 14; and Putintsev, "Talagaiskaia svad'ba," 111–12.

43. Tkachev, "Etnograficheskie ocherki," 200; ARGO, raz. 9, op. 1, d. 55, l. 4; Plikarpov, "Bytovye cherty," 14; and Putintsev, "Talagaiskaia svad'ba," 113–14.

44. Despite the legal importance of the church rite in legitimizing the union, the ritual itself received very little attention in the copious ethnographic literature on peasant wedding rituals. Worobec suggests that this imbalance in the literature is due to the greater importance of the wedding celebrations (Worobec, *Peasant Russia*, 162), but other possible reasons for this silence might include the bias of ethnographers toward nonchurch religious expression and the widespread familiarity with the church rite, which varied little regardless of its performance in village or urban churches.

45. Snesarev, "Obyknoveniia malorossian," 277.

46. Ibid., 288; Kutepov, "Sloboda Meniailova," *VGV*, no. 67, unof. pt. (1886): 3; and ibid., no. 68, unof. pt. (1886): 3.

47. ARGO, raz. 9, op. 1, d. 55, l. 1 ob.; and Putintsev, "Talagaiskaia svad'ba," 118–19.

48. Polikarpov, "Bytovye cherty," 16. On the difficult lot of peasant women, see Rose L. Glickman, "Women and the Peasant Commune," in *Land Commune*, ed. Robert Bartlett (London: Mcmillan, 1990), 321–38.

49. Polikarpov, "Bytovye cherti," 22.

50. Jacques Le Goff, *The Birth of Purgatory*, trans. Arthur Goldhammer (Chicago: University of Chicago Press, 1984), 1–2, 4; and Polikarpov, "Bytovye cherty," 25. This section is an abridged version of Chulos, "'A Place without Taverns'."

51. Russian peasants were not unique but were doing what many others had done since time immemorial. See Eliade, *Images and Symbols*, 37–38; and idem, *Eternal Return*.

52. Maksimov, *Nechistaia, nevedomaia i krestnaia sila*, 209–228; Olga Semyonova Tian-Shanskaia, *Village Life in Late Tsarist Russia*, ed. David L. Ransel, Indiana-Michigan Series in Russian and East European Studies (Bloomington: Indiana University Press, 1993), 137; Hubbs, *Mother Russia*, chap. 3; and Hellberg-Hirn, *Soil and Soul*, chap. 6.

53. The quote is from AREM, f. 7, op. 1, d. 536 (Kaluga Province, 1899), l. 1. On the location of hell, see ibid., f. 7, op. 1, d. 556 (Kaluga Province, 1898), l. 2; and B. M. Firsov and I. G. Kiseleva, comps., *Byt velikorusskikh krest'ian-zemlepashchtsev. Opisanie materialov etnograficheskogo biuro kniazia V. N. Tenisheva. (Na primere Vladimirskoi gubernii.)* (St. Petersburg: Izd-vo Evropeiskogo Doma, 1993), 147.

54. AREM, f. 7, op. 1, d. 556 (Kaluga Province, 1898), l. 1; ibid., f. 7, op. 1, ed. khr. 530 (Kaluga Province, 1898), l. 2; ibid., f. 7, op. 1, d. 484 (Kaluga Province, 1898), ll. 15–16; and Firsov and Kiseleva, *Byt velikorusskikh krest'ian-zemplepashtsev,* 145.

55. Iakovlev, "Poslovitsy, pogovorki, krylatye slova," 154.

56. The first saying is from Fon-Kremer, "Obychai pover'ia," 279; the second and third are from Iakovlev, "Poslovitsy, pogovorki, krylatye slova," 155.

57. Selivanov, "Etnograficheskie ocherki," 110; and Iakovlev, "Poslovitsy, pogovorki, krylatye slova," 155.

58. The first saying is from Selivanov, "Etnograficheskie ocherki," 110; the following is from Iakovlev, "Poslovitsy, pogovorki, krylatye slova," 155. Crossing oneself while passing a cemetery was believed to counteract the effects of any malevolent spirits lingering in the area. Ibid., 178; and Ivan Usov, "O boiazni pokoinikov," *VEV,* no. 8, unof. pt. (1901): 353.

59. Fon-Kremer, "Obychai pover'ia," 277, 280; S., "Ocherki poverii," 388; ARGO, raz. 9, op. 1, d. 55, l. 4; and Zelenin, *Vostochnoslavianskaia etnografiia,* 345–47.

60. Under no circumstances were medical authorities to tamper with the body, a custom which prevented zemstvo doctors from conducting autopsies during epidemics or following unnatural deaths. See Stolariov, *Zapiski russkogo krest'ianina,* 25.

61. Ibid.; Tkachev, "Etnograficheskie ocherki," 185; and "Etnograficheskii ocherk," 714.

62. Zelenin, *Vostochnoslavianskaia etnografiia,* 345; and Fon-Kremer, "Obychai pover'ia," 277, 280.

63. Ioann Putintsev, "Selo Dimitrievskoe, korotoiakskogo uezda," *VEV,* no. 14, unof. pt. (1868): 465; Selivanov, "Obychai pover'ia," 277, 280; S., "Ocherki poverii," 388; and ARGO, raz. 9, op. 1, d. 55, l. 4 ob.

64. Priscilla Roosevelt, *Life on the Russian Country Estate: A Social and Cultural History* (New Haven, CT: Yale University Press, 1995).

65. In his seminal work on revolutionary utopianism, Richard Stites has masterfully demonstrated that intellectual, social, and cultural thought at times sought to abolish the basic opposition of "city light and rural darkness" but could never quite shake itself entirely of the lures and influences, however indirect and distant, of peasant culture. See Richard Stites, *Revolutionary Dreams: Utopian Vision and Experimental Life in the Russian Revolution* (New York: Oxford University Press, 1989), 48. Ivan Stoliarov described the lures of the village in the familial terms of the "mother *kormilitsa*" (nourisher), whose appeal city dwellers were powerless to resist (Stoliarov, *Zapiski russkogo krest'ianina,* 72).

3: Mythical Origins, Magical Icons, and Historical Awareness

1. I use the term "collective memory" to describe how peasant communities remembered their own past. Collective reminiscence did not require special guardians but was the responsibility of what peasants referred to as "the elderly folk," the oldest living generation. I am less interested in methods of perpetuating

collective memory than in its contents. Most of the current literature on collective memory owes a debt to the fundamental ideas of Maurice Halbwachs, which date to 1925. The first English translation of his work was published as *On Collective Memory*, trans. Lewis A. Coser (Chicago: University of Chicago Press, 1992).

2. The first paragraph of Stoliarov's memoir, *Zapiski russkogo krest'ianina* (see the epigraph to this chapter), serves as the literary equivalent to the village signpost that alerts visitors to their passage from one place to another, each with its own physical and psychological boundaries. Stoliarov created a play on words by using the word "soul" *(dusha)*, which referred to the "individual male serf" before emancipation, to connote all residents of the village, male and female.

3. Villages were subjected to periodic administrative reassignment to a different township, district, or province. Village names frequently changed at the time of a community's legal establishment and entry into public records, as well as upon the subdivision of large villages into smaller units. In the latter case, the prefixes "new," "old," "big," or "little" were commonly used to distinguish between the original village and its offshoot.

4. Peasants' constant revision and preservation of inherited historical knowledge parallels the methods of today's historians, who claim to be rewriting earlier redactions of history, ever improving and refining the story into subtler and more comprehensive, as well as comprehensible, wholes. For a discussion of the similarities between collective memory and the historical profession, see Anne Ollila, ed., *Historical Perspectives on Memory*, Studia Historica 61 (Helsinki: Finnish Historical Society, 1999), especially the articles by Natalie Zemon Davis and Georg G. Iggers.

5. Absent from these tales is any mention of the influx of Old Believer refugees to the region after the schism of 1666–1667, although their influence would remain vivid in the collective memory of Orthodox leaders in Voronezh until the last days of tsarist rule.

6. "Reka Usman', proiskhozhdenie ee nazvaniia po narodnomu predaniiu," *Voronezhskii literaturnyi sbornik*, vyp. 1 (1861): 499–513. The beauty of this ill-fated Tatar princess allegedly attracted many interested suitors as she waited for true love. When the secret romance between the princess and a young man from a rival court was discovered, her father, outraged by his daughter's insubordination, killed her lover. The princess was so distraught that she drowned herself forthwith.

7. V. P. Zagorovskii, *Istoricheskaia toponimka Voronezhskogo kraia* (Voronezh: Izd-vo Voronezhskogo universiteta, 1973), 49–50, 104. On sixteenth-century Voronezh place names, see ibid., chap. 4. "Cherkassk" was a contemporary Muscovite appellation for Ukrainians.

8. Idem, "Istoriko-toponimicheskii slovar' Voronezhskogo kraia," in *Istoricheskaia toponomika*, s.v. "Kazatskoe" and "Korotoiak."

9. Documentary evidence confirms two visits by Peter the Great to Kon'-Kolodez', first in 1696 and again in 1709, but the naming legend was not recorded until 1890. Peter the Great was the subject of many popular legends that told of his helpful interaction with peasants. See Nicholas V. Riasanovsky, *The Image of Peter the Great in Russian History and Thought* (New York: Oxford University Press, 1985), 83–84.

10. Naum Akimovich Seniavin was indeed a vice admiral in Peter's navy, who owned land in the vicinity of Kon'-Kolodez'.

11. The origin legend of Kon'-Kolodez' can be found in Nik. Nikitin, "Selo Kon'-Kolodez'," *VEV*, no. 1, unof. pt. (1890): 23–33; ibid., no. 2, unof. pt. (1890): 64–75; ibid., no. 5, unof. pt. (1890): 207–213; and ibid., no. 8, unof. pt. (1890): 367–79.

12. According to an 1808 church inventory, the antimension of the wooden church contained the inscription: "Given in 1711 to the wooden Bo-goslovskaia Church of Kon'-Kolodez' Village." The inventory and antimension, however, had been lost at some point so that when a certain Nik. Nikitin recorded this legend in 1890, he relied on the testimony of the late priest of the village, Fr. Nikolai Adamov (d. 1881), who claimed to have seen the inventory before it disappeared. But even Fr. Adamov's diary had many pages missing. Nikitin was also convinced that the inscription was connected to the visit of Peter the Great to the wooden church because the Gospel's "printing, in 1711, corresponds exactly to the year . . . mentioned in the inscription on the antimension." See ibid., no. 1, unof. pt. (1890): 29. *PPBES* (St. Petersburg: Izd-vo P. P. Soikina, 1913), s.v. "antimins."

13. Neither the villagers of Kon'-Kolodez' nor Nikitin seems to have noticed that, according to the legend, Peter the Great "founded" a village that had already existed. By doing so, he established a direct relationship between empire and peasant society.

14. *PBE*, ed. A. P. Lopukhin (Petrograd [*sic*]: Prilozhenie k dukhovnomu zhurnalu, "Strannik," 1902), s.v. "Dimitrii Solunskii."

15. Putintsev, "Selo Dimitrievskoe," 462–65.

16. According to collective memory, Bol'shie Lipiagi (named after the Russian word for lime tree, *lipa*) was originally settled in the late–sixteenth century by Russian bandits seeking protection against Tatar raids.

17. N. I. Polikarpov, "Selo Bol'shie Lipiagi Valuiskogo uezda i nakhodiashcha-iasia v nem Nikolaevskaia tserkov', pervonachal'no postroennaia (1699) na pozhalovannym tsarem Petrom I sredstva v g. Valiuki. Istoriko-statisticheskii ocherk," *VEV*, no. 7, unof. pt (1899): 294–308; and *VEV*, no. 8, unof. pt. (1899): 336–56. This story was written down at the request of Archbishop Anastasii, who, during a visit to Bol'shie Lipiagi in 1897, was baffled by its ornate wooden architecture, which did not correspond to the surrounding village without a single street to organize its scattered houses.

18. According to local lore, these traders had earlier been known by the nicknames "promenivan'e," "menian'e," and "mena," each indicating movement.

19. Kutepov, "Sloboda Meniailova," *VGV*, no. 53, unof. pt. (1886): 3, and ibid., no. 54, unof. pt. (1886): 3. Another type of secular village origin legend referred to ordinary people of little historical significance beyond the local, or to features of the landscape. Some legends had nothing to do with mythic origins but were concerned instead with linguistic meanings of village names. See, for example, Polikarpov, "Bytovyia cherty," 2–3; N-ov, "Iz sela Ramen'ia Novokhoperskogo uezda," *VGV*, no. 72, unof. pt. (1867): 303; "Iz khutora Skrypnikova," *VGV*, no. 4, unof. pt. (1867): 13; and Timofei Barsukov, "Sloboda Lesnaia Ukolova," *VGV*, no. 25, unof. pt. (1865): 102–3. Other communities claimed not to have any origin legends, or at least they appeared to have faded from collective memory, although I am not entirely convinced that residents could not recall any legends. An element of "clamming up in front of strangers" was certainly at play. See Evgenii Markov, "Poezdka k kamniu Buily," *PKVG* (1894): 127–46; and idem, "Donskaia Beseda i sosedniia ei drevniia urochishcha Dona. (Putevye zametki)," *PKVG* (1896): 108–135.

20. By "patriotic" I mean the expression of local pride that acknowledged, explicitly or tacitly, the diversity of the Russian Empire.

21. R. Nozdrin, "Sloboda Alekseevka, Biriuchenskogo uezda. (Cherty iz istorii slobody i eia sovremennogo byta)," *PKVG,* part 3 (1905): 37–38. Only by an imperial decree of 1783 were Alekseevka peasants formally enserfed at the request of Empress Catherine.

22. Ibid., 41, 43, 45, 48.

23. Ibid., 39–40, 45.

24. Vera Shevzov, "Chapels and the Ecclesial World of Prerevolutionary Russian Peasants," *SR* 55, no. 3 (1996): 586.

25. Shevzov has noted that the popularity of these "promises" *(obety)* was on the rise after 1861 ("Popular Orthodoxy," 320–22). While this may have been so, memorials fulfilling these vows were common throughout rural Russia before 1861. In his description of sixteenth-century Spanish religion, William Christian described similar vows as "contracts with the divine" (*Local Religion,* 32).

26. Reverence for wondrous icons was not limited the Orthodox faithful. The national and local religious press regularly reported about Protestants, Catholics, and nonbelievers who were cured by wondrous icons.

27. The regulations on icons can be found in S. V. Kalashnikov, comp. *Alfavitnyi ukazatel' deistvuiushchikh i rukovodstvennykh kanonicheskikh postanovlenii, ukazov, opredelenii i rasporiazhenii Sviateishego Pravitel'stvuiushchego Sinoda (1721–1901 g. vkliuchitel'no) i grazhdanskikh zakonov, otnosiashchikhsia k dukhovnomu vedomstvu pravoslavnogo ispovedaniia.,* 3d ed. (St. Petersburg: Izd. knigoprodavtsa I. A. L. Tuzova, 1902), nos. 668–84, 690–94, 696–97. The official designation of icons as possessing special attributes was part of the broader censorship policy of the Holy Synod, but the regulation of sacred images also sought to prevent the distribution of non-Orthodox visual depictions created by Old Believers, sectarians, or those not properly trained. Newspaper accounts and unpublished records of the Holy Synod and Ministry of Internal Affairs suggest that these regulations were also inspired by fears about the implied subversion of peasants who attributed special sanctity to objects that were not officially registered.

28. Ordinary believers reacted to this directive with suspicion, just as they did to any form of government information gathering, because they feared that the ultimate purpose behind the list was to confiscate the icons. Consequently, only the most famous specially revered and wondrous icons, whose reputations could not be hidden, were reported to church officials. As Vera Shevzov has pointed out, these incomplete lists hinder interdiocesan comparisons of wondrous objects. See Shevzov, "Popular Orthodoxy," 416.

29. For examples of the certification process elsewhere in Russia, see ibid., chap. 4; and Minenko, *Kul'tura russkikh krest'ian,* 174–79. Icons that were not deemed to be wondrous were also returned to their home parishes, but now with the stigma of having been declared ordinary.

30. *Pravoslavnye Russkie obiteli,* 487. Shevzov calls these "epiphanic" icons and notes the belief that their appearance was divinely inspired and they thus possessed miraculous qualities. See Shevzov, "Miracle-Working Icons, Laity, and Authority in the Russian Orthodox Church, 1861–1917," *RR* 58, no. 1 (1999): 29.

31. RGIA, f. 796, op. 172, ed. khr. 1749, OSVE (1893).

32. A. G. Rashin, *Naselenie Rossii za 100 let (1811–1913): Statisticheskie ocherki* (Moscow: Gosudarstvennoe statisticheskoe izd-vo, 1956), 36–37, 208.

33. This decision was in keeping with the policy of Archbishop Anastasii and the diocesan administration to approve requests for special icon processions, blessings of the fields, and prayer services during the crop failure and cholera epidemic of 1891–1892. See RGIA, f. 796, op. 442, ed. khr. 1384, OSVE (1892).

34. Ibid., op. 172, ed. khr. 1749, OSVE (1893).

35. On the psychological process of identification, see Gellner, *Nations and Nationalism,* 7; and William Bloom, *Personal Identity, National Identity, and International Relations,* Cambridge Studies in International Relations, no. 9, ed. Stephen Smith (Cambridge: Cambridge University Press, 1990), 52.

36. Fr. M. Mar'evskii, "Chetvertyi krestnyi khod. (Iz Userda v gorod Biriuch s Tikhvinskoiu Ikonoiu Bozhiei Materi 30–go iiunia 1872 goda)," *VEV,* no. 20, unof. pt. (1872): 932–39.

37. "K stat'e: Chetvertyi krestnyi khod iz Userda v g. Biriuch 30 Iunia 1872 goda, s ikonoiu Tikhv. Bozhiei Materi," *VEV,* no. 15, unof. pt. (1873): 616–617.

38. This competitive element in the obtaining of religious objects and services has not been discussed in any study of Russian popular religion. As the district capital, Biriuch also had greater influence over diocesan authorities than the tiny, politically inconsequential Noven'kaia.

39. The Kozel'shchinskaia Mother of God icon was very old, but its miraculous powers only began in 1880 when the daughter of Count Kapnist of nearby Kozel'shchina village (Poltava province) was cured of a debilitating illness. See *PPBES,* s.v. "Kozel'shchinskaia ikona Bozhiei Materi"; and *PRO,* 500–501.

40. M. Pogrebnikov, "Vstrecha ikony," *VEV,* no. 22, unof. pt. (1895): 817–18.

41. One could add to the human attributes of this sacred image a reproductive interpretation since this icon could be considered an "offspring" of the original in Kursk.

42. General introductions to the literature on myth and history can be found in Michel de Certeau, *The Writing of History,* trans. Tom Conley (New York: Columbia University Press, 1988); Natalie Zemon Davis, *Fiction in the Archives: Pardon Tales and Their Tellers in Sixteenth-Century France* (Stanford, CA: Stanford University Press, 1987); Kirsten Hastrup, ed., *Other Histories* (London: Routledge, 1992); and Geoffrey Hosking and George Schöpflin, eds., *Myths and Nationhood* (London: Routledge, 1997).

4: Uncompromising over Parish Authority

1. The Russian words for "church," *khram* (house of worship, temple) and *sobor* (cathedral, assembly), allude to the unity and collectivity in belief and worship, which did not preclude disagreement among individual members about praxis. *Tserkov',* which also can refer to the church as a house of worship, more commonly implies the institutional organization of faith.

2. Although I found no evidence that peasants were aware of decrees on the parish, knowledge cannot be ruled out. The surviving sources in which peasants expressed their conceptions of the parish—mostly written complaints and counter-complaints to religious authorities—had no reason to refer to formal law. Juridically, the parish possessed neither the rights of ownership nor the prerogative of self-administration. Officially, the parish church was defined as a territorial unit comprising coreligionists and their respective property (churches, chapels, cemeteries, parsonages, schoolhouses), clerical personnel, and religious services. The parish possessed neither the rights of ownership nor independence in administrative matters. See *Otzyvy,* 1:135–36.

3. With the help of a local scribe, teacher, or parish elder, villagers expressed their needs and demands in formal requests *(pros'by),* complaints *(zhaloby),* and petitions *(proshcheniia)* addressed to diocesan and synodal authorities.

4. The dual image of the clergy was reflected in the honorary title peasants conferred on their priests, *batiushka,* literally, "little father." Depending on the context, *batiushka* could evoke a sense of endearment and intimacy usually reserved for family and friends, or it could refer to the social and patriarchal authority of the clergy over the laity.

5. The idea of separate religious and secular jurisdictions was borrowed from Byzantium by the Kievan princes. The history of clerical authority in the Orthodox Church is discussed in John Meyendorff, *Byzantine Theology: Historical Trends and Doctrinal Themes* (New York: Fordham University Press, 1979), 213–17. The development of church administration in Russia is discussed in Meyendorff, *Byzantium and the Rise of Russia: A Study of Byzantino-Russian Relations in the Fourteenth Century* (Crestwood, NY: St. Vladimir's Seminary Press, 1989), 11–17; A. V. Kartashev, *Ocherki po istorii Russkoi tserkvi* (Moscow: Terra, 1993), 1:157–81; and James Cracraft, *The Church Reform of Peter the Great* (London: Macmillan, 1971).

6. See Gregory L. Freeze, *The Parish Clergy in Nineteenth-Century Russia: Crisis, Reform, Counter-Reform* (Princeton: Princeton University Press, 1983), 11–50; Freeze, introduction to I. S. Belliustin, *Description of the Clergy in Rural Russia: The Memoir of a Nineteenth-Century Parish Priest,* translated and with an interpretive essay by Gregory L. Freeze (Ithaca, NY: Cornell University Press, 1985), 15–29; and I. K. Smolich, *Istoriia Russkoi tserkvi, 1700–1917,* vol. 8, pt. 1, *Istoriia Russkoi tserkvi* (Moscow: Izd-vo Spaso-Preobrazhenskogo Valaamskogo monastyria, 1997), 652–55.

7. Freeze, *Parish Clergy,* 53–54, 316; and Smolich, *Istoriia Russkoi tserkvi,* 654–55. To Freeze's and Smolich's lists of unordained clergy I have added elders, wardens, keepers of the keys, and bakers of the communion bread because these people were as important as readers and chanters to the performance of liturgy. In the following discussion I define "parish clergy" more restrictively to include only the religious personnel whose services were essential to the actual performance of rituals: all of the ordained clergy *and* psalmists. Peasants made the same distinctions.

8. An elder was a peasant selected by the parishioners for terms of three years, although, if well liked, he could serve successive terms until the end of his life. Peasants held parish elders to high standards and expected them to possess an exemplary moral character, leadership abilities, literacy skills, and economic know-how.

9. The parish council reform was introduced in 1864 (see Freeze, *Parish Clergy,* 52–101). A balanced and thorough overview of the village commune's multiple functions can be found in David Moon, *The Russian Peasantry: The World the Peasants Made* (London: Addison Wesley Longman, 1999), chap. 6. These goals were to be achieved through the formal institution of lay authority in parish functions. See Freeze, *Parish Clergy,* 252–59; Shevzov, "Popular Orthodoxy," 117–22; Glennys Young, "'Into Church Matters': Lay Identity, Rural Parish Life, and Popular Politics in Late Imperial and Early Soviet Russia, 1864–1928," *RH* 23, nos. 1–4 (1996): 368–69, 370–76; P. Nikol'skii, "K kharakteristike sovremennoi tserkovno-prikhodskoi zhizni," in *Interesy i nuzhdy eparkhial'noi zhizni* (Voronezh: Tip.-lit. V. I. Isaeva, 1902), 46; and RGIA, f. 796, op. 442, ed. khr. 1496, OSVE (1894), ll. 31, 34.

10. Peasants resisted the councils by flatly refusing to introduce them, but also in the way they talked about them, using words that implicitly referred to existing institutions—*obshchina* (commune), *prikhodskii/tserkovnyi sovet* (parish/church council), or *skhod* (assembly)—rather than by the official name, *propechitel'stvo.*

11. Brotherhoods, religious circles, and church societies combined religious self-education with social activism: they studied religio-moral texts and tended to

the needy in the community. Officially they existed at the behest of local bishops and civil authorities and were supervised by the parish clergy. See "Utverzhdennye opredeleniem Sviateishego Sinoda, ot 18–25 noiabria 1906 g. za no. 6590, pravila, opredeliaiushchiia otnosheniia tserkovnoi vlasti k obshchestvam i soiuzam, voznikaiushchim v nedrakh Pravoslavnoi tserkvi i vne eia i k obshchestvenno-politicheskoi i literaturnoi deiatel'nosti tserkovnykh dolzhnostnykh litsakh," *VEV,* no. 1, of. pt. (1907): 3–7; and Fr. Petr Feodorov, "O tserkovno-prikhodskoi obsh-chine," *VEV,* no. 1, unof. pt. (1909): 1–4. The few surviving minutes of parish meetings reveal that peasant communities assiduously managed their church affairs, allotted welfare to those in need, and organized an array of social and cultural activities for the village at large. For examples of the parish council as forum for action, see "Otchet tserkovno-prikhodskogo popechitel'stva Voronezhskoi Bogorodit-skoi 'Vzyskanie Pogibshikh', chto na Streletskom losku, tserkvi za 1885 g.," *VEV,* no. 4 of. pt. (1887): 143–51; "Otchet prikhodskogo Popechitel'stva pri Trekhsviatitel'skoi tserk. sela Rossoshei Nizhnedevitskogo uezda za 1894 goda," *VEV,* no. 18, unof. pt. (1895): 583–87; and "Otchet Krasnenskogo tserkovno-prikhodskogo Popechitel'stva za 1916 goda," *VEV,* no. 10, of. pt. (1917): 116–17.

12. Among the episcopate, the parish councils were widely declared a failure, although there were marked regional differences. One success story was the Vologda diocese, where 85 percent of parishes had an active council in 1914. See *VOOSS* (St. Petersburg: Sinodal'naia tip., 1914), supplement, 20, 114, 169; as well as Shevzov, "Popular Orthodoxy," 122.

13. Recent studies of peasant courts and conflict resolution have depicted the post-emancipation village as a cauldron of disputatious behavior. For examples, see Stephen P. Frank, "Popular Justice, Community and Culture among the Russian Peasantry, 1870–1900," *RR* 46, no. 3 (1987): 239–65; Cathy A. Frierson, "*Razdel:* The Peasant Family Divided," *RR* 46, no. 1 (1987): 35–51; and Gareth Popkins, "The Russian Peasant Volost' Court and Customary Law, 1861–1917," (Ph.D. diss., University of Oxford, 1995), chap. 3. This image of rural life as fractious contrasts with idealized notions of the harmonious and charitable peasant commune as epitomized in the practices of *krugovaia poruga* (collective responsibility), *pomochi* (communal work for the benefit of neighbors in grave hardship), and egalitarianism (land allotment and communal support that corresponded to a household's size and contribution to society). Like all other human communities, Russian peasant villages could be characterized as having alternating moments of harmony and discord. For recent examples of the harmonic interpretation, see M. M. Gromyko, "Obychai pomochei u Russkikh krest'ian v XIX v.," *SE,* no. 4 (1981): 21–38, and no. 5 (1981): 32–46; and Gromyko, *Mir Russkoi derevni,* esp. chap. 2.

14. James C. Scott has described this balancing act as a reciprocal exchange of duties and services between elites and subordinates that holds together systems of exploitation. See Scott, *Moral Economy,* 41–52, 161–82.

15. Sometimes the elder and the scribe were the same individual. Procedural blunders could be costly. Frequent errors included violation of accepted literary styles, use of ordinary paper rather than approved parchment, and failure to pay the stamp tax *(na neustanovlenoi gerbovoi bumage)* at the time of filing.

16. No general study of peasant petitions in the late imperial period has been made. An introduction to the problematics of peasant petitions can be found in a recent article by Andrew Verner, who argued that petitions both affirmed communal values and were a means of transforming the community. See his "Discursive Strate-

gies in the 1905 Revolution: Peasant Petitions from Vladimir Province," *RR* 54, no. 1 (1995): 65–90; Gregory L. Freeze, "A Case of Stunted Anticlericalism: Clergy and Society in Imperial Russia," *European Studies Review* 13, no. 2 (April 1983): 177–200; and Shevzov, "Popular Orthodoxy," 201–74. An overview of the tradition of petition writing can be found in Sheila Fitzpatrick, "Editor's Introduction: Petitions and Denunciations in Russian and Soviet History," *RH* 24, nos. 1–2 (1997), 1–9.

17. Belliustin's memoir was the first in-depth account of Russian church life at the grass-roots level. Its scandalous nature forced the author to seek a foreign publisher, although the book quickly became known in Russia. The hostile reaction to the memoir is described in Gregory L. Freeze's introduction to his translation of *Description of the Clergy in Rural Russia*, 30–48.

18. The Holy Synod introduced three major initiatives to reinvigorate *(ozhivl-lat')* parish life in the nineteenth century (1829, 1842, 1869). On these and other attempts at church reform, see Freeze, *Parish Clergy*, 66–86, 194–247, 298–326, 364–83; Freeze, "The Disintegration of Traditional Parish Communities: The Parish in Eighteenth-Century Russia," *Journal of Modern History* 48, no. 3 (July 1976): 32–50; and A. Papkov, *O blagoustroistve pravoslavnogo prikhoda. S prilozheniem proekta prikhodskogo ustava* (St. Petersburg: Sinodal'naia Tip., 1907).

19. Gregory Freeze has noted that opposition to consolidation and closure was widespread. See his *Parish Clergy*, 364–69.

20. I was able to locate petitions and complaints from more than three hundred cases involving Voronezh peasants between 1859 and 1917. These documents can be found in the archives of the Holy Synod in St. Petersburg (RGIA, ff. 796, 797, 799, 834), the Voronezh Diocesan Consistory (GAVO, f. 1-84), the Voronezh governor's office (GAVO, f. I-6), and the Voronezh Police Administration (GAVO, f. I-1). Because these represent only a portion of all complaints, the rest being lost or misfiled, it is impossible to ascertain how typical such cases were.

21. Because drunkenness was almost always linked to mistakes made while performing religious rites, the charge of "liturgical error" or "failure to perform religious services" became a kind of shorthand for "clergyman suffering from alcohol abuse."

22. RGIA, f. 796, op. 187, ed. khr. 6858.

23. Ibid., f. 797, op. 84, ed. khr. 187, 3 otd., 5 st., "Proshenie krest'ianina slob. Aleksandrovka, Borisovskoi volosti, Valuiskogo u. Theodora Koltunova."

24. All investigations of clergymen, ordained or not, included attestations of their current and previous behavior. Most of the time, clergymen were reported to have been on good or exceptionally good behavior just prior to the alleged offense. Materials for all of the cases I examined were filled with unanswered questions (why, for example, was there no police report if Savitskii had telephoned to complain about Koltunov's threatening behavior?), loose ends (what were the relations between Fr. Savitskii and Koltunov after the case had been decided?), and hearsay (whose version of the story should we believe, and why?).

25. Approximately 45 percent of the cases were solely about moral improprieties.

26. RGIA, f. 796, op. 182, ed. khr. 3906, "Po predstavlennoi . . . sv-ka Nikolaia Tairova."

27. Less than 5 percent of the cases I examined were about corruption.

28. Ibid., f. 797, op. 88, ed. khr. 256.

29. Parishioners, of course, could respond to abusive and offensive behavior in kind, but this was seldom before 1905, and it was not usually enough to prompt their clergyman to request a transfer. Only in the revolutionary years of 1905–1907

were parishioners able to force out or, after February 1917, remove unwanted clerics and replace them with their own candidates.

30. On the stereotypes of the clergy as holy or debauched, see Chris J. Chulos, "Peasant Perspectives of Clerical Debauchery in Post-Emancipation Russia," *Studia Slavica Finlandensia* 12 (1995): 33–53.

31. RGIA, f. 796, op. 182, ed. khr. 1629, "Po prosheniiu zhitelei s. Gorokhovki, Pavlovskogo uezda, Voronezhskoi eparkhii, ob osveshchenii novoi tserkvi v etom sele i o naznachenii po nei prichta." As with many of these cases, the final outcome is not known. For a discussion of the importance of church construction in post-emancipation communal identity, see Minenko, *Kul'tura russkikh krest'ian*, 150–68; and Shevzov, "Chapels and the Ecclesial World."

32. RGIA, f. 796, op. 139, ed. khr. 265, "Po pros'be doverennykh ot obshchestva sela Staroi Chigly krest'ian Semena Popova i Stepana Gnelushina o perenesenii sushchestvuiushchii v tom sele Kazanskoi tserkvi s zemlia pomeshchika Tulinova na drugoe im prinadlezhashchee, mesto." A conclusion was not included among the files.

33. No bishop could fairly claim ignorance of the miserable condition of dirt roads that plagued rural Russia, since annual visitations were always organized around the spring and autumn flooding seasons.

34. Despite the fact that petitioners and diocesan officials referred to Zaval'ska and Ostroukhova as separate villages, only the first appeared in the lists of population settlements. It is probable that both were parts of the larger, officially listed Zaval'ska, whose population is roughly the same as the other two combined.

35. Ibid., op. 182, ed. khr. 1430 (1901), "Po prosheniiu kr-n. derev'ni Zaval'skoi, Biriuchenskogo uezda, o razreshenii postroit' v etoi derene tserkov'."

36. The elaborate plans for parish reform after 1905 are the topic of chapter 7. The elective principle provided that the laity could select their own clergymen, subject to the approval of the diocesan bishop.

5: Saints, Pilgrimage, and Modern Russian Orthodox Identity

1. The theme of unity has been repeated throughout the centuries by the leading Orthodox thinkers. In the fourth century, Gregory of Nyssa explained the Eucharist (in Orthodox theology, the body and blood of Christ) as an act of spiritual unity through which God "disseminates Himself in every believer . . . blending Himself with the bodies of believers" (quoted in Meyendorff, *Byzantine Theology*, 201). The fourteenth-century Greek theologian Nicholas Cabasilas explained that "the Church is represented in the holy mysteries . . . no mere sharing of a name, or analogy by resemblance, but an identity of actuality." See Nicholas Cabasilas, *A Commentary on the Divine Liturgy*, trans. J. M. Hussey and P. A. McNulty, with an introduction by R. M. French (Crestwood, NY: St. Vladimir's Seminary Press, 1977), 91. Extending the metaphor of unity to include tradition, the twentieth-century Russian Orthodox theologian Sergius Bulgakov argued that "Orthodox unity . . . is realized in the world . . . by unity of faith, and, growing out of this, unity of life and of tradition, hence also the apostolic succession of the hierarchy." See Sergius Bulgakov, *The Orthodox Church*, translation revised by Lydia Kesich, with a foreword by Thomas Hopko (Crestwood, NY: St. Vladimir's Seminary Press, 1988), 90.

2. The process of identification during religious travel (regardless of the distance covered) is what Victor and Edith Turner have described as *communitas,* when the pilgrim "becomes increasingly capable of entering in imagination and with sympathy into the culturally defined experiences of the founder and of those persons depicted as standing in some close relationship to him" (saints, princes, and warriors). Victor Turner and Edith Turner, *Image and Pilgrimage in Christian Culture: Anthropological Perspectives* (Oxford: Basil Blackwell, 1978), 10–11. Victor Turner's model is more complex than presented here. The model can be found in his *Dramas, Fields, and Metaphors: Symbolic Action in Human Society,* Symbol, Myth, and Ritual Series, ed. Victor Turner (Ithaca, NY: Cornell University Press, 1974), 201–7. Turner's *communitas* has been criticized as simplistically harmonious and overly idealistic. See John Eade and Michael J. Snallow, "Introduction," in *Contesting the Sacred: The Anthropology of Christian Pilgrimage,* ed. John Eade and Michael J. Snallow (London and New York: Routledge, 1991). For a concise introduction to the history of pilgrimages, see Simon Coleman and John Elsner, *Pilgrimage Past and Present: Sacred Travel and Sacred Space in the World Religions* (London: British Museum Press, 1995).

3. A. Preobrazhenskii, *Etimologicheskii slovar' russkogo iazyka* (Moscow, 1910–1918), s.v. *"piligrim";* Maks Fasmer, *Etimologicheskii slovar' russkogo iazyka,* transl. O. N. Trubachev (Moscow: Progress, 1971), s.v. *"piligrim";* and H. Tegopoulos, *Elleniko lexiko: Orthografiko, ermeneutiko, etimologiko, sinonimon, antitheton, kirion onomaton,* 5th ed. (Athens: Armonia, 1992), s.v. *"proskinitis," "proskinima."* The distinction between Catholic and Orthodox pilgrimage has been discussed in Hannu Kilpeläinen, "Pilgrimage in Karelia: The Case of Valamo in the 1930s," *Byzantium and the North/Acta Byzantina Fennica* 7 (1995): 102–3; and René Gothóni, "Pilgrimage to Mount Athos as the Habit of the Laity," *Byzantium and the North/Acta Byzantina Fennica* 7 (1995): 48–53.

4. Although primarily occupied by mundane tasks related to buying and selling, ordinary Russians attending fairs and markets were also reminded of more sublime realities every time they glanced at a nearby church or monastery, overheard hymns sung during religious services, lit church candles, or offered prayers to special icons. The most famous of the fairs was in Nizhnii Novgorod and was popularly known as the "Makar'ev Fair" because of its association with the local Makar'ev Monastery and the feast of St. Makarius (25 July). For a description, see Anne Lincoln Fitzpatrick, *The Great Russian Fair: Nizhnii Novgorod, 1840–1890* (London: Macmillan, in association with St. Antony's College, Oxford, 1990).

5. Robert J. Kaiser, *The Geography of Nationalism in Russia and the USSR* (Princeton: Princeton University Press, 1994), 7.

6. Gregory L. Freeze has described the convergence of old and new cultural systems in terms of the deepening crisis in the relationship between church and state in the late-imperial period. See his "Tserkov', religiia i politicheskaia kul'tura na zakate staroi Rossii," *Istoriia SSSR,* no. 2 (March-April, 1991): 107–19. The creation of the image of a modern secular Russia in popular literature has been vividly depicted in Brooks, *When Russia Learned to Read,* chap. 6. On stunted (equivocal) nationhood, see Geoffrey Hosking, *Russia, People and Empire, 1552–1917* (London: HarperCollins, 1997).

7. A similar growth in pilgrimage to Mecca occurred among Muslims in the empire after Catherine II granted them religious freedom in 1773. See Daniel Brower, "Russian Roads to Mecca: Religious Tolerance and Muslim Pilgrimage in the Russian Empire," *SR* 55, no. 3 (1996): 566–84.

8. Similar stories appeared in the diocesan and secular provincial papers, attesting to the widespread interest in holy people.

9. "Andrei, iurodstvovavshii v gorode Meshchovske," *TL,* no. 203 (1905).

10. Brenda Meehan-Waters, "The Authority of Holiness: Women Ascetics and Spiritual Elders in Nineteenth-Century Russia," in *Church, Nation and State in Russia and Ukraine,* ed. Geoffrey A. Hosking (London: Macmillan, in association with the School of Slavonic and East European Studies, University of London, 1991), 39–43.

11. Beyond *Troitskie listki,* religious publications for more educated audiences were filled with stories of local holy people and wonderworking objects. The story of the shrine of Anna of Kashin in Tver province, which appeared in the national newspaper *Russkii palomnik* (Russian pilgrim), evoked traditionalism, as well as national symbolism. E. Poselianin, "Kashinskie torzhestva," *Russki palomnick,* no. 25 (1909): 391–402

12. The basic story of Mitrofan's canonization can be found in RGIA, f. 797, op. 87, ed. khr. 111 (1832 g); E. Golubinskii, *Istoriia kanonizatsii sviatykh v Russkoi tserkvi,* 2d ed., revised and supplemented (Moscow: Universitetskaia tipografiia, 1903), 177–78; and V. V. Litvinov, "Voronezhskii gubernator D. N. Begichev i ego rasporiazheniia pri otkrytii moshchei Sviatitelia Mitrofana i perenesenii ikh iz Arkhangel'skogo sobora Blagoveshchenskii," *VS,* no. 13 (1914): 109–21.

13. Another reason for the sudden rise in Mitrofan's popularity in 1830 was the cholera epidemic, during which the monastery compound swelled with believers seeking miraculous protection. The possible influence of the epidemic on Mitrofan's subsequent canonization is mentioned in only one obscure source: E. Sokovina, "Vospominaniia o D. N. Begicheve," *Istoricheskii vestnik,* no. 3 (March 1889): 668.

14. Litvinov, "Voronezhskii gubernator D. N. Begichev," 115–21. Although Begichev estimated attendance at sixty thousand, the number was probably higher since he counted only commoners.

15. Two early versions of the life of St. Mitrofan are *Istoricheskie svedeniia o zhizni Mitrofana, pervogo episkopa Voronezhskogo,* 2d ed. (St. Petersburg, n.p., 1832); and *Zhitie vo sviatykh ottsa nashego Mitrofana, v skhimonasekh Makariia, pervogo episkopa Voronezhskogo i novoiavlennogo chudotvortsa i skazanie o obretenii i otkrytii chestnykh ego moshchei i o blagodatnykh pri tom znameniiakh i chudesnykh istseleniiakh (izvlecheno iz aktov i donosenii imeiushchiikhsia v Sviateishem Sinode)* (Moscow: Sinodal'naia tip., 1838). Later popular versions included glorified illustrations of Mitrofan giving advice to Peter the Great. See *Sviatitel' i chudotvorets Mitrofan.*

16. Tikhon was alone and enjoying the picturesque view from the monastery's bell tower when the accident happened. At the moment that the railing gave out, Tikhon was thrust backward by a mysterious force.

17. A brief account of Tikhon's life can be found in Filaret (Gumilevskii), comp., *Zhitiia sviatykh, chtimykh pravoslavnoiu tserkoviu, so svedeniami o prazdnikakh gospodskikh i bogorodichnykh, i o iavlennykh chudotvornykh ikonakh,* 2d rev. ed. (St. Petersburg: Izd. I. L. Tuzova, 1892), 5:85–107.

18. *Proslavlenie sviatitelia Tikhona,* 2:4–5.

19. Evgenii Bolkhovitinov, *Polnoe opisanie zhizni Preosviashchennogo Tikhona, byvshago prezhde Episkopa Keksgol'mskogo i Ladozhskogo, i Vikariia Novogorodskogo, a potom Episkopa Voronezhskogo i Eletskogo, sobrannoe iz ustnykh predanii, i zapisok ochevidnykh svidetelei, s nekotorymi istoricheskimi svedeniiami, kasaiushchimisia do Novogorodskoi i Voronezhskoi Ierarkhii* (St. Petersburg: Tip. Chuzhestrannykh edinovertsov, 1796).

20. V. Litvinov, "Bibliograficheskii ukazatel' literatury o Sviatitele Tikhone Zadonskom i obzor izdanii ego tvorenii," *VS*, no. 10 (1910): 221–73. The popularity of St. Tikhon is attested by the publication numbers: By 1911, more than 400,000 copies of the life in more than four hundred editions were in circulation, making the Zadonsk holy man one of the best known saints in modern Russia.

21. Archbishop Antonii's motivations in having a second Voronezh holy man canonized raised suspicions among church elites, who tabled the matter for another fifteen years. See P. Nikol'skii, "Antonii II, Arkhiepiskop Voronezhskii (1826–1846) i obretenie moshchei Sviatitelia Tikhona," *VS*, no. 10 (1911): 19–54; E. Poselanin, "Antonii, arkhiepiskop Voronezhskii i Zadonskii," *Russkie podvizhniki. Istoriko-biograficheskie ocherki*, pt. 1 (St. Petersburg: Izd. P. P. Soikina, 1900), 46–68.

22. *Proslavlenie sviatitelia Tikhona*, 2:68–75.

23. "Ukaz Ego Imp. Velich., iz Sviat. Pravit. Sin. (ob otkrytii v g. Zadonske moshchei Sv. Tikhona, episkopa Voron.)," *VGV*, no. 29, unof. pt. (1861): 391. According to procedure, reports of uncorrupted remains and miracles attributed to them were investigated by the Holy Synod to prevent fraud and to control undesirable spontaneous religious sentiment. The Holy Synod was skeptical about such reports and hesitant about appeals for canonization. From the time of Peter the Great until the February Revolution, only ten individual national saints were canonized, compared with 146 in the Muscovite period (1549–1721). See Golubinskii, *Istoriia kanonizatsii*, 109–169, 169–223; and N. S. Torienko, *Novye pravoslavnye sviatye* (Kiev: Izd-vo Ukraina, 1991), 27–32. The particulars of the investigation of Tikhon's remains were reported in the national religious press. See "Ukaz Sviateishego Sinoda, ob otkrytii moshchei sviatitelia Tikhona, ep. Voronezhskogo," *Strannik*, 3, otd. IV (July 1861): 1–4.

24. T. Oleinikov, "Opredelenie Sv. Sinoda ob otkrytii moshchei Sv. Tikhona," *VS*, no. 10 (1911): 96–98.

25. *Proslavlenie sviatitelia Tikhona*, 2:4, 2:8–57.

26. Claims that saints demonstrated divine favor have a long history in Russia. For a recent study of a medieval saint who supported the Muscovite princes in their struggle to consolidate the scattered Russian lands, see David B. Miller, "The Cult of Saint Sergius of Radonezh and Its Political Uses," *SR* 52, no. 4 (1993): 680–99.

27. "Ukaz Ego Imp. Velich.," 389–91. The invitation to all Russians also seems to have been a subtle call to former serf owners to prepare themselves for the large number of requests they would receive from peasants wishing to attend the canonization events. According to the emancipation charter, for at least two years after freedom was declared, newly freed serfs were required to obtain permission from their former masters in order to travel away from their village.

28. Ibid., 391. An important vehicle for the dissemination of information about Tikhon was the evolving network of local and national newspapers that did not exist at the time of St. Mitrofan's canonization, six years before the Voronezh provincial gazette was established in 1838.

29. Vitalii Spasovskii, "Opisanie otkrytiia v g. Zadonske sv. Moshchei Sviatitelia i Chudotvortsa Tikhona, Episkopa Voronezhskogo," *VGV*, no. 35 (2 September 1861): 475–78; Aleksandr Kremenetskii, "Otkrytie Sviatykh moshchei Sviatitelia Tikhona, Zadonskogo Chudotvortsa, 13 avgusta 1861 g.," *VS*, no. 10 (1911): 100–101; and Oleinikov, "Opredelenie Sv. Sinoda," 98. The fact that Archbishop Iosif of Voronezh barely mentioned the events in his report for 1861 suggests that there may have been tension between members of the Synod and local religious authorities (RGIA, f. 796, op. 442, ed. khr. 46, OSVE, ll. 5 ob.–6).

30. *Proslavlenie sviatitelia Tikhona,* 2:84–85.

31. "Otkrytie sv. moshchei sviatitelia Tikhona, novoiavlennogo chudotvortsa, episkopa voronezhskogo i eletskogo (Soobshcheno P. I. Salomonom)," *Strannik,* 3, otd. 4 (September 1861): 122.

32. N. I. Polikarpov, "Proslavlenie Sviatitelia Tikona Zadonskogo i otkrytie ego sviatykh moshchei. K 50–letiiu sego sobytiia 13–go avgusta 1861–1911 gg.," *PKVG* (1911): 015–016.

33. "K 50–letiiu proslavleniia sviatitelia Tikhona Zadonskogo," *Tserkovnye vedomosti,* no. 33 (13 August 1911): 1411.

34. *Proslavlenie sviatitelia Tikhona,* 2:75.

35. More than four thousand carriages and twelve thousand wagons carried pilgrims to Zadonsk. Press coverage of the event can be found in "Opisanie torzhestva otkrytiia v Zadonske sv. moshchei sviatitelia i chudotvortsa Tikhona, episkopa Voronezhskogo," *Pravoslavnoe obozrenie,* no. 9 (September 1861): 130–35; and Salomon, "Otkrytie sv. moshchei sviatitelia Tikhona," 122–27. See also *Poezdka v Zadonsk vo vremia otkrytiia moshchei Episkopa Voronezhskogo i Eletskogo Tikhona 1–go* (Moscow: Universitetskaia tip., 1861); and *Rasskaz ochevidtsa ob otkrytii netlennykh moshchei Sviatitelia i chudotvortsa Tikhona, Episkopa Voronezhskogo 12 i 13 avgusta 1861 goda, v Zadonskom Bogoroditchnom monastyre* (St. Petersburg: Tip. Departamenta Udelov, 1861).

36. Oleinikov, "Opredelenie sv. Sinoda," 95.

37. "Slovo v den' otkrytiia sv. Moshchei sviatitelia i chudotvortsa Tikhona, skazannoe v Zadonskom monastyre sinodal'nym chlenom, Isidorom, Mitropolitom novgorodskim i s. peterburgskim," *Strannik,* 3, otd. 4 (September 1861): 131. Peter Brown has written about the unity of local and universal communities of believers around relics in early Christianity. See his *Cult of Saints: Its Rise and Function in Latin Christianity* (Chicago: University of Chicago Press, 1981), chap. 5.

38. Oleinikov, "Opredelenie sv. Sinoda," 95.

39. Salomon, "Otkrytie sv. moshchei sviatitelia Tikhona," 127.

40. William Bloom has described local identification with national imagery as critical to the process of personal and group identification that takes place as an empire or nation draws together diverse regions. See Bloom, *Personal Identity,* 55–73. See also Peter Brown's remarks on the importance of local officials in the creation and sustenance of a glorious empire in Byzantium, "A More Glorious House," *The New York Review of Books* (29 May 1997): 19–24. For a detailed description of the canonization ceremonies, see Chulos, "Religious and Secular," 35–38.

41. To accommodate the large numbers of pilgrims, a hostel, hospital, and pharmacy were built at the Zadonsk Monastery in 1863; the Mitrofanov Monastery constructed its own equivalents in 1868. See RGIA, f. 796, op. 442, ed. khr. 263, OSVE, ll. 9 ob.–10. On attendance, see ibid., ed. khr. 89, OSVE (1862), ll. 4 ob., 11; ibid., ed. khr. 1226, OSVE (1888), ll. 54 ob.–55; ibid., ed. khr. 1496, OSVE (1894), l. 8; "Mestnyi otdel'," *VGV,* no. 59, unof. pt. (1883): 6; "Mestnyi prazdnik," *VT,* no. 174 (10 August 1907): 2; "Gorodskaia zhizn'," *VT,* no. 176 (11 August 1915): 2; ibid., no. 174 (10 August 1916): 2; and A. N. Meerkova, *Otkhozhye promysly: Pereselencheskoe i bogomol'cheskoe dvizhenie v Voronezhskoi gubernii v 1911 godu* (Voronezh: Izd. Voronezhskogo gubernskogo zemstva, 1914), 57–65.

42. After 1862 miracles attributed to St. Tikhon were seldom reported in the national press. For national coverage, see "Chudesnye istseleniia, sovershivshiiasia pri otkrytii moshchei sviatitelia i chudotvortsa Tikhona, episkopa Voronezhskogo i Elet-

skogo," *Dukhovnaia beseda*, "Tserkovnaia letopis'," (25 November 1861): 717–28, reprinted in *Khristianskoe chtenie* (December 1861): 429–39; "Istseleniia, sovershivshiiasia v Zadonskom monastyre pri otkrytii moshchei sviatitelia Tikhona, Episkopa Voronezhskogo i Eletskogo," *Khristianskoe chtenie*, pt. 1 (1862): 87–95; Iosif, Arkhiepiskop Voronezhskii i Zadonskii, "Chudesnye istseleniia, sovershivshiiasia pri otkrytii moshchei sviatitelia i chudotvorsta Tikhona, Episkopa Voronezhskogo i Eletskogo," *Strannik*, supplement (May 1862): 1–35; numerous entries in *Dushepoleznoe chtenie* (October, November, December 1861, January 1862); and T. Popov, "Proslavlenie Sviatitelia Tikhona posle otkrytiia ego sviatykh moshchei," *VS*, no. 10 (1911): 126–34.

43. Spasovskii, "Opisanie otkrytiia," 45. The breakdown by social background and gender reflected the popularity of St. Tikhon among peasants (twenty-two) and women (twenty-seven, of whom sixteen were peasants). These figures were culled from the articles listed in note 48.

44. Iosif, "Chudesnye istseleniia," 721–22.

45. Iosif, "Chudesnye istseleniia," 17–20.

46. Ibid., 23–24.

47. Tat'iana Redkina, "Chesnoe istselenie," *VEV*, no. 4, unof. pt. (1868): 128–29.

48. See the episcopal reports for 1862, 1887, and 1894: RGIA, f. 796, op. 442, ed. khr. 89, OSVE, ll. 4 ob., 11; ibid., ed. khr. 1226, OSVE, ll. 54 ob.–55; and ibid., ed. khr. 1496, OSVE, l. 8. Examples from the local press can be found in: "Mestnyi otdel'," 6; "Mestnyi prazdnik," 2; and "Gorodskaia zhizn'," 2. The years 1905–1906 were exceptional for the low turnout of pilgrims, which local authorities attributed to widespread fear of public disorder wherever crowds gathered. See *VT*, no. 174 (9 August 1906): 1; and ibid., no. 174 (10 August 1907): 2. On the enduring popularity of Tikhon's shrine after 1907, see Meerkova, *Otkhozhie promysly*, 57–65.

49. G. Kaz'min, "Iz g. Zadonska," *VEV*, no. 21, unof. pt. (1897): 621–22.

50. "Mestnyi otdel," 6–7.

51. The program for the jubilee was published in *VS*, no. 9 (1909). Additional information about Zadonsk city officials' preparations can be found under the rubric "K Zadonskim torzhestvam," *VT*, nos. 173, 175, 180 (1911). The committee published a commemorative issue of its journal, *Voronezhskaia starina*, for better-educated readers, and nineteen popular leaflets *(listki)*, many of them illustrated and distributed free of charge, for the literate lower classes. Some of these leaflets were published in the commemorative issue of *Voronezhskaia starina*. See *VS*, no. 10 (1911).

52. The organizing committee did not invite members of the Holy Synod or national civil authorities, although it received official permission from the Synod for the event. See "K 50–letiiu so dnia otkrytiia moshchei Sv. Tikhona Zadonskogo," *VT*, no. 170 (1911): 2. The decision to bypass the Synod was a consequence of growing alienation between central church authorities and the parish clergy, who was becoming more vocal in its demands for a devolution of church power to the dioceses. See Chris J. Chulos, "Revolution and Grass-Roots Re-evaluations of Russian Orthodoxy, 1905–1907," in *Transforming Peasants: Society, State and Peasants, 1861–1931*, ed. Judith Pallot, Selected Proceedings of the V ICCEES Conferences, Warsaw, 1995 (London: Macmillan, 1998), 90–112. Although one senator was present, it appears that his visit was of a personal nature since he did not play any role in the ceremonies and was mentioned only incidentally. RGIA, f. 796, op. 442, ed. khr. 2445, OSVE (1911), l. 30. A list of the special guests can be found in "Programma prazdnovaniia ispolniaiushchegosia 13 avgusta sego 1911 goda piatidesiatiletiia so dnia otkrytiia netlennykh moshchei Sviatitelia Tikhona Zadonskogo," *VEV*, no. 25, of. pt. (1911): 314–15.

53. "Piatidesiatiletie otkrytiia sviatitelia Tikhona Zadonskogo (13 avgusta 1861–13 avg. 1911 g.)," *Dushepoleznoe chtenie* (July-August 1911): 433; *VOOSS* (1911–1912), 22; "V Peterburge," *VT,* no. 182 (1911): 3; and G. Th., "Iubileinyi akt. (Ot nashego spetsial'nogo korrespondenta)," *VT,* no. 185 (1911): 2. In a published list of 118 newspaper and journal articles about the event, only a handful appeard in national publications.

54. P. N., "Piatidesiatiletnii iubilei so dnia otkrytiia moshchei Sv. Tikhona Zadonskogo (13 avgusta 1911 goda)," *VS,* no. 11 (1912): 190. Press reports of the celebration appeared in *Voronezhskie eparkhial'nye vedomosti* and *Voronezhskii telegraf.*

55. See "Nuzhdy vremeni. Chem sleduet oznamenovat' 50–letnii iubilei so dnia proslavleniia Sv. Tikhona," *VEV,* no. 5, unof. pt. (1911): 123–29; "Sviatitel' Tikhon Zadonskii," *VEV,* no. 43, unof. pt. (1911): 1087–1104; and Dm. Belozerov, "Obshchestvennyi prazdnik," *VT,* no. 181 (13 August 1911): 2.

56. P. N., "Piatidesiatiletnii iubilei," 188. Although few eyewitness accounts of the jubilee noted the diversity of the crowds they encountered, participants represented a cross section of society. Archbishop Arsenii attended as a representative of St. Tikhon's native province, Novgorod.

57. Ibid., 191–204.

58. "Nakanune iubileia. (Ot nashego spetsial'nogo korrespondenta)," *VT,* no. 182 (1911): 3.

59. G. Th., "Krestnyi khod iz Voronezha v Zadonske," *VT,* no. 178 (1911): 2.

60. Ierodiakon Kornili, "K 50–letiiu proslavleniia sv. moshchei Sviatitelia Tikhona, Zadonskogo Chudotvortsa," *VEV,* no. 11, unof. pt. (1911): 354; G. Th., "Den' torzhestva," 2; RGIA, f. 796, op. 442, ed. khr. 2445, OSVE (1911), ll. 26–33; and Nikolai Okolovich, "Prazdnovanie 50–letiia so vremeni proslavleniia Sviatitelia Tikhona Zadonskogo," *VEV,* no. 35, unof. pt. (1911): 858.

61. G. Th., "Den' torzhestva," 2.

62. Robert Kaiser terms this identification "an extended family" (*Geography of Nationalism,* 12–13).

63. Viacheslav Gavrilov, "Prazdnovanie 50–letiia otkrytiia moshchei Sviatitelia Tikhona Zadonskogo v s. Iasenovke, Bogucharskogo uezda," *VEV,* no. 34 (1911): 827–28.

64. Anderson, *Imagined Communities,* 54–55.

6: The Modernizing Village

1. The secularization process is influenced by the social and cultural systems of individual countries. In Catholic and Protestant Europe and, more recently, in post-Soviet Russia, former state churches resemble private-sector charity organizations. In Scandinavia, the Lutheran Church (and in Finland, the Orthodox Church as well), like the state, has its own rights of taxation and civil-service career schemes. The effects of secularization theories on the study of peasant religion in Russia are discussed in Chulos, "Cultural Survivals," 195–96.

2. Conversions to other faiths were very low, except in regions in Russia where non-Orthodox populations had been forced to accept Orthodoxy, for example, in Karelia. See Marina Vituhnovskaja, "Cultural and Political Reaction in Russian Karelia in 1906–1907: State Power, the Orthodox Church, and the 'Black Hundreds' against Karelian Nationalism," *Jahrbücher für Geschichte Osteuropas,* 49, no. 1 (2001):

24–44. More than 99 percent of Voronezh residents were Orthodox until the last tallies were made in 1916. Among Old Believers and sectarians, a gradual shift occurred between 1870 and 1913, when the number of Old Believers closest to the Orthodox (those accepting the clergy and church rites) declined by nearly 20 percent. See statistical tables in *PKVG*, otd. II (1907): 79; ibid., otd. II (1916): xlii. The influence of Old Believers and sectarians on their surrounding communities is extremely difficult to assess and may have been disproportionate to actual numbers, which troubled clergymen throughout the Russian Empire and was the subject of many clerical reports, articles, and sermons. Between 1904 and 1913 the number of Milk Drinkers, Shtundists, Self-Castrators, and Flagellants in Voronezh Province increased by nearly 10 percent. See *VOOSS* (1905–1907): 70, 72; and ibid. (1914): 34–35, 38–39.

Because of the Orthodox Church's official status and the social pressures it was able to command, it is impossible to distinguish between required and willing participation in the ritual life of the faith, but I have found no evidence of persecution or prosecution for refusal to participate in Orthodox rituals in Voronezh province. Between 1860 and 1914 the rates of annual confession and communion among the Orthodox in Voronezh were between 75 and 78 percent, the remaining members of the faith being too young to participate, absent, or forbidden to partake in the rites due to various infractions (less than 0.5 percent of all Orthodox). For these statistics, see RGIA, f. 796, op. 142, d. 2372, (1860), l. 126; ibid., op. 151, d. 285a (1870), ll. 43–44; ibid., op. 162, ed. khr. 2327 (1880), ll. 29 ob.–30; ibid., op. 440, ed. khr. 55 (1892), ll. 83–84, 109–119; ibid., op. 182, ed. khr. 4604, ll. 109–111; and ibid., f. 797, op. 72, ed. khr. 404, 2 otd., 3 st. (1904–1913), ll. 24a-g, 36 ob.–38, 40 ob.–42, 46–47 ob., 50–50 ob., 52–52 ob., 54 ob., 56–56 ob., 58–58 ob. In terms of financial support, which could also indicate change in religious practice, tray collections, candle sales, and other donations outpaced inflation, suggesting that at least to those who participated in church services the local church continued to be relevant. See Chris J. Chulos, "Peasant Religion in Post-Emancipation Russia: Voronezh Province, 1880–1917" (Ph.D. diss., University of Chicago, 1994), 399–403.

3. This paragraph is based on Jeffrey Brooks, "The Zemstvo and the Education of the People," in *The Zemstvo in Russia: An Experiment in Local Self-Government*, ed. Terence Emmons and Wayne S. Vucinich (Cambridge: Cambridge University Press, 1982), 243–78; and Ben Eklof, *Russian Peasant Schools: Officialdom, Village Culture, and Popular Pedagogy, 1861–1914* (Berkeley: University of California Press, 1986), chap. 6. The Education Statutes of 1864 and 1866 stipulated that literacy was to be a practical means of imparting "religious and moral notions among the population and to spread useful, basic knowledge" (ibid., 53, 64).

4. *PKVG* (1905): 100–101; ibid., otd. III (1906), 58; ibid., otd. II (1915), 55; ibid., otd. III (1915): xxxviii–xxxix; *VOOSS* (1894), pril. 92; *Istoricheskii ocherk razvitiia tserkovnykh shkol za istekshee dvadtsatipiatiletie (1884–1909)* (St. Petersburg, 1909), pril. 38–39, 42–43, 46–47; *Odnodnevnaia perepis' nachal'nykh shkol v imperii proizvedennaia 18 ianvaria 1911 goda*, vyp. 13, *Khar'kovskii uchebnyi okrug, Ministerstvo narodnogo prosveshcheniia* (Petrograd: Tip. tov. "Ekateringofskoe pechatnoe delo," 1914), part 1, pp. 1, 5, 21; *Nachal'nye uchilishcha vedomstva narodnogo prosveshcheniia v 1914 godu, Departament Narodnogo Prosveshcheniia* (Petrograd: Tipo-lit. M. P. Frolovoi, 1916), 16–17, pril. II.; G. Fal'bork and V. Charnoluskii, eds., *Nachal'noe narodnoe obrazovanie v Rossii* (St. Petersburg: Tip. Narodnaia Pol'za, 1900), 2:25, 28, 34, 61, 152; S. I. Strannik, "Okhrana veroucheniia," *VEV*, no. 9, unof. pt. (1915): 227–31; and Eklof, *Peasant Schools*, 53, 483–87. In 1914 peasant literacy rates in Voronezh

reached 16 percent, well below the national average of 25 percent, which was much lower than in central, northern, and western Europe.

5. Shcherbina, "Narodnoe obrazovanie," 72–73. Another teacher added that peasants who had attended primary school looked to books as an "authority of their own."

6. Nearly 55 percent of students who had finished primary schooling between 1876 and 1893 were tested, 73 percent having finished between 1885 and 1893. See *Dolgo-li pomniat gramotu krest'iane, proshedshie nachal'nuiu narodnuiu shkolu, chitaiut li oni po vykhode iz shkoly, i chto po preimushchestvu, gde berut knigi?* (Voronezh: Tovarishchestvo Pechatnaia S. P. Iakovleva, 1894), 7–9. High retention levels (3.6 on a five-point scale) were recorded for reading and arithmetic and even some improvement was noted, whereas writing skills declined considerably. The religion test included knowledge of prayers, religious history, events from the Old and New Testaments, and the creed. High levels of literacy retention, especially of religious topics, were common throughout Russia. Testing was conducted only on students who had completed four years of primary schooling and thus reveals nothing about retention levels or reading tastes of those who did not finish the basic course of study. See Eklof, *Peasants Schools*, 394–402.

7. Despite the image of lower religiosity of men compared to women that continues to prevail in popular and scholarly literature, this study suggests that religious literature retained a powerful hold over educated peasant men. Sixty-three of the sixty-four men singled out for detailed study revealed that they read religious and moral literature. For a standard expression of the belief that literacy was the cause of men's lower church attendance, see "Letopis' Nizhned. uezda sela Rossoshei," 18.

8. Konstantin Popov, "Samoe vazhnoe delo eparkhii." *VEV*, no. 8, unof. pt. (1908): 488; RGIA, f. 796, op. 442, ed. khr. 1176, OSVE (1887), l. 37–37 ob.; ibid., ed. khr. 1226, OSVE (1888), l. 55 ob.; "Vnebogosluzhebnye sobesedovaniia i chteniia," *VEV*, no. 7, unof. pt. (1890): 313–23; and *Zhurnaly Pavlovskogo uezdnogo zemskogo sobraniia ocherednoi sessii 1902 g.* (Pavlovsk: Tip. I. P. Ivanova, 1903), 153.

9. *VOOSS* (1879–1880), 112; ibid., (1890–1891): 36; ibid., (1905–1907): 74; ibid., (1914): 14.

10. For example, the Mitrofanov Church in Karaiashnik village had a library with 674 titles, the Church of the Transfiguration in Buturlinovka had 412 publications, the Church of the Ascension in Tereshkova had 360, the Church of the Presentation in Vorontsovka had 278, and St. Nicholas Church in Turovo had 263. RGIA, f. 796, op. 442, ed. khr., OSVE (1868), ll. 20–22. Roughly 45 percent of all titles were religious periodicals.

11. Archbishop Anastasii held up as an example the diocesan brotherhood of the Ascension Mitrofanov Monastery, whose library boasted 44 out of 249 subscribers from the peasant estate. Half of the peasants with library privileges ordered books to the reading room. Ibid., ed. khr. 1328, OSVE (1890), ll. 91 ob.–95.

12. To the bewilderment of Russian elites, the relationship between the producers of literature (writers) and its consumers (readers) contradicted the more pedantic cultural ethos on which primary education rested. See Brooks, "The Educated Response: Literature for the People," in *When Russia Learned to Read*, 295–352; McReynolds, *The News*, esp. chaps. 3 and 5; and Beth Holmgren, "Gendering the Icon: Marketing Women Writers in Fin-de-Siècle Russia," in *Russia—Women—Culture*, eds. Helena Goscilo and Beth Holmgren (Bloomington: Indiana University Press, 1996), 321–46.

13. To this end, church leaders exhorted believers to shun those people who "willingly embrace . . . progressive newspapers, pamphlets, brochures, and all types of proclamations, sent and distributed for free in hundreds or thousands of copies by 'sham' benefactors of mankind." RGIA, f. 796, op. 442, ed. khr. 2139, OSVE (1906), l. 10. See also RGIA, f. 797, op. 75, ed. khr. 18b, III otd., 5. st., "O prosshestviiakh v tserkvakh i voobshche po dukhovenstvu vedomstvu (1905)," l. 34–34 ob.; GAVO, f. 1-6, op. 1, ed. khr. 1233, "Mat. ob areste kr-na derevni Zamiatinoi zadonskogo uezda Ivana Matveevicha Karlov k pogromu sostoiatel'nykh krest'ian i sviashchennikov (1907)"; and ibid., ed. khr. 1077, "Raporty gubernatory Biriuchenskogo uezdnogo ispravnika o napadenii v noch' na 24 iiunia 1907 goda na dom sviashchennika sela Piatnitskogo Nikolaia Efremova."

14. The bishops' aversion to popularizing the Scriptures was not new. Previous attempts to disseminate the Bible had been spearheaded by foreign missionaries of the Russian Bible Society, but Tsar Nicholas I deemed their activities to be treacherous enough to have them banned in 1826. Exactly fifty years later, in 1876, the Holy Synod itself issued a translated version over which it maintained exclusive publication rights, and the council of bishops grudgingly allowed free distribution of the Bible. See Stephen K. Batalden, "Colportage and the Distribution of the Holy Scripture in Late Imperial Russia," in *Christianity and the Eastern Slavs*, vol. 2, *Russian Culture in Modern Times*, ed. Robert P. Hughes and Irina Paperno (Berkeley: University of California Press, 1994), 83–92; and Brooks, *When Russia Learned to Read*, 306–8.

15. Church authorities' linkage of literacy and apostasy was not unfounded; the main heretical groups used printed materials as a chief means of propagation. RGIA, f. 796, op. 176, ed. khr. 2139 (1895), l. 5; and A. Mikulin, "Nashi zadachi v XX veke," *VEV*, no, 14, unof. pt. (1901): 627.

16. Ronald Vroon, "The Old Belief and Sectarianism as Cultural Models in the Silver Age," in *Christianity and the Eastern Slavs*, ed. Hughes and Paperno, vol. 2, *Christianity and the Eastern Slavs*, 172–90.

17. From the 1870s until 1905, followers of Pashkovitism, Tolstoyanism, Baptism, and Shtundism were among the groups that secular and religious provincial leaders considered to be subversive, if not always revolutionary. Although these groups appealed mostly to the spiritually eccentric and well-educated Russians whose revolutionary political aspirations were seldom attractive to peasants, a small, but growing, cohort of educated peasants responded favorably to alternative religious and political ideas. Beginning in the 1880s, the Voronezh diocesan journal was filled with dozens of lengthy articles about the historical background and teaching of these groups, as well as bibliographies of their key publications. For example, see A. S-skii, "K voprosu ob uchenii shtundistov," *VEV*, no. 5, unof. pt. (1887): 181–95; P. Obolenskii, "Veroizpovedanie Russkikh sektantov-ratsionalistov (dukhobortsev, molokan i shtundistov)," part 4, "Shtundisty," *VEV*, no. 1, unof. pt. (1890): 1–20; ibid., no. 5, unof. pt. (1890), 195–207; ibid., no. 6, unof. pt. (1890): 256–69; ibid., no. 9, unof. pt. (1890): 403–413; ibid., no. 10, unof. pt. (1890): 442–54; ibid., no. 12, unof. pt. (1890): 529–43; "Perechen' broshiur s tendentsiami Paskhovskogo lzheucheniia," *VEV*, no. 5, unof. pt. (1895): 191–97; I. Filipp, "Nemetskaia shtunda i khristianstvo," *VEV*, no. 34, unof. pt. (1916): 887–91; "Otzyvy pochivshego sviatitelia zatvornika Theofana o grafe L've Tolstom," *VEV*, no. 21, unof. pt. (1895): 705–7; T. Rozhdestvenskii, "Otkrytoe pis'mo 6-oe. (O Tolstovstve)," *VEV*, no. 23, unof. pt. (1897): 699–711; I. Mikhail, "Znachenie obshchestvennogo bogosluzheniia po povodu otveta L. N. Tolstogo Sv. Sinodu," *VEV*, no. 17, unof. pt. (1901): 718–27; and ibid., no. 18, unof. pt. (1901): 753–66.

18. Despite his privileged background as a member of the aristocracy, Chertkov's involvement in the populist "Going to the People" aimed at elevating peasants' awareness of their oppression and offering ways to overcome it. In 1884, Chertkov established the "Posrednik" (Intermediary) publishing house, the primary vehicle of Tolstoy's followers, which produced inexpensive works for the people. Throughout the 1890s Archbishop Anastasii began to gather incriminating evidence against Chertkov and the peasants living on his estate, who "abuse the clergy, ridicule the sacraments, mock all holy things, repudiate the church and every type of authority." See RGIA, f. 796, op. 442, ed. khr. 155, OSVE (1895), l. 52–52 ob.

19. Religious deviance and secular disloyalty prompted the governor of Voronezh to join forces with Archbishop Anastasii, and, after a long drawn-out process, Chertkov was forced into exile. Between 1897 and 1905 he resided in England, where he redoubled his efforts on behalf of Tolstoy and, through his followers in Voronezh, continued to operate a distribution network that smuggled the writer's banned works to various parts of the empire. See GAVO, f. I-6, op. 1, ed. khr. 190 (1896), l. 13–14 ob. See also ibid., ed. khr. 142 (1894); RGIA, f. 796, op. 442, ed. khr., OSVE (1901), l. 21; GAVO, f. I-6, op. 1, ed. khr. 142 (1894); GAVO, f. I-1, op. 1, ed. khr. 410 (1901–1902); ibid., ed. khr. 350 (1902–1903); and RGIA, Chital'nyi zal, "Kollekstiia pechatnykh otchetov gubernatorov," no. 18 (1914): 10.

20. GAVO, f. 277, op. 1, ed. khr. 3, "Borisoglebskoe otdelenie Voronezhskogo zhandarmskogo politseiskogo upravleniia Zheleznykh dorog (1915 g.)," ll. 434–35; and Petr Sergeev, "Nemetsko-sektantskoe zasil'e," *VEV,* no. 1, unof. pt. (1917): 3–14; ibid., no. 2, unof. pt. (1917): 40–48.

21. According to the New Israelites, the city of Bobrov was their new Bethlehem. Among the many charges against this group made by the Holy Synod, the most dangerous was that it was an Antichrist sect that propagated revolution against the regime. See RGIA, f. 796, op. 442, ed. khr., OSVE (1910), ll. 21 ob.–22; and ibid., f. 1276, op. 17, ed. khr. 421, l. 8 ob. Reginald Zelnik has called the use of standard Orthodox imagery by rebels and revolutionaries "naive Orthodoxy," because the teachings of religion inspired them to act against the government. See Reginald E. Zelnik, "'To the Unaccustomed Eye': Religion and Irreligion in the Experience of St. Petersburg Workers in the 1870s," in *Christianity and the Eastern Slavs,* ed. Hughes and Paperno, vol. 2, *Russian Culture in Modern Times,* 50.

22. Although clerical and lay initiative was behind the introduction of this form of extraliturgical preaching in the late 1860s, peasants made it a success by attending in large numbers. A critical turning point came with the establishment of the SS. Mitrofan and Tikhon Brotherhood in 1885, which served as a model for similar societies around the diocese. The brotherhood complemented its religious discussions with a wide range of activities that promoted Orthodox literacy and included the establishment of libraries and bookshops, the distribution of popular religious literature, and missionary work against sectarians and Old Believers. The popularity of these discussions resembles that of other forms of entertainment that came to the village as peasants flocked to listen to an inspired speaker, to marvel at images projected onto the wall by "magic lanterns," and to listen to the melodious voices of choirs during intermissions. Listeners willingly paid for an entrance ticket, and in 1886 alone, the SS. Mitrofan and Tikhon Brotherhood sold 16,421 tickets at a price of 5 kopeks for general seating, and 10 kopeks for the front four rows (fifty free tickets were distributed for each program). RGIA,f. 796, op. 442., ed. khr., OSVE (1875), ll. 19 ob.–20; ibid., ed. khr., OSVE (1880), ll. 18–19 ob.; and ibid., ed. khr.

949, OSVE (1882), ll. 17–18 ob.; "Vnebogosluzhebnye sobesedovaniia i chteniia," 313–23; *Otchet Voronezhskogo Bratstva sviatitelei Mitrofana i Tikhona za 1887 god* (Voronezh: Tip. V. I. Isaeva, 1888), 3; V. Drozdov, "Prostoe slovo sel'skogo pastyria," *VEV,* no. 12, unof. pt. (1890): 550–51; G. Remorov, "O propovediakh i vnebogosluzhebnykh sobesedovaniiakh v prikhodakh zarazhennykh raskolom," *VEV,* no. 14, unof. pt. (1890): 621–24; and "Otradnyi primer," *VEV,* no. 8, unof. pt. (1901): 368–70. See RGIA, f. 796, op. 442, ed. khr. 1068, OSVE (1885), l. 27 ob.; "Otchet Voronezhskogo Bratstva Svv. Mitrofana i Tikhona za 1886 god," *VEV,* no. 1, of. pt. (1887): 7–48 (which includes the programs of all Voronezh diocese brotherhoods); and "Iz zhizni 'Bratsvta sv. Nikolaia' pri Valuiskom Uspenskom monastyre," *VEV,* no. 15, unof. pt. (1916): 386–87.

23. Church leaders were often pedantic in their obsession with controlling popular culture. For example, see Fr. Nikolai Nikonov's review of the "book for the people," *Happiness Cannot Be Found in Money* (Ne v den'gakh schast'e), published by the Society of the Committee for Popular Reading (Obshchestvo pri Kommissii narodnykh chtenii). Nikonov objected to the portrayal of a main character who died without requesting a priest, an act that he interprets as anti-Christian because it suggests that there is no life after death. See "Zametka pastyria," *VEV,* no. 18, unof. pt. (1887): 737–49.

24. As Stephen Frank has suggested in his recent investigation of crime in late-tsarist Russia, statistics contributed to widespread fears among educated Russians about most spheres of peasant life, but the numbers reveal little about the levels or causes of criminal activity because the collectors and users of this new information were imprecise about the base-line society and about true causalities. See Stephen P. Frank, *Crime, Cultural Conflict, and Justice in Rural Russia, 1856–1914,* Studies on the History of Society and Culture, no. 31 (Berkeley: University of California Press, 1999), 20.

25. Joan Neuberger, *Hooliganism: Crime, Culture, and Politics in St. Petersburg, 1900–1914* (Berkeley: University of California Press, 1993), 1–8.

26. In the last two decades, a vast body of literature has mapped specific economic, social, or cultural changes in the late-tsarist village. A comprehensive mosaic approach that integrates economic, social, and cultural life of the village, similar to what Catherine Evtuhov has done in her study of Russian religious philosophy, is long overdue. See her *Cross and the Sickle: Sergei Bulgakov and the Fate of Russian Religious Philosophy, 1890–1920* (Ithaca, NY: Cornell University Press, 1997), esp. p. 4; and Zelnik, "'To Unaccustomed Eyes,'" esp. p. 72.

27. On the representation of the returning migrant worker as the conveyor of moral corruption, see Burds, *Peasant Dreams,* 30–34.

28. Quoted in Patricia Herlihy, "Joy of the Rus': Rites and Rituals of Russian Drinking," *RR* 50, no. 2 (1991): 132.

29. Quoted in Nancy Mandelker Frieden, *Russian Physicians in an Era of Reform and Revolution, 1856–1905* (Princeton: Princeton University Press, 1981), 248. The special session also called for an end to coercive administrative treatment of alcoholics (ibid., 249).

30. The effects of rising peasant alcohol consumption in Voronezh province, beginning in the 1890s, gradually took their toll, and between 1908 and 1913 deaths caused by alcoholism rose 80 percent in rural areas, and an astonishing 127 percent among women. See the statistical tables in *PKVG* otd. II (1910): 120–21; and ibid., otd. II (1915), table xxxvi. But if medical professionals and social reformers provided few solutions to the steep rise in alcoholism, the state was on slippery moral grounds

with the introduction of its liquor monopoly in 1894, which contributed to the production of moonshine, a cheaper alternative. The prominence of women in moonshine production startled educated Russians, who construed femininity to be the sacred sphere of morality. See Frank, *Crime, Cultural Conflict, and Justice*, 122–24.

31. It is important to note that peasants did not dispute the beneficial effects of reduced consumption. Instead, they opposed total abstention on the grounds that it would have turned their holiday calendar into a succession of somber events. In their eyes, the descent into drunken revelry was their just reward for hard and monotonous labor in the fields and the many related hardships of rural life.

32. RGIA, f. 796, op. 442, ed. khr., OSVE (1883), l. 12 ob.; ibid., ed. khr. , OSVE (1901), l. 18; ibid., ed. khr. 2631, l. 14; RGIA, Chital'nyi zal, kollektsiia pechatnykh otchetov gubernatorov, no. 18 (1895), l. 5; and RGIA, f. 1284, op. 17, ed. khr. 421 (1916), ll. 159–160 ob.

33. "Voronezhskaia Dukhovnaia Konsistoriia slushali Ukaz Sviateishego Pravitel'stvuiushchago Sinoda, ot 9 Dekabria 1889 goda za no. 13, sleduiushchego soderzhaniia . . ." *VEV,* no. 3, of. pt. (1890): 41–43.

34. D. Sklobovskii, "K voprosu o narodnykh razvlecheniiakh," *VEV,* no. 22, unof. pt. (1901): 950–51.

35. Petr Sergeev, "Besedy pastyria s pasomymi," *VEV,* no. 48, unof. pt. (1913): 1289. By placing alcohol in the center of their struggle to extinguish village immorality, educated Russians were merely confirming that for most peasants religion had never been, nor perhaps would ever be, a dry matter. Sermons and lessons about the dangers of alcohol and advice on how to fight abuse regularly appeared in the diocesan clerical journal, along with exhortations to the parish clergy to set the example for their flocks by avoiding excessive drinking and by organizing temperance societies. RGIA, f. 796, op. 442, ed. khr. 1226, OSVE (1888), l. 58–58 ob.; "Chto mozhet byt' sdelano dukhovenstvom k iskoreneniiu p'ianstva v narode," *VEV,* no. 5, unof. pt. (1890): 219–20; Vasilii Andreevskii, "Neotlozhnaia zadacha pastyrei," *VEV,* unof. pt (1915): 674–77; and RGIA, Chital'nyi zal, kollektsiia pechatnykh otchetov gubernatorov, no. 18 (1914), ll. 7–7 ob. (emphasis in original). The temperance movement made few inroads in Voronezh and by 1913 only fifty societies existed diocesewide. RGIA, f. 796, op. 442, ed. khr. 2572, OSVE (1913), l. 10 ob.

36. Five conflicting interest groups emerged from the debate that ensued: synodal officials, who wished to preserve the sanctity of Sundays and major feast days of the faith; government and business enterprises, who demanded fewer days on which work was forbidden; local authorities, who strove to reduce the number of days given over to revelry; moralists engaged in a battle against peasant sloth and insobriety; and local believers, who defended their perceived "right" to designate certain days of the year as sacred or festive. Synodal, diocesan, and government officials distinguished between six categories of holidays: *prestol'nye prazdniki* honored the patron saint or event to which the altar was dedicated; *prikhodskie prazdniki* were feast days of saints or events sacred to the parish; *khramovye prazdniki* celebrated the saint or event to which the church was dedicated; *derevenskie prazdniki,* which were designated by individual villages rather than parishes; *neprisutstvennye,* nonreligious public holidays, which often coincided with feast days, when government offices were closed; and *vysokotorzhestvennye dni,* marking the birthday of the emperor and empress, the heir to the throne, their name days, and the anniversary of the coronation. Peasants added their own preferences to this list, thus making any calculation of the number of days off work dependent on who was counting and for what purposes.

37. Resistance came from the peasantry as well as the clergy, who depended on the gifts they received during holiday visitations for their livelihood. See RGIA, f. 796, op. 151, ed. khr. 72, 1 st. III otd. (1870–1871), ll. 1–2. RGIA, f. 797, op. 96, ed. khr. 230 (1909), "Doklad i opravki kommissii Gosudarstvennogo Soveta ob izmenenii zakonov o prazdnichnykh dniakh i zapiski otdel'nykh lits po etomu voprosu," l. 8 ob. Olga Crisp has calculated the working year in Russia in 1900 to be 264 days. In the United States in 1900 it was 283.3 days. See her "Labor and Industrialization in Russia," *The Cambridge Economic History of Europe*, vol. 7 (Cambridge: Cambridge University Press, 1978): 380–81.

38. "Obiazatel'nye postanovleniia, izdannye po g. Voronezhu i Voronezhskoi gubernii, s noiabria 1905 g. po noiabr 1906 g.," *PKVG*, otd. 1 (1907): 43–53.

39. Public prudishness about sex was challenged by the tawdry press that thrived at the end of the nineteenth and beginning of the twentieth centuries. An excellent introduction to sexuality during Russia's struggle to modernize, and the role of the family paradigm in the new power relations and personal identity, can be found in Laura Engelstein, *The Keys to Happiness: Sex and the Search for Modernity in Fin-de-Siècle Russia* (Ithaca, NY: Cornell University Press, 1992).

40. V. Naumov, "Sovety roditeliam o vospitanii detei. (Golos pastyria k pasomym)," *VEV*, no. 12, unof. pt. (1895): 416–20; ibid., no. 13, unof. pt. (1895): 447–51; and "Obuchenii krest'ianskikh devochek gramote (V Boze pochivshogo preosviashchennogo episkopa Theofana)," *VEV*, no. 13, unof. pt. (1895): 421–24. This was reprinted from *Tserkovno-prikhodskaia shkola* (January 1895).

41. The prominent zemstvo statistician and student of peasant life, Feodor Shcherbina, did not consider the demise of the patriarchal family to be the result of a shift in morals. Instead, he attributed the high rate of household division to the emancipation, whose freedom extended to the "slavery" of the family and created the conditions for "individual initiative, independent action, personal risk, awareness of moral responsibility," all things that led to the demise of the patriarchal family. See Shcherbina, "Semeinye razdely," 55–67. An overview of the effect of household divisions on the family can be found in Frierson, *"Razdel."*

42. While prohibitions against illegitimacy remained the norm among the peasantry, it may well be that its frequency reflected a fluidity in village attitudes about sexuality. Illegitimacy figures for Voronezh can be found in *PKVG* (1870–1871), otd. II, 139–40; ibid. (1887), 438–39; ibid. (1906), 92–97; and ibid. (1916), otd. II, tables 12–17. On the reliability of illegitimacy figures, see David L. Ransel, "Problems in Measuring Illegitimacy in Prerevolutionary Russia," *Journal of Social History* 16, no. 2 (1982): 111–27.

43. Parishioners also recognized the human need for affection and physical satisfaction that did not threaten the stability of the community. Time and again peasants expressed their heartfelt sympathy for priests who, widowed or abandoned by their wives, fulfilled their physical and emotional desires or the needs of their children for a mother by taking a mistress.

44. For examples, see Tenishev Commission Questionnaire, no. 451, 452; Frank, *Crime, Cultural Conflict and Justice*, 147–59; and Burds, *Peasant Dreams*, chap. 1.

45. Burds, *Peasant Dreams*, 166–69. Late-nineteenth- and early-twentieth-century ethnographers were obsessed with peasant dress as a reflection of deeper social and cultural structures in the village. They categorized dress according to use—ceremonial, holiday, and ordinary—and found that factory-made cloth and clothing was most common in everyday attire. Ceremonial and holiday clothing was usually made by peasant

communities themselves, often using local materials. See Feodor Polikarpov, "Zhenskaia krest'ianskaia odezhda v s. Istobnom Nizhnedevitskogo u.," *TVUAK*, vyp. II (1908): 29–38.

46. Burds is less convincing in his argument that insults were part of a culture of peasant denunciation that were a reaction to the threats of urbanization, modernization, and commoditization. The evidence for villager collaboration with the state, police, and church (to anathematize peasant-workers) is thin. See his *Peasant Dreams*, chap. 7.

47. N. Generozov, "Ne prostaia sluchainost'!" *VEV*, no. 10, unof. pt. (1911): 421–22.

48. Contrary to the norm, some clergymen welcomed the "fresh forces and ideas of the youth." See Iv. Ermolaev, "'Nas davno zhdet poleznaia rabota'," *VEV*, no. 4, unof. pt. (1916): 95–98.

49. "Zhurnal zasedanii obshcheeparkhial'nogo s"ezda o.o. deputatov ot dukhovenstva Voronezhskoi eparkhii s uchastiem tserkovnykh starost 1913 goda," *VEV*, unof. pt. no. 44 (1913): 487–91.

50. Clergymen were keenly aware of their social rank and title and were loath to demean themselves by working the land, which might denigrate their status in the community. In some parishes the faithful continued to work the priest's land for free long after being emancipated, while other peasants worked as day laborers for their spiritual father.

51. RGIA, f. 1405, op. 218, ed. khr. 508.

52. Ibid., ed. khr. 1224 (1907).

53. Archbishop Nikon's opinion reflects the general aloofness within upper church circles toward the needs of the people, as well as an inability to comprehend the changing tastes of the growing working class by assuming that workers would choose to spend their precious free time in occupations more acceptable to the church. See Archbishop Nikon, "Moi dnevnik. Zrelishcha i uveseleniia bliz narodnykh sviatyn'," *Troitskoe slovo*, no. 234 (20 August 1914): 539–43; and "Moi dnevnik. Narodnye doma i narodnye sviatyni," *Troitskoe slovo*, no. 235 (27 August 1914): 555–60.

54. G. A. Khaichenko, *Russkii narodnyi teatr kontsa XIX-nachala XX veka* (Moscow: Izd-vo "Nauka," 1975), 115–16.

55. Richard Stites, *Russian Popular Culture: Entertainment and Society since 1900* (Cambridge: Cambridge University Press, 1992), 16–18. The quote is from p. 18. See also *Novyi entsiklopedicheskii slovar' Brokgauz i Efron*, s.v. "Narodnye doma" (St. Petersburg, 1898).

56. Richard Stites concludes that in 1914 cinema audiences were larger than those of all other popular entertainment (Stites, *Russian Popular Culture*, 30). For useful introductions to prerevolutionary cinema, see ibid., 27–34; Stites, "Dusky Images of Tsarist Russia: Prerevolutionary Cinema," *RR* 53, no. 2 (1994): 285–95; Peter Kenez, *Cinema and Soviet Society, 1917–1953* (Cambridge: Cambridge University Press, 1991), chap. 1; Jay Leyda, *Kino: A History of the Russian and Soviet Film*, 3d ed. (Princeton: Princeton University Press,1983), chaps. 1–5; Denise J. Youngblood, *The Magic Mirror: Moviemaking in Russia, 1908–1918* (Madison: University of Wisconsin Press, 1999); and Yuri Tsivian, *Early Cinema in Russia and Its Cultural Reception*, trans. Alan Bodger, ed. Richard Taylor, with a foreword by Tom Gunning (Chicago: University of Chicago Press, 1998).

57. Stites, *Russian Popular Culture*, 28.

58. "Razvrashchaiushchee vlianie kinematografa," *VEV*, no. 4, unof. pt. (1915): 101–2.

59. "Narodnoe razvrashchenie," *VEV*, no. 6, unof. pt. (1916): 183.

60. Mikhail Kosyrev, "Selo Krasnorechenskoe, Novokhoperskogo uezda," *VEV,* no. 19, unof. pt. (1912): 642–64.

61. V. N. Vy-kii, "V selakh i derevniakh. (Iz lichnykh vpechatlenii)," *VEV,* no. 8, unof. pt. (1911): 255–58.

7: *Failed Visions of Reform at the End of an Era*

1. Gregory Freeze has argued that specialists of late-imperial Russia erroneously rely on popular stereotypes about the church's inability to comprehend the severity of revolutionary movements around the country and the church's subservience to the state. These myths ignore the fact that a growing number of liberal, moderate, and conservative bishops responded to the political disorder between 1905 and 1917 by calling for the restoration of the patriarchate. Under a reestablished patriarch, the church would gain independence from the state and would better represent Orthodoxy's interests in a modern secular Russia. See Freeze, "Church Politics," 274. Support for a council was also widespread among the parish clergy. Even the progressive clergymen known as the "Petersburg 32" presumed that the only way to introduce reform was through a national church council. For an overview of their position, see their first article, which provoked a storm of opposition and support: "O neobkhodimosti peremen v russkom tserkovnom upravlenii. Mnenie gruppy stolichnykh sviashchennikov," *Tserkovnyi vestnik,* no. 11 (17 March 1917), cols. 322–25.

2. The psychological effect of the manifesto and the subsequent barrage of criticism of the church hierarchy proved to be more frightening to the episcopate and parish clergymen than revolutionary violence. Gregory Freeze has called the manifesto "the Church's Bloody Sunday," because it breached what had been an inviolable "social contract" with the regime. See Freeze, "Church Politics," 274.

3. John Meyendorff, "Russian Bishops and Church Reform in 1905," in *Russian Orthodoxy under the Old Regime,* ed. Robert L. Nichols and Theofanis George Stavrou (Minneapolis: University of Minnesota Press, 1978), 170–82; and S. L. Firsov, *Pravoslavnaia Tserkov' i gosudarstvo v poslednee desiatiletie sushchestvovaniia samoderzhaviia v Rossiia* (St. Petersburg: Izd-vo Russkogo Khristianskogo gumanitarnogo universiteta, 1996), 296–329.

4. A standard account of the exchanges in the press can be found in Curtiss, *Church and State,* 213–27.

5. Tomilin, "K voprosu," (1916), 1201–15; and Popov, "Mnenie sel'skogo sviashchennika," 312.

6. Between 1865 and 1881, the pages of the gazette were divided into an official section, which listed announcements for the clergy and published statistical information on local religious life, and an official part, which was filled with articles of general interest that appealed to a wide audience of priests, deacons, psalmists, and better-educated lay people. Both sections were edited by senior clergymen associated with the diocesan clerical seminary, who set the tone of the paper and served as local censors. For the next twenty-five years, stricter censorship of newspapers led the editorial staff to retreat into the safety of historical topics and esoterica that appealed to only a small group of parish clergymen. The unofficial part, which was supposed to serve as a source of information about pastoral service and issues of topical importance, soon lost its intended readership and often went unopened. The official part

changed little over the years and was widely read by the parish clergy. See Grigorii Lebedev, "Eshche k zlobodnevnomu voprosu reorganizatsii Eparkhial'nykh Vedomostei," *VEV*, no. 10, unof. pt. (1908): 598–605.

7. "Zhurnal zasedanii obshcheeparkhial'nogo s"ezda o. o. deputatov ot dukhovenstva Voronezhskoi eparkhii, sostoiavshegosia 14 fevralia 1907 goda v g. Voronezhe," *VEV*, no. 6, unof. pt. (1907): 144; P. Nikol'skii, "Liubopitnyi proekt reorganizatsii Eparkhial'nykh Vedomostei," *VEV*, no. 20, unof. pt. (1907): 677–81; and Konstantin Popov, "O reorganizatsii Eparkhial'nykh Vedomostei," *VEV*, no. 1, unof. pt. (1908): 1–18.

8. The agenda for this assembly, as well as its proceedings, can be found in "Ot Voronezhskoi Dukhovnoi Konsistorii v svedeniiu dukhovenstva eparkhii," *VEV*, no. 15, of. pt. (1917): 149–50; and "Zhurnal Voronezhskogo Eparkhial'nogo Sobraniia delegatov ot dukhovenstva i mirian," *VEV*, no. 20, of. pt. (1917): 177–206. The ideas were well known in liberal Orthodox circles. For example, see the work of Alexander Papkov (1868–1920), *O blagoustroistve pravoslavnogo prikhoda*.

9. "Ot redaktora," *VEV*, no. 25, unof. pt. (1917): 527. Proposals similar to those of the Voronezh clergy and laity were being made throughout the empire. See the collection of proposals in RGIA, f. 796, op. 445, ed. khr. 223, "O rassmotrenii proekta polozheniia o prikhode (1916–1917)."

10. The church's response to the Bolsheviks later that year expressed the same sentiment. For examples, see Orlando Figes and Boris Kolonitskii, *Interpreting the Russian Revolution: The Language and Symbols of 1917* (New Haven, CT: Yale University Press, 1999), 172–73.

11. The reforms are discussed in B. V. Titlinov, *Dukhovnaia shkola v Rossii v XIX stoletii* (Vil'na, 1908–1909; reprint, Gregg International Publishers, 1970, with an introduction by G. Florovsky), 2:231–374. The consequences of these reforms on the identity of clerical sons is discussed in Laurie Manchester, "The Secularization of the Search for Salvation: The Self-Fashioning of Orthodox Clergymen's Sons in Late Imperial Russia," *SR* 57, no. 1 (1998): 50–76.

12. Such an unruly student body did not automatically lead to a rebellious clergy, but the consequences of seminary life have been overshadowed by more famous examples of revolutionaries and later Soviet officials who, having been "groomed" as antireligeous revolutionaries in the religious seminaries, unleashed powerful forces of destruction against organized religion. Ibid., GAVO, f. I-6, op. 1, ed. khr. 1926.

13. RGIA, f. 796, op. 187, ed. khr. 6641, "Po predlozheniiu g. ob.-pr-ra o protivoprav. deiatel'nosti sviashchennikov Vor. ep . . . (1906)," ll. 2–9 ob.; GAVO, f. I-6, op. 1, ed. khr. 1459 (1908), ll. 49–50; and Stoliarov, *Zapiski russkogo krest'ianina*, 154–55, 158. It is not clear from the records whether Meretskii was returned to his parish, but, given the shortage of clergymen, it is likely that he continued to serve as a priest. At the age of thirty-nine, Meretskii, the son of a deacon, was married, had a family, and had taught religion at zemstvo schools since 1889. He had previously received two awards for service and excellent conduct and had never before been under suspicion. Meretskii, like Stoliarov, was a member of the All-Russian Peasant Union.

14. Complaints filed by peasant communities or individuals revealed a wide range of sentiment that was present in any given community, though not necessarily representative of an entire community's feelings. A useful discussion of problems of using crime reports can be found in Neuberger, *Hooliganism*, 9–24. Convincing examples of how to overcome source problems when studying groups that are either illiterate or have very low literacy levels can be found in many works of

Carlo Ginzburg and Natalie Zemon Davis; for example, Carlo Ginzburg, *The Cheese and the Worms: The Cosmos of a Sixteenth-Century Miller,* trans. John Tedeschi and Anne Tedeschi (Baltimore: Johns Hopkins University Press, 1982); Carlo Ginzburg, *The Night Battles: Witchcraft and Agrarian Cults in the Sixteenth and Seventeenth Centuries,* trans. John Tedeschi and Anne Tedeschi (Baltimore: Johns Hopkins University Press, 1983; reprint, New York: Penguin Books, 1985); Natalie Zemon Davis, *The Return of Martin Guerre* (Cambridge: Harvard University Press, 1983); and Davis, *Fiction in the Archives.*

15. These cases are the strongest evidence that peasants understood the church administrative system and the process of filing appropriate documents to initiate a case or an appeal of an unfavorable decision. These cases also demonstrate how unresponsive the Voronezh consistory and Holy Synod were to the religio-moral sensibilities of the peasants, as cleric after cleric was returned to his parish after paying a fine or performing a brief penance. Concern about the image of wayward clergy was acknowledged in Archbishop Anastasii's reply to the synodal questionnaire, *Otzyvy eparkhial'nykh arkhiereev po voprosu o tserkovnoi reforme* (St. Petersburg: Sinodal'naia tip., 1906), 1:140.

16. On the priest who fell asleep at the altar table, see RGIA, f. 796, op. 187, ed. khr. 6858 (1906). The second case can be found in ibid., op. 201, ed. khr. 232, V otd., 2d st. (1915).

17. In addition to the examples discussed in chap. 4, see RGIA, f. 1405, op. 218, ed. khr. 508 (1906); GAVO, f. I-6, op. 1, ed. khr. 930 (1906); ibid., ed. khr. 1212 (1907); and ibid., ed. khr. 1224 (1907).

18. "Dukhovenstvo i narod," *VEV,* no. 19, unof. pt. (1907): 640–50. Three neighboring settlements were known as Usman': Bol'shaia and Malaia Usman' and Usmanskie Vyselki (or Usman Settlements). Lists of villages sometimes combined the three. This case is most likely about Bol'shaia Usman' and Usmanskie Vyselki. See *Novyi entsiklopedicheskii slovar'* (Brokgaus-Efrona), (St. Petersburg: 1909–1916), s.v. "Usman'"; and *PKVG,* otd. 1(1910): 102.

19. "V Voronezhskom sovete rabochikh, soldatskikh i krest'ianskikh deputatov," *VEV,* no. 25, unof. pt. (1917): 525–57.

20. GARF, f. R-3431, op. 1, ed. khr. 273, ll. 2–2 ob.; and *VVTsE,* no. 26 (19 October 1917): 3. The decree appears to have been a compilation of widespread practice after the abdication of Tsar Nicholas II.

21. GARF, R-3431, op. 1, ed. khr. 273, ll. 64–64 ob. Unlike most prerevolutionary petitions, which were filed by a corporate group (the parish or village commune) and then signed by supporters, this petition named the senders individually. Among the complainants were the district superintendent, a priest from the Boguchar city cathedral, and several dozen school teachers, priests, and officials who appealed to Archbishop Tikhon to present their views to the national church council, to which he was a representative.

22. A review of the council's discussions can be found in *VVTsE,* no. 13 (3 August 1917): 1–4; and ibid., no. 16 (13 August 1917): 1–2. The dispute between the council and the opposition faction can be found in ibid., no. 4 (2 July 1917): 2–3; ibid., no. 5 (6 July 1917): 2–3; ibid., no. 6 (13 July 1917): 1; and ibid., no. 8 (16 July 1916): 2.

23. The custom surrounding imperial succession that expressed sorrow at the passing of one ruler and hesitant joy at the accession of a new ruler, whose reign might bring better or worse times, was expressed in the formulaic public announcement by the court: "The tsar is dead! Long live the tsar!" See Chris J. Chulos, "Festivals and Collective Memory in Imperial Russia," paper presented at the Sixth International Council for Cen-

tral and East European Studies Congress, Tampere, Finland, August 2000.

24. A general introduction to the events of spring 1917 can be found in Orlando Figes, *A People's Tragedy: The Russian Revolution, 1891–1924* (London: Jonathan Cape, 1996), 339–53, and chaps. 9–10.

25. The issues discussed in this and the following paragraph can be found in *Voronezhskii telegraf* and *Voronezhskii vestnik tserkovnogo edineniia,* February and March 1917. Ershov also argued that the nation's fate would no longer depend on a monarch but "the people" *(narod),* who would have to take credit for the revolution, as well as partial blame for the old regime's oppression.

26. *VT,* no. 71 (2 April 1917); and *VVTsE,* nos. 19, 23, and 37 (1917).

27. I. Atskii, "Tserkov' i Gosudarstvo," *Proletarii,* no. 5 (3 May 1918): 2. This newspaper was published by the Bobrov District Executive Committee, which changed the title in 1919 to *Izvestiia Bobrovskogo uezdnogo ispolnitel'nogo komiteta.* The editors proclaimed this newspaper to be "purely peasant," and they encouraged contributions from the peasantry.

28. *Izvestiia Voronezhskogo gubispolkoma sov. R.K.D. i gorod sov. R. i K.D.,* no. 8 (14 January 1919).

29. For the authors of this piece, Christmas of 1918, which, for the Orthodox who adhered to the old calendar, fell at the beginning of January 1919, marked "the nativity of brotherhood and love, equality and freedom. . . . The path from the Nativity of Christ to the approaching nativity of freedom was the thorny road of victory toward a better future for all peoples, for all of humanity." *Izvestiia Ostrogozhskogo uezdnogo ispolnitel'nogo Komiteta sovetov rabochikh i krest'ianskikh deputatov,* no. 5 (7 January 1919).

30. Ibid., nos. 76, 84.

31. *Sovetskaia gazeta,* no. 11 (2 February 1918) (emphasis in original). The authors further argued that the Bolsheviks had replaced Christ as the great teacher of socialism.

32. Field, *Rebels;* Figes and Kolonitskii, *Interpreting the Russian Revolution,* chap. 5; and Aleksei Putintsev, "Iz etnograficheskikh vpechatlenii i nabliudenii (Korotoiakskii uezd Voronezhskoi gub.)," *Voronezhskii istoriko-arkheologicheskii vestnik,* no. 2 (1921): 43–44.

33. Mikh. Gorev, "Vskrytie moshchei Tikhona Zadonskogo i Mitrofana Voronezhskogo," *Revoliutsiia i tserkov',* no. 2 (1919): 12–13. By waging their campaign against the two most sacred Voronezh holy places, local authorities implicitly acknowledged the shrines' importance to Russian Orthodoxy. The ceremony was widely described in the provincial and national press.

34. "Kukla Tikhona," *Sovetskaia gazeta,* no. 9 (31 January 1919): 1–2, which was reprinted in the next issue, no. 10 (1 February 1919), 1–2; "Kukla v monastyre. Vtoroe otkrytie 'moshchei Tikhona,'" *Sovetskaia gazeta,* no. 11 (2 February 1919): 1; GARF, f. A-353, op. 3, ed. khr. 731; and Gorev, "Vskrytie," 9–23. See also GARF, f. A-353, op. 3, ed. khr. 731; and ibid., f. A-353, op. 3, ed. khr. 736. Some of the archival material was published in D. Anashenko, V. Mandrykin, and D. Savel'ev, eds., *Voronezhskie "chudotvortsy." Sbornik statei* (Voronezh: Kommuna, 1929), 42–45; and Gorev, "Vskrytie," 11–14. Published accounts of other shrine "revelations" *(otkrytiia),* as well as scientific explanations of relics, can be found in the journal *Revoliutsiia i tserkov',* which was published by the People's Commissariat of Justice (Moscow), 1919–1924. Although I have not viewed it, a copy of the film is listed among the holdings of the Russian State Documentary Film and Photo Archive at Krasnogorsk (Rossiisskii gosudarstvenyi arkhiv kino-fotodokumentov).

35. GARF, f. R-3431, op. 1, ed. khr. 563, ll. 35–39.

36. GARF, f. A-353, op. 3, ed. khr. 763, l. 12.

37. Ibid., op. 5, ed. khr. 251, ll. 10, 11–12 ob., 15, 18. The corruption of Serafim's remains had been public knowledge since 1903, when the synodal commission investigating his sanctity made the same discovery.

38. For examples of the enlightenment approach, see "Ot redakstii," *Vestnik prosveshcheniia,* no. 1 (Voronezh 1921): 3–4; "T'ma besprosvetnaia," *Vestnik prosveshcheniia,* no. 1 (1921): 72; and Smirnov, "Zadachi vneshkol'nogo obrazovaniia," *Revoliutsiia i tserkov',* no. 2 (1919): 1–4.

39. N. Rybakov, "Tolki naroda o Tikhone," *Sovetskaia gazeta,* no. 11 (2 February 1919): 2 (emphasis in original).

40. V. N. Dunaev, "Vystuplenie krest'ian Voronezhskoi gubernii protiv reaktsionnykh deistvii dukhovenstva (mart-oktiabr' 1917 g.)," *Sbornik rabot aspirantov Voronezhskogo gosudarstvennogo universiteta,* no. 1 (1965): 143–48.

41. Many examples of Anastasii's criticism of the clergy as inadequate or bad examples of the faith can be found in his annual reports. See RGIA, f. 796, op. 442, ed. khr. 1714 (1898), l. 9 ob.; and ibid., ed. khr. 2019 (1904), l. 17.

42. One of the few exceptions was a district clerical assembly of September 1916 that decided not to make any final decisions about the reform of parish life before consulting with the parishioners. See Tomilin, "K voprosu," 1201.

43. Evtuhov's discussion of the role of the intelligentsia in this council is particularly illuminating about the importance of Orthodoxy for Russia's greatest thinkers of the time. See "The Lid Comes Off: The Church Council of 1917–1918," in *Cross and Sickle,* 189–206. The acts and decisions of the council can be found in *Deianiia Sviashchennogo Sobora Pravoslavnoi Rossiiskoi Tserkvi 1917–1918 gg.,* 3 vols. (Moscow: Izd. Sobornogo Soveta, 1918; reprint, Izd. Novospasskogo Monastyria, 1994); and *Sobranie opredelenii i postanovlenii Sviashchennogo Sobora Pravoslavnoi Rossiiskoi Tserkvi 1917–1918 gg.* (Moscow: Izd. Sobornogo Soveta, 1918; reprint, Izdanie Novospasskogo Monastyria, 1994).

44. *Sobranie opredelenii,* part 3, 13–14, 17–18. By the time that new parish regulations were issued in April 1918, Orthodox Christianity could no longer officially serve as an organizing motif in everyday life. Ironically, for the first time in Russian history, women were allowed to participate as full members of parish councils, and soon they became some of the staunchest defenders of Orthodoxy. Using their newly gained political freedoms and their new literacy, women helped to rally local religious sentiment against church closures, organized petitions to local and national authorities, and physically guarded the holy places and objects of their communities. Until the start of World War II, their actions provided a spiritual and cultural link to the past that eased the harsh transition to a Russia without a tsar and without a church.

45. This description of the Azov celebration is based on James von Geldern, *Bolshevik Festivals, 1917–1920,* Studies on the History of Society and Culture, ed. Victoria E. Bonnell and Lynn Hunt (Berkeley: University of California Press, 1993), 15–16.

Conclusion: *Religion without a Tsar or a Church*

1. Episcopal authority was under siege already in 1917 as bishops were routinely arrested for counterrevolutionary activity. The confiscation of church valuables during

the famine of 1921 and 1922 stripped the church of much of its movable wealth. The death of Patriarch Tikhon in 1925 after a series of arrests, coupled with the controversial declaration of support for the Soviet regime made by his successor, Metropolitan Sergii, in 1927, demoralized the episcopate and clergy and precipitated further schisms between opposing parties within the church.

2. Aleksandr Ch., "Paralleli," *Revoliutsiia i prosveshchenie,* no. 1 (1919): 16.

3. Peasant communities throughout the country filed petitions seeking to keep their churches open in the 1920s and 1930s. See the archives of the Permanent Central Commission on Cults, Gosudarstvennyi arkhiv Rossiiskoi federatsii, f. R-5263.

4. On the nonreligious aspects of pilgrimage, see John M. Theilmann, "Medieval Pilgrims and the Origins of Tourism," *Journal of Popular Culture* 20, no. 4 (spring 1987): 93.

5. See the incisive remarks of Laura Engelstein, "Revolution and the Theater of Public Life in Imperial Russia," in *Revolution and the Meanings of Freedom in the Nineteenth Century,* ed. Isser Woloch (Stanford, CA: Stanford University Press, 1996), 353–57.

Selected Bibliography

Archival Sources

Arkhiv Russkogo geograficheskogo obshchestva (ARGO)

Arkhiv Rossiiskogo etnograficheskogo muzeia (AREM)
- f. 7   Tenishev Bureau

Gosudarstvennyi arkhiv Rossiiskoi Federatsii (GARF)
- f. 109   Third Section of His Royal Highness's Personal Chancellery
- f. A-353   People's Commissariate of Justice
- f. R-393   People's Commissariat of Internal Affairs of the Russian Soviet Federation of Socialist Republics
- f. R-3431   All-Russian Church Council
- f. R-5263   Permanent Central Commission on Cults of the All-Russian Central Executive Committee of the Soviets.

Gosudarstvennyi arkhiv Voronezhskoi oblasti (GAVO)
- f. I-1   Voronezh Provincial Gendarmes Administration
- f. I-6   Chancellery of the Governor of Voronezh
- f. I-64   Public Schools Board
- f. I-84   Voronezh Spiritual Consistory
- f. 277   Voronezh District Gendarmes Administration
- f. 1138   Personal files
- f. 1939   Personal files

Rossiiskii gosudarstvennyi istoricheskii arkhiv (RGIA)
- f. 796   Chancellery of the Holy Synod
- f. 797   Chancellery of the Chief Procurator of the Holy Synod
- f. 802   Educational Committee of the Holy Synod
- f. 835   Photographs of the Holy Synod
- f. 1276   Council of Ministers
- f. 1405   Ministry of Justice

Contemporary Periodicals

Bogoslovskii vestnik

Don

Dukhovnaia beseda

Dushepoleznoe chtenie

Filologicheskie zapiski

Golos truda

Istoricheskii vestnik

Izvestiia Ostrogozhskogo uezdnogo ispolnitel'nogo Komiteta sovetov rabochikh i krest'ianskikh deputatov

Izvestiia Voronezhskogo gubispolkoma sov. R.K.D. i gorod sov. R. i K.D.

Khristianskoe chtenie

Pamiatnaia knizhka Voronezhskoi gubernii

Poriadok

Pravoslavnyi sobesednik

Proletarii

Revoliutsiia i tserkov'

Russkii vestnik

Soobshcheniia imperatorskogo pravoslavnogo palestinskogo obshchestva

Sovetskaia gazeta

Staroobriadcheskaia mysl'

Strannik

Troitskie listki

Troitskoe slovo

Trudy voronezhskoi uchenoi arkhivnoi komissii

Tserkov'

Tserkovnye vedomosti

Tserkovnyi vestnik

Vestnik prosveshcheniia

Voronezhskaia kooperativnaia niva

Voronezhskaia starina

Voronezhskie eparkhial'nye vedomosti

Voronezhskie gubernskie vedomosti

Voronezhskii istoriko-arkheologicheskii vestnik

Voronezhskii krai

Voronezhskii listok

Voronezhskii mysl'

Voronezhskii spravochnik

Voronezhskii telegraf

Voronezhskii vestnik tserkovnogo edineniia

Voronezhskoe slovo

Zhivaia starina

𝒫rimary Sources

Belliustin, I. S. *Description of the Clergy in Rural Russia: The Memoir of a Nineteenth-Century Parish Priest.* Translated and with an interpretive essay by Gregory L. Freeze. Ithaca, NY: Cornell University Press, 1985.

Bolkhovitinov, Evgenii. *Istoricheskoe, geograficheskoe i ekonomicheskoe opisanie Voronezhskoi gubernii sobrannoe iz istorii, arkhivnykh zapisok i skazanii.* Voronezh: Tip. Gubernskogo upravleniia, 1800.

"Chudesnye istseleniia, sovershivshiiasia pri otkrytii moshchei sviatitelia i chudotvortsa Tikhona, episkopa Voronezhskogo i Eletskogo." *Dukhovnaia beseda.* "Tserkovnaia letopis'." (25 November 1861): 717–28.

Deianiia Sviashchennogo Sobora Pravoslavnoi Rossiiskoi Tserkvi 1917–1918 gg. 3 vols. Moscow: Izd. Sobornogo Soveta, 1918. Reprint, Izd. Novospasskogo Monastyria, 1994.

Diad'kov, A. "Voronezhskii Gubernskii Muzei v 1894–1897 godakh." *PKVG*, otd. 3 (1897): 56–72.

———. "Pushkinskie prazdnestva v Voronezhskoi gubernii." *PKVG* (1900): 45–52.

Dolgo-li pomniat gramotu krest'iane, proshedshie nachal'nuiu narodnuiu shkolu, chitaiut li oni po vykhode iz shkoly, i chto po preimushchestvu, gde berut knigi? Voronezh: S. P. Iakovleva, 1894.

Dolgopolov, Vl. "Velikaia reforma. (Po povodu 50–ti letnego osvobozhdeniia krest'ian ot krepostnoi zavisimosti)." *VEV*, no. 10, unof. pt. (1911): 303–19.

Fal'bork, G., and V. Charnoluskii, eds. *Nachal'noe narodnoe obrazovanie v Rossii.* St. Petersburg: Tip. Narodnaia Pol'za, 1900.

Fon-Kremer, A. "Obychai pover'ia i predrassudki krest'ian sela Verkhotishanki." *PKVG* (1870–1871).

Gavrilov, Viacheslav. "Prazdnovanie 50–letiia otkrytiia moshchei Sviatitelia Tikhona Zadonskogo v s. Iasenovke, Bogucharskogo uezda." *VEV*, no. 34 (1911): 827–28.

Golubinskii, E. *Istoriia kanonizatsii sviatykh v Russkoi tserkvi.* 2d rev. ed. Moscow: Universitetskaia tip., 1903.

Goretskii, V., and V. Vil'k, comps. *Russkii narodnyi lechebnyi travnik i tsvetnik.* 2d ed. Moscow: Tip. V. V. Chicherina, 1892–93.

Gorev, Mikh. "Vskrytie moshchei Tikhona Zadonskogo i Mitrofana Voronezhskogo." *Revoliutsiia i tserkov'*, no. 2 (1919): 9–23.

(Gumilevskii), Filaret, comp. *Zhitiia sviatykh, chtimykh pravoslavnoiu tserkoviiu, so svedeniiami o prazdnikakh gospodskikh i bogorodichnykh, i o iavlennykh chudotvornykh ikonakh.* 2d rev. ed. St. Petersburg: Izd. I. L. Tuzova, 1892.

[Iakovlev]. "Poslovitsy, pogovorki, krylatye slova, primety i pover'ia, sobranny v slobode Sagunakyh Ostrogozhskogo uezda." *ZS* vyp. I–II (1905): 141–80.

Iakovlev, G. "Poslovitsy, pogovorki, krylatye slova, primety i pover'ia, sobrannyi v slobode Sagunakh Ostrogozhskogo uezda." *ZS* vyp. 4, otd. 2 (1906): 165–84.

Iosif, Arkhiepiskop Voronezhskii i Zadonskii. "Chudesnye istseleniia, sovershivshiiasia pri otkrytii moshchei sviatitelia i chudotvorsta Tikhona, Episkopa Voronezhskogo i Eletskogo." *Strannik*, supplement (May 1862): 1–35.

Istoricheskii ocherk razvitiia tserkovnykh shkol za istekshee dvadtsatipiatiletie (1884–1909 gg.). St. Petersburg: Sinodal'naia tip., 1909.

Istoricheskie svedeniia o zhizni Mitrofana, pervogo episkopa Voronezhskogo. 2d ed. St. Petersburg: n.p., 1832.

Izvlecheniia iz vsepoddanneishego otcheta ober-prokurora sviateishego sinoda po vedomstvu pravoslavnogo ispovedaniia. St. Petersburg: Sinodal'naia tip., 1866–1884. (See also *Vsepoddanneishii otchet Ober-Prokurora Sviateishchego Sinoda.*)

K., B. G. "Otkrytie Voronezhskoi eparkhii i Sviatitel' Mitrofan pervyi episkop ee." In *Voronezhskii iubileinyi sbornik v pamiat' trekhsotletiia g. Voronezha*, 1:5–33. Voronezh: Tip.-lit. Gubernskogo Pravleniia, 1886.

Kalashnikov, S. V., comp. *Alfavitnyi ukazatel' deistvuiushchikh i rukovodstvennykh kanonicheskikh postanovlenii, ukazov, opredelenii i razporiazhenii Sviateishego Pravitel'svuiushchego Sinoda (1721–1901 g. vkliuchitel'no) i grazhdanskikh zakonov, otnosiashchikhsia k dukhovnomu vedomstvu pravoslavnogo ispovedaniia.* 3d rev. ed. St. Petersburg: Izd. I. A. L. Tuzova, 1902.

Kanatchikov, Semën. *A Radical Worker in Tsarist Russia: The Autobiography of Semën Kanatchikov.* Ed. Reginald E. Zelnik. Stanford, CA: Stanford University Press, 1986.

Kirillov, Dimitrii. "Nabliudeniia i zametki sviashchennika." *VEV*, no. 5 (1868): 137–49.

———. "Nabliudeniia i zametki sviashchennika." *VEV*, no. 12 (1868): 345–53.

Krainskii, N. V. *Porcha, klikushi i besnovatye, kak iavleniia russkoi narodnoi zhizni.* With an introduction by V. M. Bekhterev. Novgorod: Gubernskaia Tip., 1900.

Krest'ianskii kalendar' na 1925 g. S ob"iasneniiami prazdnikov i poleznymi sovetami dlia sel'skikh khoziaev. Kazan: Izd-vo Krasnaia Tatariia i Novaia derevnia, 1925.

Litvinov, V. V. "Prazdnovanie 200–letnego iubileia Poltavskoi pobedy 27 iiunia 1909 g. v Voronezhskoi gubernii." *PKVG* otd. III (1910): 1–38.

———. "Bibliograficheskii ukazatel' literatury o Sviatitele Tikhone Zadonskom i obzor izdanii ego tvorenii." *VS*, no. 10 (1910): 221–73.

———. "Prazdnovanie 300–letiia tsarstvovaniia Doma Romanovykh v g. Voronezhe i Voronezhskoi gubernii." *PKVG* (1914): 121–57.

———. "Voronezhskii gubernator D. N. Begichev i ego rasporiazheniia pri otkrytii moshchei Sviatitelia Mitrofana i perenesenii ikh iz Arkhangel'skogo sobora Blagoveshchenskii." *VS*, no. 13 (1914): 109–21.

Maksheev, N. *Krest'ianskii i sel'sko-khoziastvennyi kalendar' 1901.* Moscow: 1901.

Maksimov, S. V. *Nechistaia, nevedomaia i krestnaia sila.* Etnograficheskoe biuro kniazia V. N. Tenisheva. St. Petersburg: R. Golike and A. Vil'borg, 1903. Reprint, St. Petersburg: "POLISET," 1994.

Markov, Evgenii. "Poezdka v Divnogor'e." *Russkii vestnik*, no. 6 (1891): 157–82.

———. "Poezdka k kamniu Builu." *PKVG* (1894): 127–46.

———. "Donskaia beseda i sosedniia ei drevniia urochishcha Dona (putevye zametki)." *PKVG* (1896): 108–35.

"Materialy po istorii staroobriadchestva." *Tserkov'* 48 (1908): 1646–48.

Meerkova, A. N. *Otkhozhye promysly: Pereselencheskoe i bogomol'cheskoe dvizhenie v Voronezhskoi gubernii v 1911 godu.* Voronezh: Izd. Voronezhskogo gubernskogo zemstva, 1914.

Nachal'nye uchilishcha vedomstva narodnogo prosveshcheniia v 1914 godu, Departament Narodnogo Prosveshcheniia. Petrograd: Tipo-lit. M. P. Frolovoi, 1916.

Nikitin, Nik. "Selo Kon'-Kolodez'. (Istoriko-statisticheskoe opisanie—tserkvi i prikhoda)." *VEV*, no. 1, unof. pt. (1890): 23–33; no. 2, unof. pt. (1890): 64–75; no. 5, unof. pt. (1890): 207–13; no. 8 (1890): 367–79.

Nikol'skii, P. *Spravochnaia kniga dlia dukhovenstva Voronezhskoi eparkhii (osoboe prilozhenie k Voronezhskim gubernskim vedomostiam za 1900 g.).* Voronezh: Tip.-lit. V. I. Isaeva, 1900.

————. *Interesy i nuzhdy eparkhial'noi zhizni.* Voronezh: Tip.-lit. V. I. Isaeva, 1902.

————. "Antonii II, Arkhiepiskop Voronezhskii (1826–1846 gg.) i obretenie moshchei Sviatitelia Tikhona." *VS,* no. 10 (1911): 19–54.

Nikonov, Th. "Opisanie Voronezhskoi eparkhii." *VEV,* no. 2 (1867): 51–55; no. 3 (1867): 75–79; no. 6 (1867): 191–97; no. 7 (1867): 219–27; no. 8 (1867): 261–69; no. 11 (1867): 354–60; no. 12 (1867): 385–90; no. 13 (1867): 436–41; no. 15 (1867): 493–98; and no. 4 (1868): 118–28.

Nozdrin, R. "Sloboda Alekseevka, Biriuchenskogo uezda. (Cherty iz istorii slobody i eia sovremennogo byta)." *PKVG,* pt. 3 (1905): 33–48.

Obolenskii, P. "Veroizpovedanie Russkikh sektantov-ratsionalistov (dukhobortsev, molokan i shtundistov)." Pt. 4. "Shtundisty." *VEV,* no. 1, unof. pt. (1890): 1–20; no. 5, unof. pt. (1890): 195–207; no. 6, unof. pt. (1890): 256–69; no. 9, unof. pt. (1890): 403–13; no. 10, unof. pt. (1890): 442–54; no. 12, unof. pt. (1890): 529–43.

Odnodnevnaia perepis' nachal'nykh shkol v imperii proizvedennaia 18 ianvaria 1911 goda. Vyp. 13. *Khar'kovskii uchebnyi okrug, Ministerstvo narodnogo prosveshcheniia.* Petrograd: Tip. "Ekateringofskoe pechatnoe delo," 1914.

Otchet Voronezhskogo Bratstva sviatitelei Mitrofana i Tikhona za 1887 god. Voronezh: Tip. V. I. Isaeva, 1888.

Otchet Voronezhskogo eparkhial'nogo uchilishchnogo soveta o sostoianii tserkovno-prikhodskikh shkol Voronezhskoi eparkhii za 1889–1890 god. Voronezh: Tip. V. I. Isaeva, 1890.

Otzyvy eparkhial'nykh arkhiereev po voprosu o tserkovnoi reforme. St. Petersburg: Sinodal'naia tip., 1906.

Papkov, A. *O blagoustroistve pravoslavnogo prikhoda. S prilozheniem proekta prikhodskogo ustava.* St. Petersburg: S.-Peterburgskaia Sinodal'naia Tip., 1907.

Poezdka v Zadonsk vo vremia otkrytiia moshchei Episkopa Voronezhskogo i Eletskogo Tikhona 1-go. Moscow: Universitetskaia tip., 1861.

Pokrovskii, I. *Russkie eparkhii v XVI–XIX vv., ikh otkrytie, sostav i predely.* 2 vols. Kazan: Tipo-lit. Imperatorskogo universiteta, 1897–1913.

Polikarpov, N. I. "25-letie pervoi sel'skoi zhenskoi shkoly Voronezhskoi gubernii (1 sentiabria 1872–1897 gg.)." *PKVG* (1897): 73–78.

————. "Prazdnovanie Sv. koronavaniia Ikh Impratorskikh Velichestv v g. Voronezhe i Voronezhskoi gubernii." *PKVG* otd. III (1897): 29–55.

————. "Poslednie dni zhizni, konchina i pogreblenie sviatitelia Mitrofana." *VS,* no. 3 (1903): 220–39.

————. "Bytovye cherty iz zhizni krest'ian sela Istobnogo, Nizhnedevitskogo uezda, Voron. Gub." *PKVG* otd. III (1906).

————. "K istorii pechatnogo dela v Voronezhe za istekshee stoletie. Voronezhskaia gubernskaia tipografiia (14 maia 1798–1898 gg.)." *TVUAK* 2 (1908): 61–86.

————. "Proslavlenie Sviatitelia Tikona Zadonskogo i otkrytie ego sviatykh moshchei. K 50–letiiu sego sobytiia 13-go avgusta 1861–1911 gg." *PKVG* (1911): 010–021.

Polnoe sobranie zakonov. 1st ser. St. Petersburg, 1830. 3d ser. St. Petersburg, 1911.

Polnyi pravoslavnyi bogoslovskii entsiklopedicheskii slovar'. St. Petersburg: Izd-vo P. P. Soikina, 1913.

Popov, G. *Russkaia narodno-bytovaia meditsina. Etnograficheskii biuro kniazia V. N. Tenisheva.* St. Petersburg: Tip. A. S. Suvorina, 1903.

Popov, T. "Proslavlenie Sviatitelia Tikhona posle otkrytiia ego sviatykh moshchei." *VS,* no. 10 (1911): 126–34.

Poselianin, E. "Antonii, arkhiepiskop Voronezhskii i Zadonskii." *Russkie podvizhniki. Istoriko-biograficheskie ocherki.* Pt. 1. St. Petersburg: Izd. P. P. Soikina, 1900.

———. "Kashinskie torzhestva." *RP,* no. 25 (1909): 391–402.

Pravoslavnaia bogoslovskaia entsiklopediia. Ed. A. P. Lopukhin. Petrograd [*sic*]: Prilozhenie k dukhovnomu zhurnalu, "Strannik," 1902.

Pravoslavnye Russkie obiteli. Polnoe illiustrirovannoe opisanie vsekh pravoslavnykh russkikh monastyrei v Rossiiskoi imperii i na Athone. St. Petersburg: Knigoizd-vo P. P. Soikina, 1910. Reprint, St. Petersburg: Izd-vo "Voskresenie," 1994.

Preobrazhenskii, A. *Etimologicheskii slovar' russkogo iazyka.* Moscow, 1910–1918.

Preobrazhenskii, I. V., comp. *Otechestvennaia tserkov' po statisticheskim dannym s 1840–41 po 1890–91 gg.* St. Petersburg: Tip. E. Arngol'da, 1897.

———, comp. *Tserkovnaia reforma. Sbornik statei dukhovnoi i svetskoi periodicheskoi pechati po voprosu o reforme.* St. Petersburg: Tip. E. Arngol'da, 1905.

Proslavlenie sviatitelia Tikhona, obretenie i otkrytie sviatykh moshchei ego. St. Petersburg: Tip. Departamenta udelov, 1862.

Rasskaz ochevidtsa ob otkrytii netlennykh moshchei Sviatitelia i chudotvortsa Tikhona, Episkopa Voronezhskogo 12 i 13 avgusta 1861 goda, v Zadonskom Bogorodichnom monastyre. St. Petersburg: Tip. Departamenta Udelov, 1861.

S., A. "Ocherki poverii, obriadov, primet i gadanii v Voronezhskoi gubernii." *Voronezhskii literaturnyi sbornik, povremennoe izdanie* 1 (1861): 373–92.

Selivanov, A. I. "Etnograficheskie ocherki Voronezhskoi gubernii." In *Voronezhskii iubileinyi sbornik v pamiat' trekhsotletiia g. Voronezha,* 2:69–117. Voronezh: Tip.-lit. Gubernskogo Pravleniia, 1886.

Semyonova Tian-Shanskaia, Olga. *Village Life in Late Tsarist Russia.* Ed. David L. Ransel. Indiana-Michigan Series in Russian and East European Studies. Bloomington: Indiana University Press, 1993.

Shcherbina, F. A., comp. *Sbornik statisticheskikh svedenii po Voronezhskoi gubernii.* N.p.: n.p., 1884.

———. Semeinye razdely u krest'ian Voronezhskoi gubernii. *PKVG* otd. 2 (1897): 55–67.

———, comp. *Svodnyi sbornik po 12 uezdam Voronezhskoi gubernii: Statisticheskie materialy podvornoi perepisi po gubernii i obzor materialov, sposobov po sobiraniiu ikh i priemov po razrabotke.* Voronezh: Tip. Isaeva, 1897.

———, comp. *Krest'ianskie biudzhety.* Voronezh: Tip. V. I. Isaeva, 1900.

Snegirev, I. M. *Russkie prostonarodnye prazdniki i suevernye obriady.* 2 vols. Moscow: Universitetskaia tip., 1837–1839.

Snesarev, Ioann. "Obyknoveniia malorossian Voronezhskoi gubernii, Biriuchenskogo uezda." Manuscript held in Biblioteka Voronezhskogo gosudarstvennogo universiteta.

Sobranie opredelenii i postanovlenii Sviashchennogo Sobora Pravoslavnoi Rossiiskoi Tserkvi 1917–1918 gg. Moscow: Izd. Sobornogo Soveta, 1918; Reprint, Izd. Novospasskogo Monastyria, 1994.

Stoliarov, Ivan. *Zapiski russkogo krest'ianina. Récit d'un paysan russe.* With a Preface by Basile Kerblay. Notes by Valérie Stoliaroff, with the assistance of Alexis Berelowitch. *Cultures et sociétés de l'est,* no. 6. Paris: Institut d'études slaves, 1986.

Sviatitel' i chudotvorets Mitrofan, pervyi episkop Voronezhskii. 2d ed. Moscow: I. D. Sytin, 1901.

"Sviatitel' Tikhon Zadonskii." *VEV,* no. 43, unof. pt. (1911): 1087–1104.

Tenishev, V. N., comp. *Programma etnograficheskikh svedenii o krest'ianakh tsentral'noi Rossii.* Smolensk: Gubernskaia tip., 1898.

Tkachev, G. "Etnograficheskie ocherki Bogucharskogo uezda." *PKVG* (1865–1866): 176–81.

Turchaninov, N. *Itogi pereselencheskogo dvizheniia za vremia s 1896 po 1909 gg. (vkliuchitel'no)*. St. Petersburg: Izd. Pereselencheskogo upravleniia, 1910.

Valukinskii, N. V. *Drevnia Voronezhskogo uezda (iz vpechatlenii khudozhnika-etnografa)*. Voronezh: Izd. Gubmuzeia i Zhurnala "Nazha rabota," 1923.

Voronezhskii iubileinyi sbornik v pamiat' trekhsotletiia g. Voronezha. 2 vols. Voronezh: Tip.-lit. Gubernskogo Pravleniia, 1886.

Vsepoddanneishii otchet Ober-Prokurora Sviateishchego Sinoda. St. Petersburg: Sinodal'-naia tip., 1886–1915. (Continuation of *Izvlecheniia iz vsepoddanneishego otcheta ober-prokurora sviateishego sinoda po vedomstvu pravoslavnogo ispovedaniia*.)

Zabylin, M., comp. *Russkii narod, ego obychai, obriady, predaniia, sueveriia i poeziia*. Moscow: Izd. M. Berezina, 1880.

Zaozerskii, N. "Chto est' pravoslavnyi prikhod i chem on dolzhen byt'?" *Bogoslovskii vestnik* (October 1911): 523–62.

Zelenin, D. K. *Vostochnoslavianskaia etnografiia*. Berlin and Leipzig, 1927; Moscow: Nauka, 1991.

Zhitie vo sviatykh ottsa nashego Mitrofana, v skhimonasekh Makariia, pervogo episkopa Voronezhskogo i novoiavlennogo chudotvortsa i skazanie o obretenii i otkrytii chestnykh ego moshchei i o blagodatnykh pri tom znameniiakh i chudesnykh istseleniiakh (izvlecheno iz aktov i donosenii imeiushchiikhsia v Sviateishem Sinode). Moscow: Sinodal'naia tip., 1838.

Zhurnaly Pavlovskogo uezdnogo zemskogo sobraniia ocherednoi sessii 1902 g. Pavlovsk: Tip. I. P. Ivanova, 1903.

Zhurnaly i protokoly zasedanii Vysochaishe uchrezhdennogo predsobornogo prisutstviia. St. Petersburg: Sinodal'naia tip., 1906–1907.

Secondary Sources

Afanas'ev, Iu. N. *Sud'by rossiiskogo krest'ianstva*. Moscow: Rossiisk. gos. gumanit. un-t., 1995.

Akin'shin, A. N. "Tragediia kraevedov (Po sledam Arkhiva KGB)." In R. V. Andreeva, ed., *Russkaia provintsiia. Zapiski kraevedov*, 220–35. Voronezh: Tsentral'no-chernozemnoe knizhnoe izd-vo, 1992.

Anashenko, D., V. Mandrykin, and D. Savel'ev, eds. *Voronezhskie "chudotvortsy." Sbornik statei*. Voronezh: Kommuna, 1929.

Anderson, Benedict. *Imagined Communities: Reflections on the Origin and Spread of Nationalism*. Rev. ed. London: Verson, 1991.

Anfimov, A. M., and P. N. Zyrianov. "Nekotorye cherty evoliutsii russkoi krest'ianskoi obshchiny v poreformennyi period (1861–1914 gg.)." *Istoriia SSSR*, no. 4 (1980): 26–41.

Antiukhin, G. V. *Ocherki istorii pechati Voronezhskogo kraia*. Voronezh: Izd-vo Voronezhskogo universiteta, 1973.

Badone, Ellen, ed. *Religious Orthodoxy and Popular Faith in European Society*. Princeton: Princeton University Press, 1991.

Baehr, Stephen Lessing. *The Paradise Myth in Eighteenth-Century Russia: Utopian Patterns in Early Secular Russian Literature and Culture*. Stanford, CA: Stanford University Press, 1991.

Barkan, Elazar, and Ronald Bush, eds. *Prehistories of the Future: The Primitivist Project and the Culture of Modernism*. Stanford, CA: Stanford University Press, 1995.

Bartlett, Roger, ed. *Land Commune and Peasant Community in Russia: Communal Forms in Imperial and Early Soviet Society*. Studies in Russia and East Europe. London: Macmillan, 1990.

Batalden, Stephen K., ed. *Seeking God: The Recovery of Religious Identity in Orthodox Russia, Ukraine, and Georgia*. DeKalb: Northern Illinois Press, 1993.

———. "Colportage and the Distribution of the Holy Scripture in Late Imperial Russia." In Robert P. Hughes and Irina Paperno, eds., *Christianity and the Eastern Slavs*. Vol. 2, *Russian Culture in Modern Times*, 83–92. Berkeley: University of California Press, 1994.

Beckford, James S. *Religion and Advanced Industrial Society*. London: Unwin Hyman, 1989.

Bernshtam, T. A. "Svadebnyi plach v obriadovoi kul'ture vostochnykh slavian (XIX–nachalo XX v.)." In T. A. Bernshtam and K. D. Chistov, eds., *Russkii sever: Problemy etnokul'turnoi istorii, etnografii, fol'kloristiki*, 82–100. Leningrad: Izd. Nauka, 1986.

———. *Molodezh' v obriadovoi zhizni russkoi obshchiny XIX–nachala XX v.: Polovozrastnoi aspekt traditsionnoi kul'tury*. Leningrad: Nauka 1988.

———. *Molodost' v simvolizme perekhodnykh obriadov vostochnykh slavian: uchenie i opyt Tserkvi v narodnom khristianstve*. St. Petersburg: Peterburgskoe Vostokovedenie, 2000.

Bloom, William. *Personal Identity, National Identity, and International Relations*. Edited by Stephen Smith. Cambridge Studies in International Relations, no. 9. Cambridge: Cambridge University Press, 1990.

Blumenfeld-Kosinski, Renate, and Timea Szell, eds. *Images of Sainthood in Medieval Europe*. Ithaca, NY: Cornell University Press, 1991.

Bohac, Rodney D. "The Mir and the Military Draft." *SR* 47, no. 4 (1988): 652–66.

Bossy, John. *Christianity in the West, 1400–1700*. Oxford: Oxford University Press, 1985.

Bradley, Joseph. *Muzhik and Muscovite: Urbanization in Late Imperial Russia*. Berkeley: University of California Press, 1985.

Breuilly, *Nationalism and the State*. 2d ed. Chicago: University of Chicago Press, 1994.

Briggs, Robin. *Witches and Neighbors: The Social and Cultural Context of European Witchcraft*. New York: Penguin Books, 1998.

Brooks, Jeffrey. "The Zemstvo and the Education of the People." In Terence Emmons and Wayne S. Vucinich, eds., *The Zemstvo in Russia: An Experiment in Local Self-Government*, 243–78. Cambridge: Cambridge University Press, 1982.

———. *When Russia Learned to Read: Literacy and Popular Literature, 1861–1917*. Princeton: Princeton University Press, 1985.

Brower, Daniel R. "Russian Roads to Mecca: Religious Tolerance and Muslim Pilgrimage in the Russian Empire." *SR* 55, no. 3 (1996): 566–84.

Brown, Peter. *The Cult of Saints: Its Rise and Function in Latin Christianity*. Chicago: University of Chicago Press, 1981.

Bruce, S. ed. *Religion and Modernization: Historians and Sociologists Debate the Secularization Thesis*. Oxford: Oxford University Press, 1992.

Buganov, A. V. *Russkaia istoriia v pamiati krest'ian XIX veka i natsional'noe samosoznanie*. Moscow: Rossiiskaia Akademiia Nauk, 1992.

Bulgakov, Sergius. *The Orthodox Church*. Translation revised by Lydia Kesich, with a foreword by Thomas Hopko. Crestwood, NY: St. Vladimir's Seminary Press, 1988.

Burds, Jeffrey. *Peasant Dreams and Market Politics: Labor Migration and the Russian Village, 1861–1905.* Pittsburgh, PA: University of Pittsburg Press, 1998.

Bushkovitch, Paul. *Religion and Society in Russia: The Sixteenth and Seventeenth Centuries.* New York: Oxford University Press, 1992.

Cabasilas, Nicholas. *A Commentary on the Divine Liturgy.* Translated by J. M. Hussey and P. A. McNulty, with an introduction by R. M. French. Crestwood, NY: St. Vladimir's Seminary Press, 1977.

Certeau, Michel de. *The Writing of History.* Trans. Tom Conley. New York: Columbia University Press, 1988.

Chicherov, V. I. *Zimnii period russkogo narodnogo zemledel'cheskogo kalendaria XVI–XIX vekov: Ocherki po istorii narodnykh verovanii.* Trudy instituta etnografii im. N. N. Miklukho-Maklaia, n.s., vol. 40. Moscow: Izd. AN SSSR, 1957.

Chistov, K. V. "Traditsiia i variativnost'." *SE,* no. 2 (1983): 14–22.

Christian, William. *Local Religion in Sixteenth-Century Spain.* Princeton: Princeton University Press, 1981.

Chulos, Chris J. "Peasant Religion in Post-Emancipation Russia: Voronezh Province, 1880–1917." Ph.D. diss., University of Chicago, 1994.

———. "Peasant Perspectives of Clerical Debauchery in Post-Emancipation Russia." *Studia Slavica Finlandensia* 12 (1995): 33–53.

———. "Orthodoxy and Nationality Among Peasants in Late Nineteenth-Century Russia." *Idäntutkimus/Finnish Journal of East European Studies* 1 (1995): 48–56.

———. "The Collective Consciousness of the Russian Peasantry." *Finnish Review of East European Studies/Idäntutkimus,* no. 1 (1995): 70–73.

———. "Myths of the Pious or Pagan Peasant in Post-Emancipation Central Russia (Voronezh Province)." *RH* 22, no. 2 (1995): 181–216.

———. "Peasants' Attempts to Reopen their Church, 1929–1936." *RH* 24, nos. 1–2 (spring–summer 1997): 203–13.

———. "Revolution and Grass-Roots Re-evaluations of Russian Orthodoxy, 1905–1907." In Judith Pallot, ed., *Transforming Peasants: Society, State and Peasants, 1861–1931,* 90–112. Selected proceedings of the V ICCEES Conferences, Warsaw, 1995, ed. Ron Hill. London: Macmillan, 1998.

———. "Religious and Secular Aspects of Pilgrimage in Modern Russia." *Byzantium and the North/Acta Byzantina Fennica,* no. 9 (1997–1998): 21–58.

———. "Friends and Foes in the Late Imperial Russian Village and the Problem of 'Otherness.'" Paper presented at the annual meeting of the American Association for the Advancement of Slavic Studies, Boca Raton, FL, September 1998.

———. "'A Place without Taverns': Village Space in the Afterlife." In Jeremy Smith, ed., *Beyond the Limits: The Concept of Space in Russian History and Culture,* 191–99. Studia Historica, no. 62. Helsinki: Finnish Historical Society, 1999.

———. "The End of Cultural 'Survivals' *(perezhitki):* Remembering and Forgetting Russian Peasant Religious Traditions." *Studia Slavica Finlandensia* 17 (2000): 190–207.

———. "Orthodox Identity at Russian Holy Places." In Chris J. Chulos and Timo Piirainen, eds., *National Identity in Contemporary Russia,* 28–50. Aldershot, England: Ashgate Press, 2000.

———. "New Religious Movements in Russia from a Historical Perspective." In Jeffrey Kaplan, ed., *Oppositional Religions in Finland,* 341–45. Helsinki: Finnish Historical Society, 2000.

———. "Festivals and Collective Memory in Imperial Russia." Paper presented at the Sixth International Council for Central and East European Studies Congress, Tampere, Finland, August 2000.

———. "Stories of the Empire: Myth, Ethnography, and Village Origin Legends in Nineteenth-Century Russia." In Chris J. Chulos and Johannes Remy, eds., *Imperial and National Identities in Pre-Revolutionary, Soviet, and Post-Soviet Russia*, 115–143. Studia Historica, no. 66. Helsinki: Finnish Literature Society, 2002.

Clay, Catherine B. "Russian Ethnographers in the Service of Empire, 1856–1862." *SR* 54, no. 1 (1995): 45–61.

Clay, J. Eugene. "The Theological Origins of the Christ-Faith *(Khristovshchina).*" *RH* 15, no. 1 (1988): 21–41.

———. "Russian Peasant Religion and Its Repression: The Christ-Faith (Khristovshchina) and the Origins of the 'Flagellant' Myth, 1666–1837." Ph.D. diss., University of Chicago, 1989.

———. "Literary Images of the Russian 'Flagellants,' 1861–1905." *RH* 24, no. 4 (1997): 425–39.

———. "Russian Israel." *Communal Societies* 18 (1998): 81–91.

Clements, Barbara Evans, Barbara Alpern Engel, and Christine D. Worobec, eds. *Russia's Women: Accommodation, Resistance, Transformation.* Berkeley: University of California Press, 1991.

Coleman, Simon, and John Elsner. *Pilgrimage Past and Present: Sacred Travel and Sacred Space in the World Religions.* London: British Museum Press, 1995.

Confino, Michael. "Present Events and the Representation of the Past: Some Current Problems in Russian Historical Writing." *Cahiers du Monde russe* 35, no. 4 (1994): 839–68.

Cooper, Frederick. "Conflict and Connection: Rethinking Colonial African History." *AHR* 99, no. 5 (1994): 1516–45.

Cracraft, James. *The Church Reform of Peter the Great.* London: Macmillan, 1971.

Crisp, Olga. *Studies in the Russian Economy Before 1914.* London: Macmillan, 1976.

———. "Labor and Industrialization in Russia." *The Cambridge Economic History of Europe*, 7:308–415. Cambridge: Cambridge University Press, 1978.

Curtiss, John Shelton. *Church and State in Russia: The Last Years of the Empire, 1900–1917.* New York: Columbia University Press, 1940.

Davis, Natalie Zemon. "Some Tasks and Themes in the Study of Popular Religion." In *The Pursuit of Holiness in Late Medieval Renaissance Religion.* Papers from the University of Michigan Conference, ed. Heiko A. Oberman, 10:307–336. Studies in Medieval and Reformation Thought. Leiden, Netherlands: E. J. Brill, 1974.

———. *The Return of Martin Guerre.* Cambridge: Harvard University Press, 1983.

———. *Fiction in the Archives: Pardon Tales and Their Tellers in Sixteenth-Century France.* Stanford, CA: Stanford University Press, 1987.

Devlin, Judith. *The Superstitious Mind: French Peasants and the Supernatural in the Nineteenth Century.* New Haven, CT: Yale University Press, 1987.

Dixon, Simon. "How Holy Was Holy Russia? Rediscovering Russian Religion." In Geoffrey Hosking and Robert Service, eds., *Reinterpreting Russia*, 21–39. London: Edward Arnold, 1999.

Dobbelaere, Karel. "Secularization: A Multi-Dimensional Concept." *Current Sociology* 29 (1981).

———. "Some Trends in European Sociology of Religion: The Secularization Debate." *Sociological Analysis* 48 (1987): 107–37.

Dunaev, V. N. "Vystuplenie krest'ian Voronezhskoi gubernii protiv reaktsionnykh deistvii dukhovenstva (mart-oktiabr' 1917 g.)." *Sbornik rabot aspirantov Voronezhskogo gosudarstvennogo universiteta,* no. 1 (1965): 143–48.

———. "Taktika Pravoslavnykh tserkovnikov voronezhskoi i sosednikh gubernii posle okonchaniia grazhdanskoi voiny." In V. P. Zagorovskii, ed., *IIVK,* 5:15–26. Voronezh: Izd-vo Voronezhskogo universiteta, 1975.

Eade, John, and Michael J. Snallow, eds. *Contesting the Sacred: The Anthropology of Christian Pilgrimage.* London and New York: Routledge, 1991.

Economakis, Evel G. *From Peasant to Petersburger.* London: Macmillan, 1998.

Eklof, Ben. *Russian Peasant Schools: Officialdom, Village Culture, and Popular Pedagogy, 1861–1914.* Berkeley: University of California Press, 1986.

Eklof, Ben, John Bushnell, and Larissa Zakharova, eds. *Russia's Great Reforms, 1855–1881.* Bloomington: Indiana University Press, 1994.

Eliade, Mircea. *The Sacred and the Profane: The Nature of Religion.* Trans. Willard R. Trask. New York: Harcourt Brace Jovanovich, Harvest Books, 1959.

———. *The Myth of the Eternal Return, or Cosmos and History.* Trans. Willard R. Trask. Bollingen Series, no. 46. Princeton: Princeton University Press, 1954; Princeton/Bollingen Paperbacks, 1991.

———. *Images and Symbols: Studies in Religious Symbolism.* Trans. Philip Mairet. Princeton: Princeton University Press, 1991.

Emeliakh, L. I. *Antiklerikal'noe dvizhenie krest'ian v period pervoi russkoi revoliutsii.* Moscow and Leningrad: Izd-vo Nauka, 1965.

Emmons, Terence, and Wayne S. Vucinich, eds. *The Zemstvo in Russia: An Experiment in Local Self-Government.* Cambridge: Cambridge University Press, 1982.

Engel, Barbara Alpern. "The Woman's Side: Male Out-Migration and the Family Economy in Kostroma Province." *SR* 45, no. 2 (summer 1986): 257–71.

———. "Peasant Morality and Pre-marital Relations in Late Nineteenth-Century Russia." *Journal of Social History* 23, no. 4 (1990): 695–714.

———. *Between the Fields and the City: Women, Work, and Family in Russia, 1861–1914.* Cambridge: Cambridge University Press, 1995.

Engelstein, Laura. *The Keys to Happiness: Sex and the Search for Modernity in Fin-de-Siècle Russia.* Ithaca, NY: Cornell University Press, 1992.

———. "Revolution and the Theater of Public Life in Imperial Russia." In Isser Woloch, ed., *Revolution and the Meanings of Freedom in the Nineteenth Century,* 353–57. Stanford, CA: Stanford University Press, 1996.

———. "Rebels of the Soul: Peasant Self-Fashioning in a Religious Key." *RH* 22, nos. 1–4 (1996): 197–213.

———. "Paradigms, Pathologies, and Other Clues to Russian Spiritual Culture: Some Post-Soviet Thoughts." *SR* 57, no. 4 (winter 1998): 864–77.

———. *Castration and the Heavenly Kingdom: A Russian Folktale.* Ithaca, NY: Cornell University Press, 1999.

Engelstein, Laura, and Stephanie Sandler, eds. *Self and Story in Russian History.* Ithaca, NY: Cornell University Press, 2000.

Etkind, Aleksandr. *Khlyst: Sekty, literatura i revoliutsiia.* Moscow: Novoe literaturnoe obozrenie, 1998.

Evtuhov, Catherine. "The Church in the Russian Revolution: Arguments for and against Restoring the Patriarchate at the Church Council of 1917–1918." *SR* 50, no. 3 (1991): 497–511.

———. *The Cross and the Sickle: Sergei Bulgakov and the Fate of Russian Religious*

Philosophy, 1890–1920. Ithaca, NY: Cornell University Press, 1997.

Farnsworth, Beatrice. "The Litigious Daughter-in-Law: Family Relations in Rural Russia in the Second Half of the Nineteenth Century." *SR* 45, no. 1 (spring 1986): 49–64.

Farnsworth, Beatrice, and Lynne Viola, eds. *Russian Peasant Women.* New York: Oxford University Press, 1992.

Field, Daniel. *Rebels in the Name of the Tsar.* Boston: Unwin Hyman, 1989.

Figes, Orlando. *A People's Tragedy: The Russian Revolution, 1891–1924.* London: Jonathan Cape, 1996.

———. "The Russian Revolution of 1917 and Its Language in the Village." *RR* 56, no. 3 (July 1997): 323–45.

Figes, Orlando, and Boris Kolonitskii. *Interpreting the Russian Revolution: The Language and Symbols of 1917.* New Haven, CT: Yale University Press, 1999.

Firsov, B. M. "Teoreticheskie vzgliady V. N. Tenisheva." *SE,* no. 3 (1988): 14–27.

———. "'Krest'ianskaia' programma V. N. Tenisheva i nekotorye rezul'taty ee realizatsii." *SE,* no. 4 (1988): 38–49.

Firsov, B. M., and I. G. Kiseleva, comps. *Byt velikorusskikh krest'ian-zemlepashchtsev. Opisanie materialov etnograficheskogo biuro kniazia V. N. Tenisheva. (Na primere Vladimirskoi gubernii.)* St.Petersburg: Izd-vo Evropeiskogo Doma, 1993.

Firsov, S. L. *Pravoslavnaia Tserkov' i gosudarstvo v poslednee desiatiletie sushchestvovaniia samoderzhaviia v Rossii.* St. Petersburg: Izd-vo Russkogo Khristianskogo gumanitarnogo universiteta, 1996.

Fitzpatrick, Sheila. *Stalin's Peasants: Resistance and Survival in the Russian Village after Collectivization.* New York: Oxford University Press, 1994.

———. "Editor's Introduction: Petitions and Denunciations in Russian and Soviet History." *RH* 24, nos. 1–2 (1997): 1–9.

Frank, Stephen P. "Popular Justice, Community and Culture among the Russian Peasantry, 1870–1900." *RR* 46, no. 3 (1987): 239–65.

———. "Confronting the Domestic Other: Rural Popular Culture and Its Enemies in Fin-de-Siècle Russia." In Frank and Steinberg, eds., *Cultures in Flux: Lower Class Values, Practices, and Resistance in Late Imperial Russia,* 75–107. Princeton: Princeton University Press, 1994.

———. *Crime, Cultural Conflict, and Justice in Rural Russia, 1856–1914.* Studies on the History of Society and Culture, no. 31. Berkeley: University of California Press, 1999.

Frank, Stephen P., and Mark D. Steinberg, eds. *Cultures in Flux: Lower-Class Values, Practices, and Resistance in Late Imperial Russia.* Princeton: Princeton University Press, 1994.

Freeze, Gregory L. "The Disintegration of Traditional Parish Communities: The Parish in Eighteenth-Century Russia." *JMH* 48, no. 3 (July 1976): 32–50.

———. "A Case of Stunted Anticlericalism: Clergy and Society in Imperial Russia." *European Studies Review* 13, no. 2 (April 1983): 177–200.

———. *The Parish Clergy in Nineteenth-Century Russia: Crisis, Reform, Counter-Reform.* Princeton: Princeton University Press, 1983.

———. "Handmaiden of the State? The Orthodox Church in Imperial Russia Reconsidered." *Journal of Ecclesiastical History* 36 (1985): 82–102.

———. "The Soslovie (Social) Estate Paradigm and Russian Social History." *American Historical Review* 91, no. 1 (1986): 11–36.

———. "The Rechristianization of Russia: The Church and Popular Religion, 1750–1850." *Studia Slavica Finlandensia* 7 (1990): 101–36.

———. "Tserkov', religiia i politicheskaia kul'tura na zakate staroi Rossii." *Istoriia SSSR*, no. 2 (1991): 107–19.

———. "Subversive Piety: Religion and the Political Crisis in Late Imperial Russia." *JMH* 68 (1996): 308–50.

———. "Church Politics in Late Imperial Russia: Crisis and Radicalization of the Clergy." In Anna Geifman, ed., *Russia under the Last Tsar: Opposition and Subversion, 1894–1917*, 269–97. Oxford: Blackwell, 1999.

Frieden, Nancy Mandelker. "Child Care: Medical Reform in a Traditionalist Culture." In David L. Ransel, ed., *The Family in Imperial Russia: New Lines of Historical Research*, 236–59. Urbana: University of Illinois Press, 1978.

———. *Russian Physicians in an Era of Reform and Revolution, 1856–1905*. Princeton: Princeton University Press, 1981.

Frierson, Cathy A. "*Razdel:* The Peasant Family Divided." *RR* 46, no. 1 (1987): 35–51.

———. "Crime and Punishment in the Russian Village: Rural Concepts of Criminality at the End of the Nineteenth Century." *SR* 46, no. 1 (1987): 55–69.

———. *Peasant Icons: Representations of Rural People in Late-Nineteenth-Century Russia*. New York: Oxford University Press, 1993.

———. "'I Must Always Answer to the Law. . . .' Rules and Responses in the Reformed *Volost'* Court." *SEER* 75, no. 2 (April 1997): 308–34.

Geertz, Clifford. *The Interpretation of Cultures: Selected Essays*. New York: Basic Books, 1973.

Geldern, James von. *Bolshevik Festivals, 1917–1920*. Studies on the History of Society and Culture. Ed. Victoria E. Bonnell and Lynn Hunt. Berkeley: University of California Press, 1993.

———. "Life In-Between: Migration and Popular Culture in Late Imperial Russia." *RR* 55, no. 3 (1996): 365–83.

Gellner, Ernest. *Nations and Nationalism: New Perspectives on the Past*. Ed. R. I. Moore. Oxford: Basil Blackwell, 1983.

Ginzburg, Carlo. *The Cheese and the Worms: The Cosmos of a Sixteenth-Century Miller*. Trans. John Tedeschi and Anne Tedeschi. Baltimore: Johns Hopkins University Press, 1982.

———. *The Night Battles: Witchcraft and Agrarian Cults in the Sixteenth and Seventeenth Centuries*. Trans. John Tedeschi and Anne Tedeschi. Baltimore: Johns Hopkins University Press, 1983; Reprint, New York: Penguin Books, 1985.

Glasner, Peter E. *The Sociology of Secularization: A Critique of a Concept*. London: Routledge and K. Paul, 1977.

Glickman, Rose L. *Russian Factory Women: Workplace and Society, 1880–1914*. Berkeley: University of California Press, 1984.

———. "Women and the Peasant Commune." In Roger Bartlett, ed., *Land Commune*, 321–38. London: Macmillan, 1990.

———. "The Peasant Woman as Healer." In Barbara Evans Clements, Barbara Alpern Engel, and Christine D. Worobec, eds., *Russia's Women: Accommodation, Resistance, Transformation*, 148–62. Berkeley: University of California Press, 1991.

———. "'Unusual Circumstances' in the Peasant Village." *RH* 23, nos. 1–4 (1996): 215–29.

Goscilo, Helena, and Beth Holmgren, eds. *Russia. Women. Culture*. Bloomington: Indiana University Press, 1996.

Gothóni, René. "Pilgrimage to Mount Athos as the Habit of the Laity." *Byzantium and the North/Acta Byzantina Fennica* 7 (1995): 48–53.

Grinkova, N. P. "Obriad 'vozhdenie rusalki' v sele V. Vereika Voronezhskoi oblasti." *SE*, no. 1 (1947).

Gromyko, M. M. "Obychai pomochei u Russkikh krest'ian v XIX v." *SE*, no. 4 (1981): 21–38; and no. 5 (1981): 32–46.

———. *Traditsionnye normy povedeniia i formy obshcheniia russkikh krest'ian XIX v.* Moscow: Nauka, 1986.

———. "Sem'ia i obshchina v traditsionnoi dukhovnoi kul'ture russkikh krest'ian XVIII–XIX vv." In Gromyko and Litova, eds., *Russkie,* 7–24.

———. *Mir russkoi derevni.* Moscow: Molodaia Gvardiia, 1991.

———. "O narodnom blagochestii u russkikh XIX veka." In M. M. Gromyko, ed., *Pravoslavie i russkaia narodnaia kul'tura,* 1:5–30. Moscow: n.p., 1994.

Gromyko, M. M., and T. A. Listova, eds. *Russkie: Semeinyi i obshchestvennyi byt.* Moscow: Nauka, 1989.

Gromyko, M. M., S. V. Kuznetsov, and A. V. Buganov. "Pravoslavie v russkoi narodnoi kul'ture: napravlenie issledovanii." *EO*, no. 6 (1993): 60–84.

Gromyko, M. M., ed. *Pravoslavie i russkaia narodnaia kul'tura.* Nauchnyi sbornik 1. Moscow: Koordinatsionno-metodicheskii tsentr prikladnoi etnografii In-ta etnologii i antropologii RAN, 1994.

Halbwachs, Maurice. *On Collective Memory.* Trans. Lewis A. Coser. Chicago: University of Chicago Press, 1992,

Hammond, Phillip, ed. *The Sacred in a Secular Age.* Berkeley and Los Angeles: University of California Press, 1985.

Hastrup, Kirsten, ed. *Other Histories.* London: Routledge, 1992.

Hellberg-Hirn, Elena. *Soil and Soul: The Symbolic World of Russian.* Aldershot, England: Ashgate, 1998.

Hellie, Richard. *Enserfment and Military Change in Muscovy.* Chicago: University of Chicago Press, 1971.

Heretz, Leonid. "The Practice and Significance of Fasting in Russian Peasant Culture at the Turn of the Century." In Musya Glants and Joyce Toomre, eds., *Food in Russian History and Culture.* Bloomington: Indiana University Press, 1997.

Herlihy, Patricia. "Joy of the Rus': Rites and Rituals of Russian Drinking." *RR* 50, no. 2 (1991).

Herrlinger, Kimberly Page. "Class, Piety, and Politics: Workers, Orthodoxy, and the Problem of Religious Identity in Russia, 1881–1914." Ph.D. diss., University of California, Berkeley, 1996.

Hilton, Alison. *Russian Folk Art.* Bloomington: Indiana University Press, 1995.

Hobsbawm, Eric, and Terence Ranger, eds. *The Invention of Tradition.* Cambridge: Cambridge University Press, Canto, 1992.

Hoch, Stephen L. *Serfdom and Social Control in Russia: Petrovskoe, a Village in Tambov.* Chicago: University of Chicago Press, 1986.

Holmgren, Beth. "Gendering the Icon: Marketing Women Writers in Fin-de-Siècle Russia." In Helena Goscilo and Beth Holmgren, eds., *Russia. Women. Culture,* 321–46. Bloomington: Indiana University Press, 1996.

Hosking, Geoffrey. *Russia, People and Empire, 1552–1917.* London: HarperCollins, 1997.

Hosking, Geoffrey, and George Schöpflin, eds. *Myths and Nationhood.* London: Routledge, 1997.

Hroch, Mirslav. *Social Preconditions of National Revival in Europe.* Cambridge: Cambridge University Press, 1985.

Hubbs, Joanna. *Mother Russia: The Feminine Myth in Russian Culture*. Bloomington: Indiana University Press, 1988.

Hughes, Robert P., and Irina Paperno, eds. *Christianity and the Eastern Slavs*. Vol. 2, *Russian Culture in Modern Times*. Berkeley: University of California Press, 1994.

Hutchinson, John F. "'Who Killed Cock Robin?' An Inquiry into the Death of Zemstvo Medicine." In Susan Gross Solomon and John F. Hutchinson, eds., *Health and Society in Revolutionary Russia*, 3–26. Bloomington: Indiana University Press, 1990.

Hutton, Ronald. *The Stations of the Sun: A History of the Ritual Year in Britain*. Oxford: Oxford University Press, 1996.

"Istinno-pravoslavnye v Voronezhskoi eparkhii: Publikatsiia M. V. Shkarovskogo." *Minuvshee: Istoricheskii al'manakh* 19 (1996): 320–56.

Ivanits, Linda J. *Russian Folk Belief*. Armonk, NY: Sharpe, 1989.

Iz istorii voronezhskogo kraia: Sbornik statei. 7 vols. Voronezh: Izd-vo Voronezhskogo universiteta, 1961–1977; Voronezh: Regional'nyi tsentr "Uchebnaia literatura," 1998.

Johnson, Robert E. *Peasant and Proletarian: The Working Class of Moscow in the Late Nineteenth Century*. New Brunswick, NJ: Rutgers University Press, 1979.

Kääriäinen, Kimmo, and D. E. Furman. "Veruiushchie, ateisty i prochie (Evoliutsiia rossiiskoi religioznosti)." *Voprosy filosofii*, no. 6 (1997): 35–52.

Kaiser, Robert J. *The Geography of Nationalism in Russia and the USSR*. Princeton: Princeton University Press, 1994.

Kartashev, A. V. *Ocherki po istorii Russkoi tserkvi*. Vol. 1. Moscow: Terra, 1993.

Kharkhordin, Oleg. *The Collective and the Individual in Russia: A Study of Practices*. Berkeley: University of California Press, 1999.

Kilpeläinen, Hannu. "Pilgrimage in Karelia: The Case of Valamo in the 1930s." *Byzantium and the North/Acta Byzantina Fennica* 7 (1995).

Kingston-Mann, Esther. "Breaking the Silence: An Introduction." In Esther Kingston-Mann and Timothy Mixter, eds., *Peasant Economy, Culture, and Politics of European Russia, 1800–1921*, 3–19. Princeton: Princeton University Press, 1991.

Kingston-Mann, Esther, and Timothy Mixter, eds. *Peasant Economy, Culture, and Politics of European Russia, 1800–1921*. With the editorial assistance of Jeffrey Burds. Princeton: Princeton University Press, 1991.

Kizenko, Nadieszda. "Ioann of Kronstadt and the Reception of Sanctity, 1850–1988." *RR* 57, no. 3 (1998): 325–44.

———. *A Prodigal Saint: Father John of Kronstadt and the Russian People*. University Park: Pennsylvania State University Press, 2000.

Klibanov, A. I. *Istoriia religioznogo sektantstva v Rossiia (60-e gody XIX v.–1917 g.)*. Moscow: Nauka, 1965.

Kotsonis, Yanni. *Making Peasants Backward: Agricultural Cooperatives and the Agrarian Question in Russia, 1861–1914*. Houndmills, Basingstoke, England: Macmillan, 1999.

Kremleva, A. "Ob evoliutsii nekotorykh arkhaichnykh obychaev u russkikh." In M. M. Gromyko and T. A. Litova, eds., *Russkie: Semeinyi i obshchestvennyi byt*, 248–64. Moscow: Nauka, 1989.

Kriukova, T. A. "'Vozhdenie rusalki' v sele Os'kine Voronezhskoi oblasti." *SE*, no. 1 (1947): 185–92.

Krukones, James H. "To the People: The Russian Government and the Newspaper *Sel'skii vestnik* ('Village Herald'), 1881–1917." Ph.D. diss., University of Wisconsin, 1983.

Kselman, Thomas A. *Death and the Afterlife in Modern France*. Princeton: Princeton University Press, 1993.

——, ed. *Belief in History: Innovative Approaches to European and American Religion*. Notre Dame, IN: University of Notre Dame Press, 1991.

Kurilo, O. V. "Tserkovnye prazdniki liuteranskogo naseleniia Rossii (XIX–XX vv.)." *EO*, no. 2 (1997): 99–111.

Lasunskii, O. G. A. M. *Putintsev—istorik literatury, fol'klorist i etnograf. Kratkii ocherk deiatel'nosti i bibliografii trudov*. Voronezh: Izd-vo Voronezhskogo universiteta, 1969.

Laue, Theodore H. von. "Russian Labor Between Field and Factory, 1892–1903." *California Slavic Studies* 3 (1964): 33–65.

Lazutin, S. G. *Voprosy poetiki literatury i fol'klora*. Voronezh: Izd. Voronezhskogo universiteta, 1977.

Lebedeva, A. A. "Znachenie poiasa i polotentsa v russkikh semeino-bytovykh obychaiakh i obriadakh XIX–XX vv." In M. M. Gromyko and T. A. Listova, eds., *Russkie: Semeinyi i obshchestvennyi byt*, 229–47. Moscow: Nauka, 1989.

Le Goff, Jacques. *The Birth of Purgatory*. Trans. Arthur Goldhammer. Chicago: University of Chicago Press, 1984.

Lehning, James R. *Peasant and French: Cultural Contact in Rural France during the Nineteenth Century*. Cambridge: Cambridge University Press, 1995.

Leont'eva, T. G. "Vera ili svoboda? Popy i liberaly v glazakh krest'ian v nachale XX v." In P. V. Volobuev, ed., *Revoliutsiia i chelovek. Sotsial'no-psikhologicheskii aspekt*, 92–114. Moscow: Institut Rossiiskoi istorii RAN, 1996.

——. "Byt, nravy i povedenie seminaristov v nachale XX veka." In P. V. Volobuev, ed., *Revoliutsiia i chelovek. Byt, nravy, povedenie, moral'*, 20–38. Moscow: Rossiiskaia Akademiia Nauk, 1997.

——. "Byt prikhodskogo pravoslavnogo dukhoventstva v poreformennoi Rossii (Po dnevnikovym zapisiam i memuaram)." *Iz arkhiva tverskikh istorikov*, 28–49. Tver', 1999.

Levin, Eve. "*Dvoeverie* and Popular Religion." In Stephen K. Batalden, ed., *Seeking God: The Recovery of Religious Identity in Orthodox Russia, Ukraine, and Georgia*, 31–52. DeKalb: Northern Illinois Press, 1993.

——. "Religious Revival: The History of Religion in the Post-Cold Era." *RR* 58, no. 1 (1999): vi–vii.

Levitt, Marcus C. *Russian Literary Politics and the Pushkin Celebration of 1880*. Ithaca, NY: Cornell University Press, 1989.

Lewin, Moshe. *The Making of the Soviet System: Essays in the Social History of Interwar Russia*. New York: Parthenon Books, 1985.

Linëva, E. E. *Velikorusskie pesni v narodnoi garmonizatsii*. St. Petersburg: Imperatorskoi Akademii Nauk, 1904–1909.

——. *The Peasant Songs of Great Russia as They Are in the Folk's Harmonization*. St. Petersburg: Imperial Academy of Sciences, 1905.

Listova, T. A. "Russkie obriady, obychai i pover'ia, sviazannye s povival'noi babkoi (vtoraia polovina XIX–20-e gody XX v.)." In M. M. Gromyko and T. A. Listova, eds., *Russkie: Semeinyi i obshchestvennyi byt*, 142–70. Moscow: Nauka, 1989.

Löwe, Heinz-Dietrich. "Differentiation in Russian Peasant Society: Causes and Trends, 1880–1905." In Roger Bartlett, ed., *Land Commune and Peasant Community in Russia: Communal Forms in Imperial and Early Soviet Society*, 165–95. Studies in Russia and East Europe. London: Macmillan, 1990.

Manchester, Laurie. "The Secularization of the Search for Salvation: The Self-fashioning of Orthodox Clergymen's Sons in Late Imperial Russia." *SR* 57, no. 1 (1998): 50–76.

Martin, David. *A General Theory of Secularization.* New York: Harper and Row, 1978.

(Maslov), Skhiarkhimandrit Ioann. *Sviatitel' Tikhon Zadonskii i ego uchenie o spasenii.* Moscow: Izdatel'skii otdel Moskovskogo Patriarkhata, "Mir Obshchestva," 1993.

McDaniel, Tim. *The Agony of the Russian Idea.* Princeton: Princeton University Press, 1996.

McReynolds, Louise. *The News Under Russia's Old Regime: The Development of a Mass-Circulation Press.* Princeton: Princeton University Press, 1991.

Meehan, Brenda. "Popular Piety, Local Initiative, and the Founding of Women's Religious Communities in Russia, 1764–1907." In Stephen K. Batalden, ed. *Seeking God: The Recovery of Religious Identity in Orthodox Russia, Ukraine, and Georgia,* 83–105. DeKalb: Northern Illinois University Press, 1993.

Meehan-Waters, Brenda. "The Authority of Holiness: Women Ascetics and Spiritual Elders in Nineteenth-Century Russia." In Geoffrey A. Hosking, ed., *Church, Nation and State in Russia and Ukraine.* London: Macmillan, in association with the School of Slavonic and East European Studies, University of London, 1991.

———. "To Save Oneself: Russian Peasant Women and the Development of Women's Religious Communities in Prerevolutionary Russia." In Beatrice Farnsworth and Lynne Viola, eds., *Russian Peasant Women,* 121–33. New York: Oxford University Press, 1992.

Mellon, Florencia E. "The Promise of Subaltern Studies: Perspectives from Latin American History." *AHR* 99, no. 5 (1994): 1491–1515.

Meyendorff, John. "Russian Bishops and Church Reform in 1905." In Robert L. Nichols and Theofanis George Stavrou, eds., *Russian Orthodoxy under the Old Regime,* 170–82. Minneapolis: University of Minnesota Press, 1978.

———. *Byzantine Theology: Historical Trends and Doctrinal Themes.* New York: Fordham University Press, 1979.

———. *Byzantium and the Rise of Russia: A Study of Byzantino-Russian Relations in the Fourteenth Century.* Crestwood, NY: St. Vladimir's Seminary Press, 1989.

Michels, Georg. "The Violent Old Belief: An Examination of Religious Dissent on the Karelian Frontier." *RH* 19, nos. 1–4 (1992): 203–29.

———. *At War with the Church: Religious Dissent in Seventeenth-Century Russia.* Stanford, CA: Stanford University Press 1999.

Miller, David B. "The Cult of Saint Sergius of Radonezh and Its Political Uses." *SR* 52, no. 4 (1993): 680–99.

Minenko, N. A. *Kul'tura russkikh krest'ian zaural'ia XVIII–pervaia polovina XIX v.* Moscow: Nauka, 1991.

Mironov, Boris. "The Russian Peasant Commune after the Reforms of the 1860s." *SR* 44, no. 3 (1985): 438–67.

———. *Russkii gorod v 1740–1860e gody.* Leningrad: Nauka, 1990.

Moon, David. *Russian Peasants and Tsarist Legislation on the Eve of Reform: Interaction between Peasants and Officialdom, 1825–1855.* Houndmills, Basingstoke, England: Macmillan, 1992.

———. "Peasants into Russian Citizens? A Comparative Perspective." *Revolutionary Russia* 9, no. 1 (1996): 43–81.

———. *The Russian Peasantry: The World the Peasants Made.* London: Addison Wesley Longman, 1999.

Muir, Edward. *Ritual in Early Modern Europe.* Cambridge: Cambridge University Press, 1997.

Muir, Edward, and Guido Ruggiero, eds. *Microhistory and the Lost Peoples of Europe.* Trans. Eren Branch. Baltimore: Johns Hopkins University Press, 1991.

Neuberger, Joan. *Hooliganism: Crime, Culture, and Politics in St. Petersburg, 1900–1914.* Berkeley: University of California Press, 1993.

Nolan, Mary Lee, and Sidney Nolan. *Christian Pilgrimage in Modern Western Europe.* Ed. Charles H. Long. Studies in Religion. Chapel Hill and London: University of North Carolina Press, 1989.

Nora, Pierre, ed. *Realms of Memory: The Construction of the French Past.* Vol. 1, *Conflicts and Divisions.* Ed. Pierre Nora, with a foreword by Lawrence D. Kritzman. Trans. Arthur Goldhammer. Paris: Editions Gallimard, 1992; New York: Columbia University Press, 1996.

Obelkevich, James, ed. *Religion and the People, 800–1700.* Shelby Cullom Davis Center for Historical Studies, Princeton University. Chapel Hill: University of North Carolina Press, 1979.

Ollila, Anne, ed. *Historical Perspectives on Memory.* Studia Historica, no. 61. Helsinki: Finnish Historical Society, 1999.

Pallot, Judith. *Land Reform in Russia, 1906–1917: Peasant Responses to Stolypin's Project of Rural Transformation.* Oxford: Clarendon Press, 1999.

Peris, Daniel. *Storming the Heavens: The Soviet League of the Militant Godless.* Ithaca, NY: Cornell University Press, 1998.

Phillips, Laura L. "Message in a Bottle: Working-Class Culture and the Struggle for Revolutionary Legitimacy, 1900–1929." *RR* 56, no. 1 (1997): 25–43.

Popkins, Gareth. "The Russian Peasant Volost' Court and Customary Law, 1861–1917." Ph.D. diss., University of Oxford, 1995.

——. "Code *versus* Custom? Reading Peasant *Volost'* Court Appeals, 1889–1917." *RR* 59, no. 3 (2000): 408–424.

——. "Peasant Experiences of the Late Tsarist State: Legal Appeals to the District Congresses and Provincial Boards, 1891–1917." *SEER* 78, no. 1 (January 2000): 1–25.

Prakash, Gyan. "Subaltern Studies in Postcolonial Criticism." *AHR* 99, no. 5 (December 1994): 1475–90.

Propp, V. *Russkie agrarnie prazdniki (opyt istoriko-etnograficheskogo issledovaniia).* Leningrad: Izd-vo Len. un-ta, 1963.

Pypin, A. N. *Istoriia russkoi etnografii.* Vol. 1, *Obshchii obzor izuchenii narodnosti i etnografiia velikorusskaia.* Moscow: Tip. M. M. Stasiulevicha, 1890.

Ramer, Samuel C. "Childbirth and Culture: Midwifery in the Nineteenth-Century Russian Countryside." In David L. Ransel, ed., *The Family in Imperial Russia: New Lines of Historical Research,* 218–35. Urbana: University of Illinois Press, 1978.

——. "Traditional Healers and Peasant Culture in Russia, 1861–1917." In Esther Kingston-Mann and Timothy Mixter, eds., *Peasant Economy, Culture, and Politics of European Russia, 1800–1921,* 207–32. Princeton: Princeton University Press, 1991.

——. "Childbirth and Culture: Midwifery in the Nineteenth-Century Russian Countryside." In Beatrice Farnsworth and Lynne Viola, eds., *Russian Peasant Women,* 107–120. New York: Oxford University Press, 1992.

Ransel, David L. "Problems in Measuring Illegitimacy in Prerevolutionary Russia." *Journal of Social History* 16, no. 2 (1982): 111–27.

——. "Infant-Care Cultures in the Russian Empire." In Barbara Evans Clements, Barbara Alpern Engel, and Christine D. Worobec, eds., *Russia's Women: Accommodation, Resistance, Transformation.* Berkeley: University of California Press, 1991.

Rashin, A. G. *Naselenie Rossii za 100 let (1811–1913 gg.): Statisticheskie ocherki.* Moscow: Gosudarstvennoe statisticheskoe izd-vo, 1956.

Redfield, Robert. *The Little Community: Peasant Society and Culture.* Chicago: University of Chicago Press, 1960.

Riasanovsky, Nicholas V. *The Image of Peter the Great in Russian History and Thought.* New York: Oxford University Press, 1985.

Rieber, Alfred J. "The Sedimentary Society." In Edith W. Clowes, Samuel D. Kassow, and James L. West, eds., *Between Tsar and People: Educated Society and the Quest for Public Identity in Late Imperial Russia,* 344–66. Princeton: Princeton University Press, 1991.

Robson, Roy R. "Liturgy and Community among Old Believers, 1905–1917." *SR* 52, no. 4 (1993): 713–24.

———. *Old Believers in Modern Russia.* DeKalb: Northern Illinois University Press, 1995.

Roosevelt, Priscilla. *Life on the Russian Country Estate: A Social and Cultural History.* New Haven, CT: Yale University Press, 1995.

Rumiantsev, N. *Pravoslavnye prazdniki ikh proiskhozhdenie i klassovaia sushchnost'.* Moscow: Gosudarstvennoe ntireligioznoe izd-vo, 1933.

Ruud, Charles A. *Russian Entrepreneur: Publisher Ivan Sytin of Moscow, 1851–1934.* Montreal: McGill–Queen's University Press, 1990.

Saunders, David. "What Makes a Nation a Nation? Ukrainians since 1600." *Ethnic Groups* 10, nos. 1–3 (1993): 101–24.

Scott, James C. *The Moral Economy of the Peasant.* New Haven, CT: Yale University Press, 1976.

Shanin, Teodor. *The Awkward Class: Political Sociology of Peasantry in a Developing Society, Russia 1910–1925.* Oxford: Clarendon Press, 1972.

Shevzov, Vera. "Popular Orthodoxy in Late Imperial Rural Russia." Ph.D. diss., Yale University, 1994.

———. "Chapels and the Ecclesial World of Prerevolutionary Russian Peasants." *SR* 55, no. 3 (1996): 585–613.

———. "Miracle-Working Icons, Laity, and Authority in the Russian Orthodox Church, 1861–1917." *RR* 58, no. 1 (1999): 26–48.

Shuliakovskii, E. G., ed. *Ocherki istorii Voronezhskogo kraia s drevneishikh vremen do velikoi oktiabr'skoi sotsialisticheskoi revoliutsii.* 2 vols. Voronezh: Izd-vo. Voronezhskogo universiteta, 1961–1967.

Slavianskaia mifologiia: Entsiklopedicheskii slovar'. Moscow: Ellis Lak, 1995.

Slocum, John W. "Who, and When, Were the *Inorodtsy?* The Evolution of the Category of 'Aliens' in Imperial Russia." *RR* 57, no. 2 (1998): 173–90.

Smith, Anthony. *Theories of Nationalism.* London: Duckworth, 1971.

Smolich, I. K. *Istoriia Russkoi tserkvi, 1700–1917.* Vol. 8, pt. 1, *Istoriia Russkoi tserkvi.* Moscow: Izd-vo Spaso-Preobrazhenskogo Valaamskogo monastyria, 1997.

Sokolova, V. K. *Vesenne-letnie kalendarnye obriady russkikh, ukraintsev i belorusov.* Moscow: Nauka, 1979.

Steinberg, Mark D. *Moral Communities: The Culture of Class Relations in the Russian Printing Industry, 1867–1907.* Berkeley: University of California Press, 1992.

———. "Workers on the Cross: Religious Imagination in the Writings of Russian Workers, 1910–1924." *RR* 53, no. 2 (1994): 213–39.

Stepanovna, Tat'tiana Eremina. *Bogoslovie v obraze.* Moscow: Vlados, 1994.

Stevens, Carol Belkin. *Soldiers on the Steppe: Army Reform and Social Change in Early*

Modern Russia. DeKalb: Northern Illinois University Press, 1995.

Stites, Richard. *The Women's Liberation Movement in Russia: Feminism, Nihilism, and Bolshevism, 1860–1930.* Princeton: Princeton University Press, 1978.

———. *Revolutionary Dreams: Utopian Vision and Experimental Life in the Russian Revolution.* New York: Oxford University Press, 1989.

———. *Russian Popular Culture: Entertainment and Society since 1900.* Cambridge: Cambridge University Press, 1992.

———. "Dusky Images of Tsarist Russia: Prerevolutionary Cinema." *RR* 53, no. 2 (1994): 285–95.

Stocking, George W., Jr. *The Ethnographer's Magic and Other Essays in the History of Anthropology.* Madison: University of Wisconsin Press, 1992.

Struve, A. "Bytovye osnovy religioznykh verovanii russkogo krest'ianstva." *Ateist,* no. 32 (1928): 1–57.

Taradin, I. *"Zolotoe Dno": Ekonimika, istoriia, kul'tura i byt volosti tsentral'no-chernozemnoi oblasti.* Voronezh: Izd. Voronezhskogo kraevedcheskogo obshchestva, 1928.

Theilmann, John M. "Medieval Pilgrims and the Origins of Tourism." *Journal of Popular Culture* 20, no. 4 (spring 1987).

Thomas, Keith. *Religion and the Decline of Magic: Studies in Popular Beliefs in Sixteenth- and Seventeenth-Century England.* New York: Scribner, 1971.

Thompson, Ewa M. *Understanding Russia: The Holy Fool in Russian Culture.* Lanham, MD, New York, London: University Press of America, 1987.

Titlinov, B. V. *Dukhovnaia shkola v Rossii v XIX stoletii.* 2 vols. With an introduction by G. Florovsky. Vil'na, 1908–1909; Reprint, Fannborough, England: Gregg International Publishers, 1970.

Tokarev, S. A. *Religioznye verovaniia vostochnoslavianskikh narodov XIX–nachala XX v.* Moscow: Izd. AN SSSR, 1957.

Tonkov, V. A., and O. G. Lasunskii, eds. *Ocherki literaturnoi zhizni Voronezhskogo kraia (XIX–nachalo XX v.).* Voronezh: Tsentral'no-chernozemnoe knizhnoe izd-vo, 1970.

Torienko, N. S. *Novye pravoslavnye sviatye.* Kiev: Izd-vo Ukraina, 1991.

Tsekhanskaia, K. V. "Ikona v russkom dome." *EO,* no. 4 (1997): 71–85.

Tsypin, Vladislav. *Istoriia Russkoi tserkvi 1917–1997.* Vol. 9, *Istoriia Russkoi tserkvi.* Moscow: Izd-vo Spaso-Preobrazhenskogo Valaamskogo monastyria, 1997.

Tul'tseva, L. A. "Chernichki." *Nauka i religiia,* no. 11 (1970): 80–82.

———. "Religioznye verovaniia i obriady russkikh krest'ian na rubezhe XIX i XX vekov. (Po materialam srednerusskoi polosy)." *SE,* no. 3 (1978): 31–46.

Turner, Victor. *Dramas, Fields, and Metaphors: Symbolic Action in Human Society.* Ed. Victor Turner. Symbol, Myth, and Ritual Series. Ithaca: Cornell University Press, 1974.

Turner, Victor, and Edith Turner. *Image and Pilgrimage in Christian Culture: Anthropological Perspectives.* Oxford: Basil Blackwell, 1978.

Verner, Andrew. "Discursive Strategies in the 1905 Revolution: Peasant Petitions from Vladimir Province." *RR* 54, no. 1 (1995): 65–90.

Vituhnovskaja, Marina. "Cultural and Political Reaction in Russian Karelia in 1906–1907: State Power, the Orthodox Church, and the 'Black Hundreds' against Karelian Nationalism." *Jahrbücher für Geschichte Osteuropas* 49, no. 1 (2001): 24–44.

Voronina, T. A. "Problemy etnograficheskogo izucheniia russkogo pravoslavnogo posta." *EO,* no. 4 (1997): 85–95.

Vroon, Ronald. "The Old Belief and Sectarianism as Cultural Models in the Silver

Age." In Robert P. Hughes and Irina Paperno, eds. *Christianity and the Eastern Slavs*, vol. 2, *Russian Culture in Modern Times*, 172–90. Berkeley: University of California Press, 1994.

Vucinich, Alexander. *Science in Russian Culture*. Stanford, CA: Stanford University Press, 1970.

———. *Social Thought in Tsarist Russia*. Chicago: University of Chicago Press, 1976.

Weber, Eugen. *Peasants into Frenchmen: The Modernization of Rural France, 1870–1914*. Stanford, CA: Stanford University Press, 1976.

Weber, Max. *The Protestant Ethic and the Spirit of Capitalism*. 2d ed. Trans. Talcott Parsons. London: George Allen and Unwin, 1948.

Werth, Paul. "Baptism, Authority, and the Problem of *Zakonnost'* in Orenburg Diocese: The Induction of over Eight Hundred 'Pagans' into the Christian Faith." *SR* 56, no. 3 (1997): 456–80.

Wigzell, Faith. *Reading Russian Fortunes: Print Culture, Gender and Divination in Russia from 1765*. Cambridge: Cambridge University Press, 1998.

Wilbur, Elvira M. "Peasant Poverty in Theory and Practice: A View from Russia's 'Impoverished Center' at the End of the Nineteenth Century." In Esther Kingston-Mann and Timothy Mixter, eds., *Peasant Economy, Culture, and Politics of European Russia, 1800–1921*, 101–27. Princeton: Princeton University Press, 1991.

Wilson, Bryan. *Religion in Secular Society*. New York: Penguin Books, 1969.

Wirtschafter, Elise Kimmerling. *Structures of Society: Imperial Russia's "People of Various Ranks."* DeKalb: Northern Illinois University Press, 1994.

———. *Social Identity in Imperial Russia*. DeKalb: Northern Illinois University Press, 1997.

Worobec, Christine D. *Peasant Russia: Family and Community in the Post-Emancipation Period*. Princeton: Princeton University Press, 1991; DeKalb: Northern Illinois University Press, 1995.

———. "Witchcraft Beliefs and Practices in Prerevolutionary Russian and Ukrainian Villages." *RR* 54, no. 2 (1995): 165–87.

———. *Possessed: Women, Witches, and Demons in Imperial Russia*. DeKalb: Northern Illinois University Press, 2001.

Wortman, Richard. "'Invisible Threads': The Historical Imagery of the Romanov Tercentenary." *RH* 16, nos. 2–4 (1989): 389–408.

———. "Nikolai II i obraz samoderzhaviia." *Voprosy istorii*, no. 2 (1991): 119–28.

———. *Scenarios of Power: Myth and Ceremony in Russian Monarchy*. Vols. 1–2. Princeton: Princeton University Press, 1995, 2000.

Yaney, George L. *The Systematization of Russian Government: Social Evolution in the Domestic Administration of Imperial Russia, 1711–1905*. Urbana: University of Illinois Press, 1973.

———. *The Urge to Mobilize: Agrarian Reform in Russia, 1861–1930*. Urbana: University of Illinois Press, 1982.

Young, Glennys. "'Into Church Matters': Lay Identity, Rural Parish Life, and Popular Politics in Late Imperial and Early Soviet Russia, 1864–1928." *RH* 23, nos. 1–4 (1996): 367–84.

———. *Power and the Sacred in Revolutionary Russia: Religious Activities in the Village*. University Park: Pennsylvania State University Press, 1997.

Zagorovskii, V. P. *Istoricheskaia toponimka Voronezhskogo kraia*. Voronezh: Izd-vo Voronezhskogo universiteta, 1973.

———. "Vozniknovenie g. Zemlianska i zaselenie Zemlianskogo uezda v XVII veke." In V. P. Zagorovskii, ed., *IIVK*, 6:39–48. Voronezh: Izd-vo Voronezhskogo universiteta, 1977.

————. *Istoriia Voronezhskogo kraia ot A do Ia*. Voronezh: Tsentral'no-chernozemnoe knizhnoe izd-vo, 1982.

Zelnik, Reginald E. "'To the Unaccustomed Eye': Religion and Irreligion in the Experience of St. Petersburg Workers in the 1870s." In Robert P. Hughes and Irina Paperno, eds., *Christianity and the Eastern Slavs*. Vol. 2, *Russian Culture in Modern Times*, 49–82. Berkeley: University of California Press, 1994.

Zol'nikova, N. D. *Sibirskaia prikhodskaia obshchina v XVIII veke*. Novosibirsk: Nauka, Sibirskoe otdelenie, 1990.

Zyrianov, P. N. *Pravoslavnaia tserkov' v bor'be s revoliutsiei 1905–1907 gg*. Moscow: Izd-vo Nauka, 1984.

————. *Krest'ianskaia obshchina evropeiskoi Rossii 1907–1914 g.g.* Moscow: Nauka, 1992.

Index